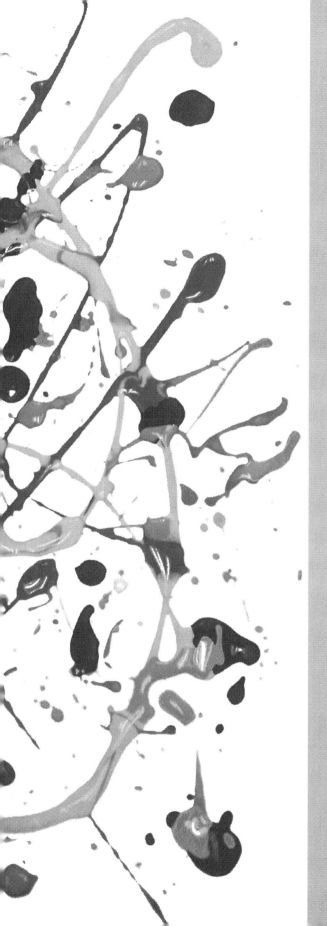

Child and adolescent mental health today:

a handbook

Edited by Catherine Jackson,
Kathryn Hill and Paula Lavis

Child and adolescent mental health today:
a handbook

Edited by Catherine Jackson, Kathryn Hill and Paula Lavis

Mental Health Foundation

YoungMinds
for children's mental health

Pavilion

Child and Adolescent Mental Health Today
A handbook

Published by:
Pavilion Publishing (Brighton) Ltd
Richmond House
Richmond Road
Brighton BN2 3RL
Tel: 01273 623222
Fax: 01273 625526
Email: info@pavpub.com
Web: www.pavpub.com

First published 2008.

ISBN: 978 1 841962 26 9

Pavilion is the leading training and development provider and publisher in the health, social care and allied fields, providing a range of innovative training solutions underpinned by sound research and professional values. We aim to put our customers first, through excellent customer service and good value.

Editors: Catherine Jackson, Kathryn Hill and Paula Lavis
Cover design: Faye Thompson
Page layout and typesetting: Faye Thompson
Printing: Ashford Press (Southampton)

Contents

Foreword

It is frequently, and rightly, said that children's mental health is everybody's business. Even without expert analysis, it is clear that many children and young people in our society are suffering from mental health problems that need to be tackled. That so many highly vulnerable children end up in care, experiencing early pregnancy, misusing substances or in prison, shows how important it is that we address early on the underlying causes of their vulnerability.

The increased focus on the mental health of the infant is welcome, given the growing body of evidence that illustrates all too starkly the impact of poor attachment on the developing infant brain. That much can be done in schools to promote emotional well-being and resilience once children start school is now recognised, as all schools start to adopt the Healthy Schools model and as they offer additional services as extended schools. Embedding primary mental health workers in schools will help to provide the support that is needed not only early on but particularly during adolescence. This will particularly be the case where they work as one component of a multidisciplinary team whose focus is on identifying the child who is experiencing difficulties, and meeting that child's needs.

There is no doubt that much has been and is being done, at government level and in local authorities, primary care trusts and mental health trusts, as well as many voluntary organisations, to improve children's mental health. There has been positive development in the last five years. A clear target for a comprehensive child and adolescent mental health service, with appropriate funding alongside it, has been established, and a standard was included in the National Service Framework for Children, Young People and Maternity Services. The effort that has gone into mapping services has undoubtedly raised the profile of, and the attention paid to, these important issues. However, given that there was previously such a scarcity of services, it is perhaps not surprising that there is still much more to be done in order to meet the needs of all children and young people with mental health problems, including many who are in evident distress. In some parts of the country there are still lengthy waiting times, and there can be a reluctance to refer to services that may be ill-equipped to deal with the specific needs of every child.

In my travels around the country, I see many children and young people who have overcome considerable adversity but for whom we could be doing far more in terms of tailoring services to their individual needs. What I want to see as Children's Commissioner, and I hope this book will help to achieve this aim, is a society that recognises the importance and centrality of children's mental health to all aspects of their current and future lives.

Sir Al Aynsley-Green
Children's Commissioner for England
11 MILLION

Contributors

Jane Barlow is a professor of public health in the early years at the University of Warwick. Her main research interest is the role of parenting in the aetiology of mental health problems, and in particular the evaluation of early interventions aimed at improving parenting practices, particularly during the formative years. Her programme of research focuses on interventions that are provided around infancy, and she is currently undertaking long-term follow-up (at age three years) of an intensive home visiting programme that was provided by health visitors to vulnerable women during pregnancy and the postnatal period. She is currently developing the Warwick Infant and Family Wellbeing Unit, which will provide training and research in innovative evidence-based methods of supporting parenting during pregnancy and the early years to a wide range of early years and primary care practitioners.

Mary Bunting qualified as a social worker in the early 1970s and has extensive experience in generic social work, adoption and fostering, and specialist CAMHS teams. As a child protection training manager in the early 1990s, Mary developed and delivered a range of training to staff in a large social services department, before returning to CAMHS as a clinician. For several years she held the position of service manager in a community health trust, where she was closely involved in developing effective multi-agency structures to deliver a more accessible service to children and their families. Since 2001, Mary has developed her own training and consultancy business, which specialises in children's services, with a particular focus on the mental health and emotional needs of children and young people and safeguarding. For several years she has worked as a trainer and consultant for YoungMinds, and is the lead on their Looked After Children Project. It is a project dear to her heart as over the years she has met so many children and young people in the care system who, despite their negative life experiences, have developed a resilience and positive attitude to life that is inspirational.

Roger Catchpole is the principal consultant at YoungMinds. He specialises in inter-professional working, learning and development in child and adolescent mental health. Having trained as a social scientist at the University of Essex, he worked in social services in London as a consultant/trainer and then training manager, before becoming a freelance consultant in 1998, and joining the staff of YoungMinds in 2004. He has led consultancy and training projects in all four countries of the UK, and has worked on a number of national training and development programmes, including Behaviour and Education Support Teams (BEST) and Sure Start in England and, in partnership with the Scottish Development Centre for Mental Health, implementation of the Framework for Child and Adolescent Mental Health in Scotland. With YoungMinds colleagues David Goosey and Mary Webb, he developed a national inter-agency training resource in Scotland. He is a visiting lecturer at City University in London, where he has been part of the development of an MSc in Inter-professional Practice in

Child and Adolescent Mental Health. Roger was a member of the national reference group developing occupational standards in mental health, is a member of the CAMHS Trainers' Forum, and has sat on Open College accreditation panels for mental health programmes.

Andy Cotgrove is clinical director and consultant in adolescent psychiatry at Pine Lodge Young People's Centre in Chester, where he has worked since 1993. He trained in Sheffield and worked in general medicine and general practice before training in psychiatry. His specialist training in child and adolescent psychiatry was at the Tavistock Clinic in London, where he also gained an MSc in family therapy. In addition to his clinical work, he is interested in service development and service improvement. He is also interested in research and is currently developing a randomised controlled trial for a treatment intervention for young people who self-harm. He was a member and topic group leader in the guideline development group for the NICE guideline on depression in children and young people (2002–2005), and expert adviser to the NICE self-harm guideline. He is a member of the NICE Mental Health Topic Selection Panel.

Jill Davies has worked with people with learning disabilities for over 20 years, and has mainly worked with children and families during this time. She has a background in learning disability nursing and moved to London many years ago to work at a unit for children with challenging behaviour and mental health problems at the South London and Maudsley NHS Trust. More recently, she worked part-time for a north west London child and adolescent mental health team. She also developed a family support service for children with autism at Bromley Autistic Trust, working there for over seven years. In 2002 Jill joined the Foundation for People with Learning Disabilities as research programme manager. Much of her focus at the Foundation has been on the mental health needs of young people with learning disabilities. This has included running a programme of research called *Making Us Count*, consulting with children and young people to get their views on CAMHS, co-running action learning sets to support more inclusive CAMHS, and managing a project called What About Us? that is addressing the needs of pupils with learning disabilities attending mainstream secondary schools.

Eric Davis is visiting professor of mental health at the University of the West of England. His current research interests include vocational activity and early intervention in psychosis. He has published widely on psychosis in peer-reviewed journals and textbooks, and is co-editor of *Changing Outcomes in Psychosis*, published in 2007. He is also a consultant clinical psychologist and previously worked for the Gloucestershire Partnership NHS Mental Health Trust, where he was project lead for the implementation of early intervention in psychosis services. The Gloucestershire service was recognised for its clinical effectiveness in the CSIP/NIMHE *10 High Impact Changes* report, in 2006. He was a founder member of the Early Psychosis Declaration, which was ratified by the World Health Organisation and Royal College of Psychiatrists, and has been a member of the

Initiative to Reduce the Impact of Schizophrenia (IRIS) working group since 1997. He has contributed extensively to training staff and others in various aspects of psychosis and was a co-founder of the Thorn course in Gloucestershire in 1995, and also the national early intervention in psychosis training programme (CD-rom) developed in 2007.

Alison Giraud-Saunders is co-director, Foundation for People with Learning Disabilities, which she joined from the Institute for Applied Health and Social Policy at King's College London. Previously she worked in the NHS in both commissioning and trust roles, supporting the development of joint commissioning and person-centred services for people with learning disabilities. She took project management responsibility for major change programmes and promoted the involvement of self advocates and family carers in service planning. Alison has worked with health and social services across England on the organisational and service development agenda for change in line with the aims of *Valuing People*, including supporting the development of partnership boards and working with a number of authorities on community team reviews. She led the Valuing People theme for the 2006/07 Beacon Scheme and continues to work on the ways that councils as a whole can make sure they improve opportunities for their citizens who have learning disabilities.

Paula Lavis is a library and information professional, who specialises in children's mental health. She has held the post of policy and knowledge manager at YoungMinds for the last nine years. She also works for the CAMHS Evidence-Based Practice Unit, and is commissioned by the National CAMHS Support Service (NCSS) in an information and research support capacity.

Tim McDougall was formerly nurse advisor for CAMHS at the Department of Health in England, and is a nurse consultant in Tier 4 CAMHS. Tim has worked in a range of CAMHS settings, including community child mental health teams, adolescent inpatient services, and secure adolescent forensic services. Tim has a national profile in CAMHS. He has spoken at numerous national and European conferences, and has published over 70 journal articles and book chapters about the mental health of children and adolescents. Tim has visited CAMHS in several European countries, and services for young offenders in Australia. Clinical interests include working with violent children and young people, and early onset psychosis. Tim was responsible for founding a number of key networks, including the National Nurse Consultants in CAMHS Forum and the Adolescent Forensic Services Professional Network. Tim also helped develop the National Institute for Clinical Excellence (NICE) guideline for bipolar disorder. In his spare time, Tim is writing another book on children and young people with ADHD and enjoys cooking Mediterranean food and visiting Greek islands with his family.

Kim Penketh is a research assistant at the Mental Health Foundation. Kim's experience as a service user of the mental health system led her to take the role of a young persons consultant at the Mental Health Foundation in 2003, where she has been a significant driving force in promoting young people's service user involvement. Kim has since developed her skills and knowledge within the mental health research field and is now a research assistant. Kim's main role is working on the Foundation's children and young people projects, which aim to improve the mental and emotional well-being of all children and young people across the UK. A key part of her role is to promote and raise awareness of holistic and creative ways to involve young people in research and practice development at all levels. Kim is studying a childhood and youth studies degree with the Open University.

Kathryn Pugh works part time with the Care Services Improvement Partnership (CSIP) child and families programme as a CAMHS regional development worker in London. Prior to this, she worked for YoungMinds for almost three years, leading the Stressed Out and Struggling Project, which aimed to improve services for and awareness of the mental health needs of 16–25 year olds. As head of policy for YoungMinds, she led for the Mental Health Alliance and a number of children's charities in lobbying for changes to the Mental Health Act, culminating in the introduction by the government of a range of amendments to protect children and young people, including amendments to ensure an age appropriate environment for children and young people requiring inpatient care. Kathryn worked for 12 years in the NHS, first in primary care management and then in commissioning. Her commissioning experience includes acute general and community care, mental health and substance misuse commissioning for all care groups, and specialist commissioning for Tier 4.

Carly Raby is young people's participation manager at YoungMinds. She obtained her Masters in Education in Integrated Therapeutic Arts from the Institute of Child Mental Health/Institute of Therapeutic Arts in London. Carly is a qualified psychotherapist and has also specialised in a range of specific areas in relation to supporting children and young people with mental health difficulties. Carly previously co-ordinated a project for children permanently excluded from mainstream services, and was director of Luna, an organisation that operates nationally and across sectors to ensure that children and young people are central to decision-making within organisations created to meet their needs.

Sam Raby has worked for over 10 years with children and young people. Previously, he has run a project for children and young people permanently excluded from mainstream services, and co-ordinated play centres in deprived areas. With a background in psychology, Sam has also trained children's services employees to listen to children and young people with additional needs. Currently he co-ordinates the Children's Voices Project for Luna, which champions the voice of children and young people at risk of exclusion. He is director of Luna Training. Luna works to ensure that children and young people can participate in services, and that their views are heard at the heart of services.

Marion Roberts completed her undergraduate and graduate psychology studies at Victoria University of Wellington, New Zealand. She taught in the psychology department at Victoria University for a year, before moving to London to study for her Doctorate under Professor Janet Treasure at the Institute of Psychiatry, King's College London.

Kapil Sayal is a consultant and senior lecturer in child and adolescent psychiatry. His research focuses on the recognition of children with mental health problems in primary care and schools, and their access to services. Current research includes intervention and follow-up studies investigating the identification of children with hyperactivity in schools and the development of quality standards for access to care through primary care. He is a member of the NICE attention deficit/hyperactivity disorder (ADHD) guideline development group.

Jude Sellen has worked in the health and social care field since 1982. Her roles have included practitioner, manager and senior policy officer, primarily focusing on meeting the mental health needs of children, young people and their carers. She has particular skills and knowledge in working with addiction, eating disorders, aggressive behaviours and self-harm, and has an MSc in Health & Social Care. Since 2000 Jude has worked as an independent young people's mental health consultant and trainer. She continues to run one and two-day self-harm training courses for frontline staff across the UK and supports areas with developing local self-harm protocols. She is currently developing self-harm training materials for use in schools.

Mike Shooter has been part of mental health services in every sense. For 25 years he was a consultant in child and adolescent psychiatry, helping lead multidisciplinary teams working with deprived families in Cardiff and the old mining valleys of South Wales. He is the immediate past-president of the Royal College of Psychiatrists, having previously been its registrar and director of public education. In 'retirement' he has become chair of YoungMinds, of Children-in-Wales and of the Princess Royal Trust for Carers in Wales, chair-elect of the Mental Health Foundation, a trustee of the National Children's Bureau, and a vice-president of the British Association for Counselling and Psychotherapy. Mike has a recurrent depressive disorder of his own, that first occurred when he was a student, and has needed regular help since. He has always been wonderfully cared for by service colleagues, by friends and most of all by his family.

Cathy Street is a freelance health researcher and consultant. She has researched and published widely on a range of topics concerning the provision of child and adolescent mental health services (CAMHS) – in particular, Tier 4 inpatient services and services for children with learning disabilities. As research consultant at YoungMinds from 2000–2007, Cathy managed a number of national projects, including service user involvement in CAMHS, access to public services by young people from black and minority ethnic groups, developments in inpatient care, and using drama as a way of sharing information about CAMHS with young people from

BME communities. She also led the YoungMinds consultancy team that worked on the Pushed into the Shadows report for the Children's Commissioner for England, which explored inappropriate admissions of young people to adult inpatient wards.

Janet Treasure is a professor of psychiatry at Guy's, King's & St Thomas' Medical School, London, and a consultant psychiatrist who has specialised in the treatment of eating disorders for more than 25 years. She is director of the Eating Disorder Unit at the South London and Maudsley NHS Foundation Trust, a leading centre for training and the clinical management of eating disorders. She chaired the physical treatment section of the committee that produced the NICE clinical guideline on eating disorders. She is the chief medical advisor for bEAT (formerly the Eating Disorder Association, the main UK eating disorder charity), and is the patron of the Sheffield Eating Disorders Association. She is on the Academy of Eating Disorders accreditation committee and is an Academy fellow. She is the medical advisor for the Capio Nightingale Hospital. In 2004 she was awarded the Academy for Eating Disorders (AED) Leadership Award in Research.

Jo Tunnard works as an independent researcher, writer and editor for a range of statutory and non-governmental organisations, including both adult and children's divisions of the Department of Health. She has 25 years experience of working in third sector organisations concerned with advising families about their legal rights and enabling families to have a voice in decisions about their children, young relatives and themselves. She is a founder member of RTB (www.ryantunnardbrown.com), and an associate of YoungMinds, the National Children's Bureau, and Research in Practice. She has conducted several service reviews of child and adolescent mental health services, and has developed and delivered training on child and adult participation in CAMHS planning and evaluation. Recent commissions from the Department of Health, the Department for Children, Schools and Families, the Ministry of Justice and the Youth Justice Board have included a national mapping exercise of needs and interventions in the secure children's estate, a commissioning framework for good practice in delivering mental health services to young people in custodial and secure welfare settings, and a health and social care strategy for children and young people involved with the youth justice system in custodial and community settings.

Angela Underdown is a public health adviser to the NSPCC. Angela originally trained as a health visitor and has a long standing interest in supporting infant mental health within family relationships. Angela has been researching infant massage interventions in the UK and has recently completed a Cochrane systematic review exploring the effects of infant massage on the mental and physical health of infants under six months of age. Angela is working on developing the Warwick Infant and Family Wellbeing Unit, which will provide training and research in innovative evidence-based methods of supporting parenting during pregnancy and the early years to a wide range of early years and primary care practitioners.

Christina Vasiliou Theodore is a senior researcher at the Mental Health Foundation. Christina trained in research methods, statistics and clinical neuropsychology. She began by working with children and young people with learning and behavioural needs and mental health problems, across the mainstream education sector. She then went on to work as a psychologist for Harrow adult mental health services, while undertaking relevant clinical research work. Christina joined the Mental Health Foundation in 2004, where she has been the lead on a number of projects, in collaboration with external key stakeholders, on the mental health and well-being of children and young people. As part of her role, Christina works with Kim Penketh on developing, supporting and promoting young person user involvement in research and practice development. In addition, she provides service evaluation consultancy for voluntary sector organisations across the UK.

Katherine Weare is professor of education at the University of Southampton and a consultant on emotional and social aspects of learning. Originally a teacher, her field is emotional well-being and emotional and social learning, on which she has researched and written extensively. Her recent publications include *Developing the Emotionally Literate School* (Sage), which is one of the leading books on the subject. She has advised the Department for Children, Schools and Families on policy on social and emotional aspects of learning (SEAL) – her report to the Department for Education and Skills on What Works in Promoting Children's Emotional and Social Competence was a significant catalyst in the development of primary SEAL and she was a key contributor to the writing and development of secondary SEAL. She is currently helping various national and international agencies to develop their education and mental health services. This includes work with the EU to develop an international database of effective mental health programmes for Europe, with the Scottish Executive to develop national policy and practice for mental health, and with the Welsh Assembly to review their National Healthy Schools programme. She has three children aged nine, 13, and 14, who help ground this in reality.

Richard Williams has been a child and adolescent psychiatrist for more than 30 years and a strategic leader in health care service design and delivery for the last 15 years. He is the professor of mental health strategy at the University of Glamorgan, honorary professor of child and adolescent mental health at the University of Central Lancashire, and a consultant child and adolescent psychiatrist with Gwent Healthcare NHS Trust. He is an active clinician. Richard Williams' research and writing is in health care policy and strategy, service design, clinical governance, modern professionalism and user and carer participation. He is co-editor of a text, published in 2005, on strategic approaches to developing child and adolescent mental health services. Much of his current work is on the psychosocial impacts of adversity, disasters, conflict and terrorism. He is a member of the Department of Health's Emergency Planning Clinical Leadership Advisory Group, and a member of the UK government's Committee on the

Ethical Aspects of Pandemic Influenza. He is advising the UK government and NATO's Joint Medical Committee on psychosocial resiliency and managing the mental health aspects of major incidents of all kinds.

Peter Wilson is a consultant child psychotherapist. Having worked initially as a social worker in England and the US, he trained to be a child psychotherapist in 1967 and qualified in 1971. For the next 20 years he worked in a variety of settings in London, including the Brixton, Hoxton and Camberwell child guidance clinics. He became principal child psychotherapist in Camberwell Health Authority, and senior clinical tutor at the Institute of Psychiatry, Maudsley Hospital Children's Department. Later, he became consultant psychotherapist at the Peper Harow therapeutic community and director of the Brandon Centre, a psychotherapy and counselling centre for young people. From April 1992 until his retirement in February 2004, he was director of YoungMinds, the children's mental health charity, which he co-founded. He has served on numerous committees and inquiries on national developments in child and adolescent mental health provision, and lectured widely. He currently serves as clinical adviser to The Place2Be, a voluntary organisation providing a comprehensive counselling service mostly in primary schools in England and Scotland. He has written numerous papers and chapters in various journals and books. He is the author of *Young Minds in Our Schools*, published by YoungMinds in 2003.

Introduction

Children and young people's mental health matters – it's a truism, but no less true for that. Our healthy mental and emotional development in infancy, childhood and adolescence largely shapes our mental health and well-being throughout our adulthood. Any trauma we experience in our formative years will echo through the rest of our life, and our abilities to handle stressful and traumatic incidents in later life will often depend on the resilience we built up in those first two decades.

Happily, the importance of this period for later mental health is increasingly recognised at government policy-making levels. So we have parenting support programmes to help parents provide their child with an emotionally nurturing environment; we have a national strategy for ending child poverty that should mean fewer children and young people grow up in the adverse circumstances that, as research repeatedly shows, can impact on mental health, and result in reduced capacity to achieve their full potential; and we have initiatives in schools for developing children and young people's emotional literacy and competence.

At the same time, however, there are growing numbers of children and young people who have a diagnosed mental health problem, and need treatment from the specialist child and adolescent mental health services (CAMHS). Not so long ago, children and young people's mental health services operated in a silo, with very little engagement with other services working with their patients – notably, with the education system and children's social services, and with the voluntary sector. To a large extent, this remains true – thus the resolve in the new *Children's Plan* (Department for Children, Schools and Families, 2007), published late in 2007, to review CAMHS, with the aim to ensure greater partnership working with other agencies. To treat children and young people in a bubble, divorced from their family, school and social environments, makes no sense.

Thus, the publication of this handbook. Many professionals and others working with children and young people outside the immediate CAMHS circle need to know about mental health issues, in order both to provide appropriate support to those who are struggling, and to engage with the wider mental health promotion and well-being agenda. This book is intended for that wide range of workers who are specialists in their own fields but would find an introduction to mental health helpful. It is intended too for students and trainees, as a broad introduction to the main issues and current knowledge about children and young people's mental health.

The book is in five parts: an overview of mental health, policies and service structures; infant mental health; children's mental health; adolescent mental health, and diagnoses and treatments. It starts with Mike Shooter's excellent introduction to understanding mental health, mental illness, its causes and the different models of treatment. Paula Lavis then sets out the main policies in England and Wales governing public sector activity related to children and young people's mental health. Next, Roger Catchpole examines a crucial feature in today's CAMHS – partnership working, and how the different agencies concerned can be enabled to work together for children and young people's mental health. Finally, in this section, Cathy Street addresses another very crucial issue: how we respond to children and young people from different cultures and minority ethnic groups, and the importance of ensuring services are sensitive to their different needs and circumstances. She emphasises that we must involve children and young people, their families, and their communities more generally in developing and delivering services if they are to be genuinely culturally appropriate.

In part II Jane Barlow and Angela Underdown provide two linked chapters on infant development and parenting support. Using the attachment model, they explain the mechanisms whereby the relationship between parent and infant – the parent's responsiveness to the infant – builds the infant's emotional resilience and ability to relate to others. They go on to describe the range of parenting support programmes that have proved it is possible to turn around the lives both of parent and child, and ensure children grow to achieve their full potential despite adverse early beginnings.

In part III these themes are continued, first in Carly Raby and Sam Raby's discussion of risk and resilience in childhood, and the factors that contribute to a child's ability to survive adversity and challenge both in their early years and in later life. Key to this resilience is the presence of a consistent, supportive mentor figure who can provide positive feedback and nurture the young person's self-esteem and sense of self.

Peter Wilson then describes initiatives in our primary schools that both seek to teach children emotional literacy skills – how to recognise and express their emotions healthily and positively, and respond to others – and to support those who are struggling with emotional distress and behavioural problems. Mary Bunting continues the theme in her chapter on the mental health needs of looked after children, whose repeatedly disrupted lives and lack of a secure, loving family environment have rendered them much more vulnerable to mental health and behavioural difficulties, in childhood and adulthood. She welcomes new government initiatives to improve their life chances as the single most effective way to prevent the disproportionate incidence of mental distress among this group.

Similarly often affected by their environments as well as their special needs are children with learning disabilities, whose mental and emotional health problems may easily be overlooked as an expression of their learning difficulties. Jill Davies and Alison Giraud-Saunders outline the challenges many of them face, and the need for joined-up, multi-agency approaches and equal access to specialist mainstream CAMHS to ensure their needs are accurately identified, understood, and met.

Part IV concerns the mental health of adolescents. It starts with Richard Williams' review of the most recent research into resilience, the factors involved, and the still unanswered question why some young people, despite massive disadvantage and trauma in their early life, are able to survive, and even flourish on challenge in later life.

Next, Kathryn Pugh describes findings from a YoungMinds project to explore what young people themselves say they find difficult in the key transitional years between childhood and adulthood. Too often young people aged 16–17 fall into a gap between the child and adult services – too old for the former, but too incomprehensible to the latter. She stresses the importance of joint working between the statutory and voluntary sectors, as the voluntary sector is frequently better able to respond to young people's needs because of its greater flexibility and because it may be less intimidating and stigmatising to access. On a similar theme, Christina Vasiliou Theodore and Kim Penketh report on a Mental Health Foundation initiative to support young people's participation in service design and development. The Foundation resourced eight voluntary sector projects to explore mechanisms for consulting with and involving young people in their activities and structures, and this chapter reports on the key findings. They outline the benefits of young people's participation, chief of which is that children and young people are likely to more readily engage with their care and treatment, and so achieve better outcomes. But participation has to be genuine; young people quickly spot tokenist, patronising and empty gestures, they warn.

Next Katherine Weare, who herself played a central part in its development, outlines the government's social and emotional aspects of learning (SEAL) programmes for primary and secondary schools. SEAL is already in place in some two-thirds of primary schools and is, she reports, already having a positive impact on social and emotional learning, behaviour and on pupils' reading and learning outcomes. Secondary SEAL is currently being rolled out, with, it is to be hoped, similar positive effects. She presents the underpinning research that demonstrates conclusively the benefits to all young people, with and without mental health difficulties, and to the school community, of a whole-school approach to promoting mental health and well-being.

Finally in this section, Jo Tunnard addresses the particular, and all-too-often unmet needs of young people who get into trouble with the law and end up in a young offenders institute. Here again is a group of already very troubled young people whose difficulties can be directly linked to their childhood and upbringing, and whose experiences in custody are unlikely to help them recover a place in society and achieve their potential. These young people need intensive support, she writes, including practical support with housing, education, training and employment. Above all, they need consistent support and continuity of care, through custody and following their release.

Part V introduces some of the main mental illnesses as they affect children and young people. These include the classic illnesses of adulthood, such as depression and bipolar disorder and psychosis, whose effects and treatment will be subtly different for age-related reasons, and also disorders that are more likely to affect children and young people: attention deficit/hyperactivity disorder (ADHD), eating disorders, and self-harm. These chapters are all written by experts with many years' experience of working with children and young people, some of whom have been involved in drawing up the NICE guideline on their particular area of expertise. Andrew Cotgrove and Tim McDougall outline the identification, diagnosis and current NICE guidance on treatment (with talking treatments and medication) of depression and bipolar disorder. Eric Davis uses his own experiences with the Gloucester Recovery in Psychosis early intervention service to explain the need for a prompt and age-appropriate response to young people when they first experience psychosis. Kapil Sayal tackles the controversial issue of ADHD, acknowledging the contested nature of the diagnosis and summarising current recommended best practice in its psychological and medical treatment. Jude Sellen's chapter on self-harm explores how those working with vulnerable children and young people can be better supported so they can themselves respond in more appropriate ways to those in their care. Telling a young person to stop self-harming will not help; staying alongside them as they work through the experiences and emotions that lead to self-harm is going to be far more effective, but will exact its toll on the worker. They will need not just training but ongoing support and opportunities to explore their own feelings in safety.

Last, Marion Roberts and Janet Treasure summarise the latest research on eating disorders. They report what research tells us about what causes a child or young person to develop an eating disorder, and why they struggle to let it go. They also point to the key role of the family, and ways in which family members can be helped to support the child or young person in their home environment, and so provide a stronger foundation for recovery and continued management of their difficulties.

This book could not hope to be fully comprehensive; undoubtedly there are areas and specialisms we have missed, but we hope it will provide an accessible, interesting and, above all useful introduction to a topic that definitely concerns us all.

Catherine Jackson
Kathryn Hill
Paula Lavis

Reference

Department for Children, Schools and Families (2007) *The Children's Plan: building brighter futures*. London: Department for Children, Schools and Families.

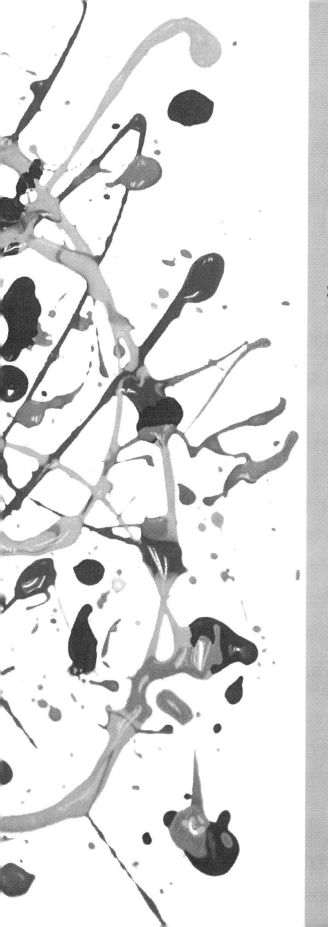

Part I

Mental health, policies and service structures

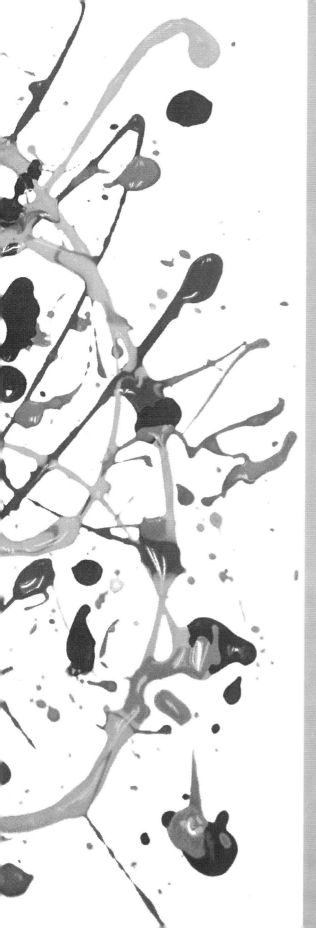

What is mental health?

Mike Shooter

Key points

- Most adult and adolescent mental ill health originates in childhood

- Mental ill health derives from genetic (nature) and environmental (nurture) influences

- Mental health is more than the absence of mental illness; it is a positive sense of psychological well-being

- Lasting recovery from mental ill health and disturbed behaviours requires more than medical treatment for the surface symptoms; attention must be paid to the child's social and emotional situation

- Children have a right to a voice and to have that voice heard in decisions and interventions that affect their lives.

Key words
Mental health; Mental illness; Biological causes; Environmental influences; Children's rights

Despite the stigma that still surrounds mental illness, its sufferers and those who care for them, there is an increasing recognition of its impact on all our lives (Thornicroft, 2006). One in four of us will develop a mental health problem in our lifetime; every family in the land will be touched by it in one way or another. Mental illness is now the biggest cause of days off work in the western world; the more insightful companies have policies to address it, and governments are spending more and more money on services to help people with mental health problems.

Since it is well established that the antecedents of most adult and adolescent mental illness begin in childhood (Smith, 2006), it makes sense to ask if there is anything that can be done in early life to prevent all this social and individual suffering later on. From there, it is just a short step to the concept of promoting mental health as an essential component of total well-being – but here we run up against a problem: what is mental health and how does it relate to mental illness?

If this was the physical world we were talking about, the answer would be relatively clear. Occasionally we imagine that we are ill when we are not; occasionally we are harbouring an illness when we feel perfectly healthy. But, by and large, we are familiar with the processes of physical illness and health in our bodies, and everything that implies. Physical illness, for example, usually has a specific bodily cause – disease or injury. It gives rise to patterns of symptoms that can be diagnosed with reasonable accuracy by medical experts, backed up by technological investigations. Diagnosis enables treatment, targeted and well researched. If the treatment is properly applied, we can usually predict the course of the illness – its prognosis.

Some of us will have an increased risk of genetically inherited problems, but if we know the causes of physical illnesses we can often avoid them, by social improvements, sensible lifestyles, and a bit of luck. This is the basis of mass public health measures like vaccination and sanitation, and of campaigns to improve individual health by encouraging regular exercise, a nutritious diet and avoiding habits that have a negative impact on health such as smoking and excessive alcohol consumption. The concern for health services then becomes not only how to treat the sick, but how to reach those who are unable or unwilling to take responsibility for keeping themselves healthy.

Mental ill health

There are some analogies here for mental illness and mental health, but the situation is rarely so straightforward. To begin with, there are rival schools of thought about the causes of mental illness, each tenaciously held and with varying degrees of evidence to back them up. The biological model focuses on inherited chemical imbalances within the brain that lead to defective transmission of nerve impulses and are rectifiable, at least in part, by drugs designed to restore those balances (Nutt, 2007).

Others point out that what we are born with – 'nature' – can only account for some of our vulnerability, even in these illnesses. The rest is down to 'nurture' – our life experiences and the way we are brought up. Psychodynamic models identify the origins of mental disorder in a conflict between the various developing parts of our psychology, the defences we erect against those conflicts, the abnormal patterns of behaviour this can cause, and the way they interfere with human relationships. Treatment might require lengthy 'talking therapy' to analyse those conflicts and free their sufferer from having to repeat them in their daily lives.

Behavioural models propose that we learn from the examples we see around us and the conditioning we receive over the years to act as we do. They argue that it is not necessary to delve into feelings; we can change things by withholding rewards from unwanted behaviours and by offering pleasant rewards for behaviours we wish to encourage. Cognitive behavioural therapy (CBT) works by challenging the negative thoughts a person develops about him or herself and the outside world and the safety-seeking social withdrawal they may lead to (Williams, 2007).

In all of these models, the relationship between the therapist and the patient will be an important factor in whether the patient gets better. In the humanistic model, that relationship is the stuff of treatment itself. People are born good, with the potential for personal growth if met by the right sort of unconditional love from their carers – namely, self-actualisation. The therapist aims to repair this process in those for whom it has been thwarted, by offering positive regard, genuineness, honesty and empathy of approach within the therapy, and encouragement to take responsibility for life outside it (Freeth, 2007).

But mental disorders can rarely be accounted for by one of these models alone. They are more likely to be complex jigsaws of interlocking factors in which the emotional and behavioural consequences are the final common outcome, rather than specific symptoms identifiable by fine diagnosis and laboratory tests. Treatment would therefore require the combined efforts of many people with a diverse range of medical, therapeutic, social and educational skills. So, if mental illness is so complicated, where does that leave mental health?

Mental health

Mental health has been defined as 'the strength and capacity of our minds to grow and develop, to be able to overcome difficulties and challenges and to make the most of our abilities and opportunities' (YoungMinds, 2006). This would certainly imply an absence of the sort of mental illnesses that would interfere with that capacity, but it is something more: a positive sense of psychological well-being. And here we have to beware of too close an analogy with physical health.

All of us can be helped to build our emotional strengths in ways that can increase our sense of well-being and sustain our relationships with others (Butler & Hope, 2007), but those of us with enduring mental illnesses may still suffer relapses, however well we manage our lives. Just as someone with diabetes can learn how to manage their illness so that it affects their life as little as possible, so someone with a mental illness can take steps to delay the onset of relapse and hasten recovery from each episode. But they should not be made to feel guilty if they fall ill again because they have 'not done it right'. We have fought hard to be part of the campaign for public health: 'there can be no health without mental health' (YoungMinds, 2007). But its achievement is not as simple as giving up smoking or not putting on excessive weight.

What does all this mean for individual children and adolescents in psychological trouble? How should we interpret what is happening to them? How can we build on the strengths in their lives, whatever the circumstances? And what can we draw from individual experiences in the way of general 'rules'? Take, for example, the two young people described below, whose names and details are fictitious but whose stories are only too true to life.

Anne-Marie's story

Anne-Marie was 15 years old when she was referred to the child and adolescent mental health service by her general practitioner. He had already diagnosed her as depressed and had started her on antidepressant medication, with little effect.

There were poor relationships at home. Her mother had postnatal depression after Anne-Marie's birth, and had been depressed on and off ever since. She said she had given up her academic career to look after her family, but her illness had probably prevented her studying consistently. Her father was under pressure at work, and was clearly drinking heavily, despite his denials.

Anne-Marie's parents quarreled frequently, and there were suspicions of physical violence from the father, though her mother had always said her bruises were due to 'accidents'. Her older brother was a good sportsman, heading for university and doted on by his father. Her mother just told her it's 'a man's world'; a woman's lot is to produce babies, and Anne-Marie's achievements at school were 'useless'.

Anne-Marie used to have a few close friends but was now withdrawing from them. She was sleeping poorly, overeating and putting on weight. She thought she was ugly and unpopular, and increasingly took time off school with 'stomach aches'. These had been investigated, but the paediatrician could find nothing wrong and wondered (not so secretly) if she was 'putting it all on'.

The referral was prompted by her mother finding Anne-Marie's diary, and reading 'I wish I was dead!' Everyone was worried that she might commit suicide.

Damian's story

Damian was referred to the child and adolescent mental health service by the educational psychologist. He was eight years old, and the school staff were convinced that he had attention deficit/hyperactivity disorder (ADHD). The psychologist pleaded that he should be put on Ritalin (methylphenidate, an amphetamine-based medication commonly used to treat ADHD) 'or he will be chucked out of school'.

His mother was struggling to bring up three children from different fathers on her own, including a six-month old baby, whose father had recently left her for another woman. Her middle child had regular contact with his father, who was both interested and supportive. Damian's own father had been killed in a road traffic accident. 'He was drunk as usual,' said Damian's mother; 'It was good riddance to bad rubbish as far as I was concerned. Damian is just like him.'

The family lived on a dilapidated housing estate in a poor area of town with little or no community support. The streets were full of violence, crime, drugs and alcohol addiction, and few households had anyone in a regular job.

Damian had moderate learning disabilities, a slight speech impediment and wet his bed – all untreated. He was often unkempt and smelly, and had few friends. Social services had once considered taking him into care on grounds of neglect but felt it would be too difficult to prove.

The school staff were finding it difficult to control him because of his poor attention span, his impulsive disregard for danger, and the way he disrupted the class by playing the fool. He had already been banned from going on any school trips. Damian had a good relationship with just one person, a young male probationary teacher, who thought that he was 'brilliant at art'.

Interpretations
The mental illness model

The general practitioner had good reason to diagnose Anne-Marie as being depressed. She had a heavy genetic loading from her mother's history, and was showing symptoms that would satisfy any system of classification – tearfulness, poor sleep, social withdrawal, a distorted view of herself arising from her black mood, and overeating as a comfort against her unhappiness. Her bodily aches and pains could be seen as the 'depressive equivalents' so common in children, in which emotional pain is translated into physical symptoms that are no less real just because they don't show up on an x-ray.

No wonder Anne-Marie's diary so worried all the adults around her. It was quite right that she should be referred for psychiatric assessment, and any child and adolescent mental health team worth its salt would be able to offer that, as a matter of urgency. The case for putting a child on antidepressants is less clear in the light of recent controversy. They would appear to be less effective and have more, and more dangerous, side effects than has been claimed (Whittington *et al*, 2004). Putting her on antidepressants on the off-chance would be bad medical practice, if an understandable response to the pressure to 'do something'. CBT might help, but would it be available? The long waits for talking treatments within the NHS are notorious.

Similarly, in Damian's case the school staff and the educational psychologist were convinced that his behaviour was due to an organic problem, attention deficit/ hyperactivity disorder. Again, this is an understandable diagnosis in the light of his typical symptom cluster of overactive, disorganised behaviour, poor attention span and dangerous impulsivity, apparently pervasive across all the contexts in which he lived – home, school and community (Goodman & Scott, 1997).

It has to be asked why the situation had been allowed to get to the point where he was in danger of being thrown out of school before help was sought. The time needed for medication (Ritalin) to be considered seriously, explained to Damian and his family, introduced, and then monitored over a trial period would be unlikely to satisfy the urgency of his situation. What's more, such medication would have to be an adjunct to a behavioural programme, with rewards for good behaviour that would challenge the negative attitudes of both Damian's mother and the school staff.

The problem in both cases is that there are equally valid interpretations for the children's symptoms that have as much to do with their circumstances as any organic mental illness. Both Anne-Marie and Damian could be seen as making a cry for help with a problem that should not be dismissed as theirs alone, rather than one created by their circumstances, and treated with medication. There is no doubt that depression and attention deficit disorders have both been under-recognised in the past, to the detriment of the child's education and future. But there is an equal danger that they are now being over-diagnosed in order to avoid tackling the deeper issues.

Individual psychodynamic models

The depression she suffered at the time of her birth may well have affected Anne-Marie's mother's whole relationship with her daughter. Certainly, Anne-Marie seems to have grown up with a very shaky sense of self-worth, constantly undermined by her mother's attitudes and influences and her father's neglect of her in favour of her brother. It is not surprising that she has developed such negative views of herself, and overeating and social withdrawal will have compounded them: 'I'm fat and ugly and nobody wants to be my friend.'

Put like this, her symptoms are an argument for a deeper exploration and repair of her unhappiness through psychotherapy; treatment based on a medical illness model would merely touch on the surface manifestations and leave the deeper trouble stored up for the future. Anne-Marie's diary could be seen as her way of expressing a need for help, carefully left for her mother to find and act on, rather than any warning of immediate suicidal intent. But any therapist would have to be brave to take that risk and carve out the space for psychotherapy amidst the surrounding anxieties.

Damian's sense of himself was blighted from the start by physical and learning difficulties, each of which might have seemed minor and unworthy of treatment on its own, but which in combination have proved quite devastating to his morale. With one obvious exception, he has been rejected by family, peer group and school staff in ways that can only have confirmed his opinion of himself. His only way to get any sense of identity has been to play the fool. Better to be punished for it, as usual, than be ignored.

Again, this might argue for psychotherapy rather than organic treatment – for a restorative model set in the here-and-now of a warm, empathic and encouraging therapeutic relationship, rather than an analytical exploration of feelings: 'I care for the person you are, though I may not care for what you have done.' The danger, both for a therapist doing that more formally and for the young male teacher doing it informally within the school day, is that it could be easy to slip into becoming the 'good' father that Damian lacks, with the risk of another 'desertion' when the relationship has to come to an end.

Children do not live in a vacuum. Important though these individual interpretations may be, they must be set in the context of family and community that may themselves be under stress. Children's symptoms may reflect what is going on around them, rather than any deep-seated internal conflicts.

Family psychodynamic models

It would be strange if Anne-Marie were not worried about what was happening in her family – her mother's depression, her father's drinking and the violent rows between them. Her stomach aches could be seen as both a direct sign of her anxiety and as an indirect way of doing something about it. By giving her an excuse to stay home from school, they enable her to protect her mother by getting in between her and the father's assaults, and this is reinforced by her mother's own depressive needs and the scorn she pours on Anne-Marie's school career.

Wherever there is mental or physical illness in a family, it is natural that children should want some sort of role in looking after the sufferer, but this should not be at the expense of their own childhood; we know the consequences of that in later life (Aldridge & Becker, 2003). The school's job would be to ensure that Anne-Marie attends school, for her educational and social good, while adult social services tackle the parents' needs and relieve their daughter of the sense of responsibility for looking after them. Whether the school could be helped to cope with Anne-Marie's stomach aches or the parents persuaded to look at their own problems is another matter.

In Damian's case, his mother still seems to be working through her feelings about his father through her attitude towards their son. If he has been told that he is 'just like his father' often enough, it is not surprising that he has begun to live up to his reputation. Damian has no other male role models, except bad ones in the estate on which they live, and must resent the close and positive relationship his younger brother enjoys with his father.

On a deeper level, it is doubtful whether Damian has ever been allowed to grieve the loss of his own father, or will ever be allowed to do so while his mother is so negative about him. Damian will certainly be angry with his father for leaving him, but will have loving feelings too that his mother would find difficult to tolerate. The young school teacher and any therapist who became involved would have to be careful lest these strong, conflicting feelings were projected onto them in turn.

Both the individual children at the centre of it all and the family around them are surrounded by the wider 'family' of the professional and voluntary services. Such services have their own internal and external dynamics that may reflect and reinforce the dynamics at every other level, helping or hindering in the process (Shooter, 2005).

Service system models

In both Anne-Marie's and Damian's situations, there is real or potential conflict between the services: between general practitioner, paediatricians and therapist over the nature of Anne-Marie's depression and what is needed in the way of treatment, and between school and therapist over how to treat Damian's behaviour. Such conflict could easily have compounded the rows in Anne-Marie's family and her own internal ambivalence. In Damian's case, living in such poor socio-economic circumstances, aggravated by rejection all round, he would have had to be pretty 'mad', you might think, not to behave in the way that he does.

Such conflict often revolves around the issue of risk. This is understandable in the litigious society in which we live and work, but we seldom agree on the degree of risk presented, the level of deprivation or danger against which we are seeking to protect the child, or even their definition (Department of Health, 2003). Damian's is a classic case of disadvantage, and yet the local authority social services have been prevented from becoming involved, it seems, by difficulties over 'proving' individual neglect in the midst of social chaos. The emotions within Anne-Marie's house are certainly abusive, and just as damaging in the long term as physical or sexual assault, but the local authority would have been loath to intervene in a middle-class, professional family. At some level, the services' helplessness has tuned into the helplessness of the children themselves.

All these models, both biological and psychodynamic, are based on a perception of illness, of things having gone wrong, of the vulnerability of the children involved, of the need for treatment of some sort to be delivered by services to passive recipients, whether they want it or not. But there is a different way of seeing situations even as dire as those of Anne-Marie and Damian: a model of mental health. How can we seek out and build on the natural resilience of children and help them to realise the potential they will retain, however deeply it may be buried beneath the horrors of what they are going through?

Models of mental health

Normally, a child's well-being is the product of healthy individual development within a sympathetic environment. Physical maturation is matched by the successful completion of cognitive, emotional, social and spiritual 'tasks' appropriate to each age group and described by such writers as Piaget, Erikson and Fowler. This is empowered by good relationships with family, peers and community, in a mutually reinforcing cycle. From it, the mentally healthy child emerges with a clear sense of identity and self-worth, effective problem-solving skills, motivational drive, the ability to recognise, label and manage his or her own emotions, and a respect for the feelings of others – the 'theory of mind' that children on the autistic spectrum find so difficult to master.

Children have a right to such self-fulfillment; it is the responsibility of adults to uphold this right, to free the children from the burdens that might weigh down their lives, and to encourage their talents to flourish. Anne-Marie showed great academic potential when she attended school regularly, and had a small but close circle of friends for which no Facebook/MySpace virtual contacts in the loneliness of her bedroom could ever be a substitute. Damian's talents would have been more difficult to uncover, but his teacher was able to find at least one, his artistic ability. Once encouraged in this, no doubt others would have emerged too. The school's task would be to avoid excluding such children, to protect them from the bullying that is so often inflicted on young carers like Anne-Marie (Crabtree & Warner, 1999) or children from poor homes like Damian, and build up and on their self-respect.

But the services are made up of people who may themselves need help before they can help others. Thus, the role of schools in promoting the well-being of their pupils has been central to the drive towards 'emotional literacy', to the PSE (personal and social education) and SEAL (social and emotional aspects of learning) programmes based on it, and to the *Every Child Matters* agenda (Department for Education and Skills, 2004). But this comes at the point where schools have been led to believe that their success will be judged on numbers of exam passes, and more holistic approaches have been stripped from their training. Unless teachers are themselves freed from this academic strait-jacket, troublesome children like Anne-Marie and Damian will not be in school to benefit from anything.

Similarly, there is no shortage of advice to social workers about how to handle the difficult behaviour of disadvantaged children, in or out of residential care. They are exhorted to meet such behaviour with understanding of its cause, forgiveness for its effects, an unconditional generosity that expects no reward, and the offer of new ways of expressing feelings that free the children from old battles. But all that is easier said than done by social workers who resent being preached at from the safety of academic ivory towers and may be so ground down by statutory tasks and anxieties that they cannot give quality time to individual clients. Being too busy to bolster a child's self-worth can be a defence against a social worker's own unhappiness: an 'intentional strategy of avoidance' (Anglin, 2002).

In other words, it may be impossible for services to promote the mental health of the children in their care if their own staff do not feel cared for, in turn. Just like parents in embattled families, workers under stress may project their unhappiness onto the children, label the children's behaviour as pathological, and send them off for treatment. Anyone suggesting that such children are basically healthy and that the problem lies in the contexts in which they live might receive short shrift. It may be far more comfortable for their families and services to see Anne-Marie and Damian as ill, whatever the model used, than to work to promote their mental health by examining their own shortcomings.

Implications for practice

The concepts outlined above have many implications for services designed to help children and adolescents. Here are half a dozen of the more important ones. The list is not exclusive and none of them is independent of the rest.

- Mental health problems are caused by many factors, acting together on the vulnerable child. Even where the problem is a clearly defined mental illness with a biological basis and a strong genetic component, that illness will be a product of the susceptibility with which the child is born and the stresses in life to which the child is subjected – nature and nurture. Help therefore needs to combine many approaches in a package tailored to the circumstances of the individual child. None of the theoretical models is an answer in itself. They are merely tools in a kit from which that package can be constructed.

- Ideally, this would require services that are comprehensive in every sense (Kurtz *et al*, 2006). The many different agencies involved with the welfare of children, both professional and voluntary, should act in concert to tackle the particular profile of problems in their area. They should be jointly commissioned, jointly resourced and jointly implemented. They should be universal in scope, rather than targeted at particular problem groups in a way that so often fails to reach children like Anne-Marie and Damian. And they should offer support to the whole trajectory of a vulnerable child's life. Too often, services become involved at flashpoints, then disappear again when the immediate crisis is over.

- There are good grounds for believing that there is a spectrum of mental health among the UK's 11 million children and adolescents, stretching from those who are mentally healthy, to the one-fifth who develop problems sufficient to interfere with the normal enjoyment of their life, to the one-half of that one-fifth who go on to develop frank mental disorders identifiable by any system of classification (Green *et al*, 2005). If there is a flow from one end of that spectrum to the other, it would make sense for services to put most of their effort into preventing problems arising in the first place, or at least into stopping them getting worse, rather than 'firefighting' disorders once they occur.

- This might be done by building upon the child's active strength and resilience, their mental health, rather than waiting for them to become the passive recipients of service help, and that might need a clarification of our attitudes to risk. Obviously, there should be clear and rapid channels of protection for those at risk of harm in all its guises, from the oppressive sterility and distorted expectations of Anne-Marie's family to the neglectful chaos of Damian's home and community. But children will not develop healthily unless they are allowed to take proper risks in their life, through play and experiment (Jennings, 2005).

- Having said all this, recent reports have warned that mental health problems in children and adolescents seem to be increasing, and that we are responding to them with little more than medication. Some of this may be a reflection of social inequalities: the gap between the haves and have-nots of this world is as wide as ever (Dorling *et al*, 2007). But the definition of deprivation covers Anne-Marie just as much as Damian. The UK is simply the least happy of all the world's 21 richest nations (UNICEF, 2007) in which to be brought up as a child. The remedy for that lies in public, press and political attitudes to children, not services.

- Children have a right to a voice and to have that voice heard in the design and practice of anything that affects their life (UNICEF, 1992). Nowhere is this more vital than in child and adolescent mental health services. Their views of what they want from such services may be very different from what adults feel they need. And such services, after all, rely on the co-operation of those they care for. Perhaps we as a society should ask ourselves if we really like children, if we respect their views, or if we would prefer children to be seen but not heard. If children feel unvalued for their own sake, we can hardly be surprised if they find their own sense of self-worth in behaviours society rejects, such as teenage pregnancy and gang culture.

All these issues, and more, will be examined in later chapters of this book.

References

Aldridge J, Becker S (2005) *Children caring for parents with mental illness*. Bristol: Policy Press.

Anglin JP (2002) *Pain, normality and the struggle for congruence*. New York: Haworth Press.

Butler G, Hope T (2007) *Manage your mind: the mental fitness guide*. Oxford: Oxford University Press.

Crabtree H, Warner L (1999) *Too much to take on*. London: Princess Royal Trust for Carers.

Department for Education and Skills (2004) *Every child matters: next steps*. Nottingham: DfES Publications.

Department of Health (2003) *The Victoria Climbié inquiry: report of an inquiry by Lord Laming*. London: The Stationery Office. www.victoria-climbie-inquiry.org.uk/finreport/finreport.htm (accessed November 2007).

Dorling D, Rigby J, Wheeler B, Ballas D, Thomas B, Fahmy E, Gordon D, Lupton R (2007) *Poverty, wealth and place in Britain, 1968 to 2005*. Bristol: Policy Press.

Freeth R (2007) *Humanising psychiatry and mental health care*. Oxford: Radcliffe Publishing.

Goodman R, Scott S (1997) *Child psychiatry* (chapter 5: Hyperactivity). Oxford: Blackwell Science.

Green H, McGinnity A, Meltzer H, Ford T, Goodman R (2005) *Mental health of children and young people in Great Britain, 2004*. Basingstoke: Palgrave Macmillan.

Jennings S (2005) *Creative play with children at risk*. Brackley: Speechmark Publishing.

Kurtz Z, Lavis P, Miller L, Street C (2006) *Developing comprehensive CAMHS: a guide*. London: YoungMinds.

Nutt D (2007) Medication. In: Persaud R (ed) *The mind: a user's guide*. London: Royal College of Psychiatrists/Bantam Press.

Shooter M (2005) Children and adolescents who have chronic physical illness. In: Williams R, Kerfoot M (eds) *Child and adolescent mental health services: strategy, planning, delivery and evaluation*. Oxford: Oxford University Press.

Smith M (2006) Early interventions with young children and their parents in the UK. In: McAuley C, Pecora P, Rose W. *Enhancing the well-being of children and families through effective interventions: international evidence for practice*. London: Jessica Kingsley.

Thornicroft G (2006) *Shunned: discrimination against people with mental illness*. Oxford: Oxford University Press.

UNICEF (2007) *Child poverty in perspective: an overview of child well-being in rich countries*. Florence: UNICEF Innocenti Research Centre.

UNICEF (1992) *United Nations Convention on the Rights of the Child*. www.unicef.org/crc (accessed November, 2007).

Whittington CJ, Kendall T, Fonagy P, Cottrell D, Cotgrove A, Boddington E (2004) Selective serotonin reuptake inhibitors in childhood depression: systematic review of published versus unpublished data. *Lancet* **363**: 1342–1345.

Williams C (2007) Cognitive behavioural therapy. In: Persaud R (ed) *The mind: a user's guide*. London: Royal College of Psychiatrists/Bantam Press.

YoungMinds (2006) *Looking after your mental health*. Information sheet. London: YoungMinds.

YoungMinds (2007) *No health without mental health*. Annual report 2006–2007. London: YoungMinds.

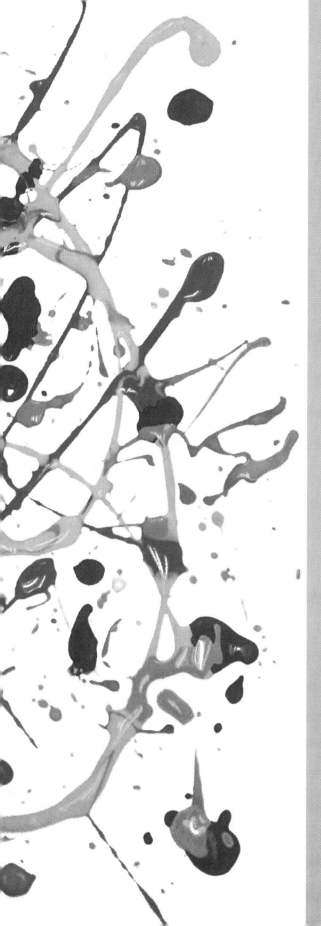

Child and adolescent mental health service (CAMHS) structures and policy

Paula Lavis

Key points

- Child and adolescent mental health services are organised in four tiers, ranging from interventions in primary care through to specialist inpatient services

- CAMHS provision is governed by the standards in the National Service Framework for Children, Young People and Maternity Services

- Government policy requires the co-ordination and collaboration of all public service sectors concerned with children and young people's well-being

- In England the *Children's Plan* recognises the rights of children to develop to their best potential

- The *Children's Plan* states the need to shape health services around the needs of children and young people, not around professional roles and boundaries.

Key words
Government policy; CAMHS; National Service Framework; Children's Plan; Joint working

This chapter will briefly describe how child and adolescent mental health services (CAMHS) are structured, and outline relevant policy concerning children's mental health and well-being in England and Wales.

CAMHS refers to the range of services available within a specific area that provide support and treatment to children and young people who are experiencing mental health difficulties. Sometimes the term 'comprehensive CAMHS' is used, and has the same meaning, in that it describes every service and agency that provides a service that contributes to the mental health and well-being of a child or young person.

CAMHS is also widely used to refer to the specialist team of mental health professionals, often led by a consultant child psychiatrist, who work with children and young people with mental health problems. This group is also referred to as specialist CAMHS.

The concept of CAMHS was first described in the now seminal NHS Advisory Service report *Together We Stand* (Williams & Richardson, 1995). CAMHS are structured in four tiers of provision:

- **Tier 1** – universal services provided by GPs, health visitors, Sure Start, voluntary organisations, teachers
- **Tier 2** – services provided by professionals working in primary care – for example, paediatricians, educational psychologists, primary mental health workers
- **Tier 3** – specialised multidisciplinary teams who deal with more severe, complex and persistent problems
- **Tier 4** – highly specialised services, ie. inpatient units.

There have been some misconceptions about the tiered model: that children enter at Tier 1 and work up towards Tier 4, for example. In fact, a child may require services from more than one tier simultaneously, and Tier 1 workers might be supported by workers from Tier 2 or 3.

Despite devolution, all four countries of the UK still refer to the tiered model in their CAMHS policy documents. There has been some variation in how this framework has been developed and applied across the UK, but it has created a common language for describing and commissioning services.

Government policy – England
National Service Framework
The new model of comprehensive CAMHS provision is set out in the National Service Framework for Children, Young People and Maternity Services (NSF), published jointly by the Department of Health and the then Department for Education and Skills in 2004. There are 11 standards in all; children's mental health is incorporated into all of the standards, but standard nine is specific to CAMHS

(Department of Health, 2004). An interim report on progress towards standard nine has been published (Department of Health, 2006), as well as a progress report on the NSF as a whole (Shribman, 2007).

Standard nine: the mental and psychological well-being of children and young people

The vision
We want to see:

- An improvement in the mental health of all children and young people.

- Multi-agency services, working in partnership, promote the mental health of all children and young people, provide early intervention and also meet the needs of children and young people with established or complex problems.

- All children, young people and their families have access to mental health care based upon the best available evidence and provided by staff with an appropriate range of skills and competencies.

Standard nine
All children and young people, from birth to their 18th birthday, who have mental health problems and disorders, have access to timely, integrated, high quality, multidisciplinary mental health services to ensure effective assessment, treatment and support, for them and their families.

CAMHS are undergoing a fundamental change. The traditional model of the specialist children's mental health service had hospital-based child psychiatry as its core, with patchily available, multidisciplinary child guidance teams offering community-based provision. The service was viewed, both from within and by others, as a relatively small specialty for a discrete group of children.

The emerging model of comprehensive CAMHS is based on the now established understanding that mental health is an integral part of children's and young people's health, development and well-being, and that CAMHS provision needs to be embedded in a wider range of services for young people. This means that, as well as comprising a range of specialist teams, providers of CAMHS work as part of universal health promotion and prevention programmes, in primary care, in schools and social care, in community child health services, and in targeted provision for vulnerable groups, and draw on a range of training, skills and approaches.

Thus, CAMHS in the 21st century addresses a range of outcomes that are not all purely health-focused, and works within a range of settings, not all of which are concerned with health care. CAMHS are increasingly seen as providing mainstream provision for children:

- as a specialist service that has as its primary function the provision of mental health care to children and young people by those with specialist training
- as a component of universal services for young people that specifically addresses their mental health needs.

Every Child Matters

Another key policy stratum is *Every Child Matters* (ECM) (Department of Health, 2003; 2004). This is a cross-government initiative, led by the Department for Children, Schools and Families (DCSF), which aims to build services around the needs of children and young people. This programme conceptualises outcomes for children across five domains:

- be healthy
- stay safe
- enjoy and achieve
- make a positive contribution
- achieve economic well-being.

The contribution of CAMHS to all five ECM domains is increasingly acknowledged: for example, it is recognised that early intervention with children with mental health problems can improve their educational attainment and ultimately their ability to achieve economic well-being.

Children's trusts

Children's trusts are a key feature of the government's partnership agenda for children's well-being. They were introduced in response to Lord Laming's report of the inquiry into the death of Victoria Climbié (Department of Health, 2003), which highlighted the importance of better working together and communication. Children's trusts are not new organisations. They have been created to address the fragmentation of responsibilities for children's services and bring together all the services and agencies in a locality that are concerned with children's well-being. They build upon, bring together and formalise the joint work that is already taking place in many local areas.

Local authorities are required by the Children Act 2004 to have in place arrangements that produce integrated working at all levels, from planning through to delivery, with a focus on improving outcomes. Local authorities may choose not to call this a 'children's trust', but the important point is that the way of working is in place and there is commitment to it. The Joint Planning and Commissioning Framework for Children, Young People and Maternity Services, published by the then Department for Education and Skills and Department of Health in March 2006, sets out a framework to help children's trusts move towards a comprehensive and integrated system of support for children, young people and their families. It is expected that services for children and young people and maternity services will increasingly be commissioned from pooled resources, including finances, capital and staff (the Children Act 2004 includes a new enabling power to pool budgets).

CAMHS provision

The current Public Service Agreement (PSA) on child and adolescent health and well-being (HM Government, 2007), which extends to 2009, highlights the following as priorities:

- development and delivery of CAMHS for children and young people with learning disabilities
- appropriate accommodation and support for 16/17 year olds
- availability of 24-hour cover to meet urgent mental health needs
- joint commissioning of early intervention support.

From 2009 the intention is to replace these measures of public sector performance with the 'value added' score from the Strengths and Difficulties Questionnaire (SDQ), to enable CAMHS to measure the success of their work by improvements in children's mental and emotional well-being. Broader measure of children's emotional well-being will also be gained through a number of questions in the Tellus 2 national survey of children and young people's views.

In line with overall government policy, the 2007 PSA requires other partners to play their part.

- Strategic health authorities (SHAs)/government offices are to:
  - promote effective practice, facilitate cross-sector working and provide intensive support for areas.

- Primary care trusts (PCTs) and local authorities are to:
  - identify co-ordinated actions to promote mental health and early intervention in universal and mainstream services and develop more targeted support services and CAMH services in PCTs' local plans, the Children and Young People's Plan, and, where appropriate, the local area agreement
  - commission comprehensive CAMHS through robust joint strategic needs analysis as part of their remit within the CAMHS Partnership Board
  - identify and address the needs of vulnerable groups such as children in care
  - performance manage delivery of community-based and specialist CAMHS.

- Children's centres are to:
  - recruit and retain vulnerable parents and support their emotional well-being
  - identify and offer additional support for children displaying early signs of mental health problems, including early intervention group work and referral to more specialist services.

- Schools (including Healthy Schools) are to:
  - implement the Social and Emotional Aspects of Learning (SEAL) programme by 2012 (all primary schools and 50% of secondary schools)
  - promote children's emotional well-being and early intervention work for those children and young people at risk of experiencing mental health problems
  - increase numbers of schools delivering school-based mental health support.

The Children's Plan

This document, published late in 2007, sets out a new, 10-year strategic plan for how government will develop all children's services, including CAMHS (Department for Children, Schools & Families, 2007).

The following five principles underpin the Children's Plan:

- government does not bring up children – parents do, so government needs to do more to support parents and families
- all children have the potential to succeed and should go as far as their talents can take them
- children and young people need to enjoy their childhood as well as grow up prepared for adult life
- services need to be shaped by and responsive to children, young people and families, not designed around professional boundaries
- it is always better to prevent failure than tackle a crisis later.

With regards to CAMHS, the Children's Plan sets out the government's intention to review existing CAMHS provision, improve collaboration between the NHS and schools and other agencies around children and young people's mental and emotional health, increase the number of specialist CAMHS beds for those with greatest need, and end the inappropriate use of adult psychiatric wards for children and young people aged under 16 (as required by the Mental Health Act 2007), and issue statutory guidance for health services and local authorities on how they should improve the health of children in care, including their mental health.

Government policy – Wales

The policy agenda in Wales is similar to England, but Wales has its own CAMHS strategy, *Everybody's Business*, published in September 2001, which sets out its plans to develop CAMHS (National Assembly for Wales, 2001). The Welsh Assembly Government also has a holistic understanding of CAMHS, and uses the term to refer to all services that involve or affect the mental health of children and young people. A core principle of their approach is: 'That no sector or component of a sector should be absolved from playing its full part in CAMHS.'

In 2004, the Welsh Assembly Government published its own National Service Framework for Children, Young People and Maternity Services (Welsh Assembly

Government, 2005). The standards concerning children's mental health state:

'Children and young people have equitable access to a comprehensive range of services according to assessed needs, delivered in a co-ordinated manner.'

'Children and young people with identified mental health problems or disorders receive services to meet their needs which are timely, effective and co-ordinated.'

Conclusion

Children's mental health remains high on the national policy agenda in England and Wales. There is an increasing understanding that the emotional well-being of adults is laid down in childhood, and that children's emotional and mental well-being requires input in every aspect of their lives – from parents, schools, health services and local authorities, working in partnership across all agencies and sectors.

This chapter draws heavily on Kurtz Z, Lavis P, Miller L, Street C (2006) Developing comprehensive CAMHS: a guide. London: YoungMinds.

References

Department for Children, Schools and Families (2007) *The Children's Plan: building brighter futures.* London: Department for Children, Schools and Families.

Department for Education and Skills (2003) *Every child matters* (green paper). London: The Stationery Office.

Department for Education and Skills (2004) *Every child matters: change for children.* London: The Stationery Office.

Department for Education and Skills/Department of Health (2006) *Joint planning and commissioning framework for children, young people and maternity services.* London: Department for Education and Skills.

Department of Health (2003) *The Victoria Climbié inquiry: report of an inquiry by Lord Laming.* London: The Stationery Office.

Department of Health (2004) *The mental health and psychological well-being of children and young people. Standard nine of the national service framework for children, young people and maternity services.* London: Department of Health.

Department of Health (2006) *Promoting the mental health and psychological well-being of children and young people: report on the implementation of standard nine of the NSF for children, young people and maternity services.* London: Department of Health.

Department of Health/Department for Education and Skills (2004) *National service framework for children, young people and maternity services.* London: The Stationery Office.

HM Government (2007) *PSA delivery agreement 12: improve the health and wellbeing of children and young people.* London: HM Treasury.

National Assembly for Wales (2001) *Child and adolescent mental health services. Everybody's business: strategy document.* Cardiff: National Assembly for Wales.

Shribman S (2007) *Children's health, our future: a review of progress against the national service framework for children, young people and maternity services 2004.* London: Department of Health.

Welsh Assembly Government (2005) *National service framework for children, young people and maternity services in Wales.* Cardiff: Welsh Assembly Government.

Williams R, Richardson G (eds) (1995) *Together we stand: the commissioning, role and management of child and adolescent mental health services. An NHS Health Advisory Service (HAS) thematic review.* London: HMSO.

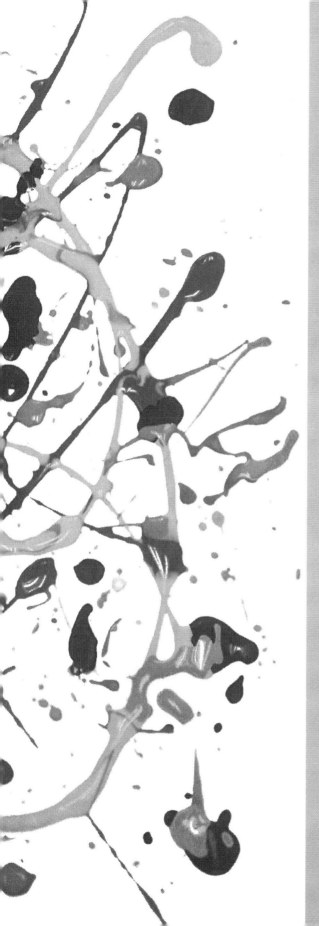

Working together for children's mental health

Roger Catchpole

Key points

- Children and young people's mental health is everyone's business

- Joined up, multidisciplinary and multi-agency working is key to successful services for children and young people

- Successful multidisciplinary working requires good management, good leadership, and clarity of purpose

- Leaders may need to learn from martial arts to work with the grain of resistance, to re-align the energy of opposition behind the purpose of the team

- Conflict should be seen not as an obstacle but as an untapped resource waiting to be harnessed.

Key words

Multidisciplinary; Multi-agency; Inter-professional practice; Leadership; Resistance

The national policy message could not be much clearer: our objective in child and adolescent mental health is an integrated, joined up, multidisciplinary and multi-agency service. Children's mental health is everybody's business, and all practitioners have a role to play in a co-ordinated system of services that promote emotional health and well-being, identify and intervene early where there are problems, and ensure continuing care and treatment for those who are most unwell.

However, the underlying rationale for this approach is sometimes less well articulated; practice-based evidence of how to work together more effectively is only slowly emerging. This chapter looks briefly at what is expected of services for children and young adults in terms of working together, and in more depth at why this is so important and how we can get better at inter-professional practice.

Every Child Matters: Change for children (Department for Education and Skills, 2004) describes a 'shared national programme of change', including the improvement and integration of universal services in early years settings, schools and the health service, alongside the development of a 'shared sense of responsibility across agencies for safeguarding children and protecting them from harm'. The National Service Framework for Children, Young People and Maternity Services (Department of Health, 2004) identifies a range of areas requiring multi-agency working, including, but not exclusively, children in care, youth justice services, paediatric liaison, early intervention for psychosis, highly complex and challenging young people, and services for black and minority ethnic groups.

Mental health and well-being are intrinsic to the five outcomes that are at the core of current policy towards children and were given statutory force in the Children Act 2004. These are: being healthy; staying safe; enjoying and achieving; making a positive contribution, and achieving economic well-being (Department for Education and Skills, 2004). Each of the outcomes is underpinned by good mental health, and each has the potential to contribute to achieving and maintaining good mental health. Success in relation to the five outcomes is not about achieving improvement in any one domain alone, but about a more holistic approach to understanding and meeting children's needs. The challenge is to find ways to support children and young people to develop physically, psychologically, emotionally, educationally, socially and spiritually. Since each dimension impacts on the others, it is a comprehensive model, requiring a comprehensive system of universal and targeted services, working towards the same outcomes. But this is a radical idea that creates real challenges in practice.

Experience tells us that working together is difficult, and that getting better at it takes time, discipline and a willingness to challenge sometimes deeply held beliefs and long established ways of working. In mental health, perhaps more than any other area, there are powerful factors that can inhibit us from taking shared responsibility for outcomes. Mental health is a contentious (and much misunderstood) term, and what we mean by it remains the subject of debate between the disciplines. That debate, well facilitated, can be a key part of creating the foundations for effective working together, but often our differences are played out in less constructive ways.

Ultimately, mental health is something that we all have a personal involvement in – we all have mental health. That can be a basis for common ground and shared understanding, but it can also touch on deep and distressing territory. Our own level of mental health is central to our ability to promote emotional well-being and provide support for children in need, but different disciplines, agencies and institutions have very different cultures when it comes to acknowledging this and working with it. Accepting that our own mental health is a legitimate, indeed essential, element in the mix can be challenging.

Perhaps we should not be surprised, then, that inter-professional practice in children's mental health remains 'work in progress'. We can allow ourselves to be frustrated by the distance we have yet to travel, or we can celebrate how far we have come. This chapter suggests that a fuller understanding of how we got here and some reflection on what has helped or hindered the journey to date is what is now needed.

Why working together?

The post-war development of the welfare state was based on an analysis that identified significant barriers to social change, and sought to put in place services to overcome them. There was a problem called 'disease', and the solution was to create a national health service. There was a problem called 'ignorance', and, if we could build a good enough education system, that could be solved. A similar approach to 'idleness', 'squalor' and 'want' saw the introduction of unemployment benefit, and vocational training, public and environmental health and housing services, and the social security system. But these were specific, largely self-contained responses to identified problems. The key agencies, locally and nationally, were established to tackle specific problems and were, perhaps inevitably, problem focused.

As professionals, we have tended to specialise in our particular problems: a child's physical health, her family circumstances, the inadequate housing she and her family live in, the fact that she is having problems in school or that she is in trouble with the police. We developed our skills in working with our specific problem, based our approach on our theoretical understanding of it, and built a professional identity and status that was distinct from those of colleagues in other agencies. And we perpetuated that way of working for 50 years. We did not, and were not expected to, talk to our colleagues in other agencies and disciplines, much less seek to achieve a shared understanding of children's needs, or discover ways of working together.

We did things to, or at best for, children and families, and, although we focused on the child who was our concern, it tended to be through our educational lens or our health care lens or our social work lens. While this produced a very detailed picture of part of the child, it usually failed to see the whole child or to recognise the value of other practitioners' pictures.

Of course, these are broad generalisations. Deep down we all knew that families' experience of disadvantage was multi-factorial, and that the connections between our services were important. When this realisation started to be articulated through social exclusion theory, the stage was set for a paradigm shift. If poverty, poor educational achievement, poor physical health and low levels of mental health and well-being were mutually reinforcing, then policy makers and practitioners looking to bring about improvement in any of these dimensions had to look to more co-ordinated interventions, involving a number of agencies and services.

Individuals can and do make a difference in children's lives, but on our own none of us can be fully effective in meeting children's mental health needs. To come together in a collaborative and co-ordinated network of services – a truly comprehensive child and adolescent mental health service, for example – we may have to be prepared to make some significant changes in our thinking and our practice, and be prepared to let go of some cherished ideas.

What enables working together?

Research (for example, Atkinson *et al*, 2002) has highlighted a range of important issues that need to be addressed for multi-agency working to be effective. These include:

- a clear vision
- a common understanding of purpose and aims
- leadership
- clarity about roles
- clear systems and procedures
- access to appropriate resources
- attention to team development
- training.

Research on multidisciplinary teams also suggests a number of factors that contribute to their success or failure (a good overview can be found in Leathard, 2000). Most of these issues fall into two broad categories. Some refer directly to the management process – that is, the deployment of physical and human resources, systems and procedures. Others refer to what can be defined as the function of leadership – holding of vision, clarity of purpose and aims, and the capacity to engage team members effectively in working on a task that meets that purpose and vision.

YoungMinds' experience demonstrates time and time again that the majority of difficulties experienced in multi-agency and/or multidisciplinary working can be traced back to a lack of clarity of vision and purpose. This focus on vision and purpose is crucial if leaders are going to lead with authority from a firm base. It enables leaders to deal with the inevitable differences and conflicts that emerge when human beings interact with each other in performing a joint task. Indeed, a team is usually defined as 'a group of people working together towards a common purpose'. That common purpose cannot be assumed, and must be consistently reiterated. In the case of children's mental health, the common purpose must be built on a child-centred approach.

Purpose is more than a goal or an objective. It is the reason why a team, or other system, exists. Purpose is a systemic concept. It can only be understood in relation to a group or institution's active engagement with their context. Purpose describes the final outcome of the process through which that active engagement takes place. A statement of purpose seeks to put into the public domain what the system is doing to contribute to the health and well-being of the community within which it exists. Because human beings bring their whole selves (hands, hearts and minds) to the system they work in, the system's purpose enables those internal resources of energy to be made available and aligned creatively, with the result that the whole can become greater than the sum of the parts.

Rawson (2000) identifies two distinct versions of the effects of inter-professional teamwork: the additive effect, and the multiplicative effect. In the former, individual contributions are simply added together. The input of the school staff is added to the input of, for example, the social worker and the primary mental health worker (PMHW). At best, the total output will be the sum of those individual contributions. What's more, there is a real danger of cancelling out and/or duplication, with the result that the actual achievement is less than the sum of the parts. In the multiplicative model, 'efforts are combined to achieve more than is possible by simply adding contributions together'. Multidisciplinary work generates creativity and new potential, and releases untapped resources. In this case, the school staff, the social worker and the PMHW, working together, generate an output that is both quantitatively and qualitatively different from what any of them could achieve alone. However, in this model the danger is that attempts to work together can become not multiplicative but literally divisive, resulting in fragmentation and unproductive conflict. It is the understanding and application of purpose that make the difference.

A shared understanding of purpose is a necessary condition if a team is to survive. To be effective, teams must identify and work on tasks that serve the shared purpose. This requires access to resources, and a system that does not have a purpose will die, because the context will not make available the resources necessary for its survival. A team has to convince its context that it has something of value to offer. Without a statement of purpose that is widely understood, within the team and within the context, leadership and management cannot be offered in ways that maximise the potential of a team. Members cannot take up roles that serve the purpose of the team while that purpose remains undefined or poorly understood. Within the comprehensive CAMHS, finding purpose requires ongoing dialogue about the nature of mental health and well-being in children and the development of a common language through which to articulate shared accounts of children's needs.

Systems need to be sensitive to questions of humanity. Teams are groups of people, and the context within which a team operates is made up of people. In order to sustain purpose, teams need to pay attention to the needs, perceptions, motivations and feelings of people within the team, and within the wider context. Unless this happens, the team will not win the hearts and minds of those who work within it, and it will not convince people in the context that it has anything to offer them. Because the personnel may change over time, and because the needs, perceptions, motivations and feelings of the people involved may also change over time, it is necessary to continually work at purpose. Each change in the team or in the context requires new effort to sustain the shared understanding of purpose that is vital to the life of the team.

Clarity of purpose is a defining characteristic of a team. It can also be a challenge to others. In situations where radical change is required – for example, in creating a comprehensive CAMHS – having a purpose can be seen as an act of defiance: defiance of elements in the surrounding culture that militate against establishing something shared and multi-agency. Sometimes deliberately and sometimes unwittingly, many forces will resist, subvert or obstruct the attempt to work collaboratively to a shared purpose. Professional or territorial rivalries, attempts to conceal lack of competence in specific areas, and previous unproductive attempts at working together are all examples of such forces.

The principle, found in many martial arts, of working with the force of opposition and deflecting or redirecting that force may be of value here. Multidisciplinary teams encounter resistance both from their members within and from the wider context, precisely because they represent an attempt to do things differently. A head-on challenge to powerful and long-established ways of thinking and behaving may succeed, but is likely to bruise and damage all involved. The critical challenge for leaders is to develop their capacity to work with the grain of resistance, understanding the origins and drivers of the opposition they face and finding ways to re-align that energy behind the purpose of the team. Understanding why, for example, a teacher may be reluctant to use consultation offered by a Tier 3 service allows the team to anticipate the resistance and position itself (through its actions) to redirect that opposition in a more positive direction. A similar approach is essential to engaging with families who may have a range of reasons why they are reluctant for their child to attend an appointment with a mental health service.

Purpose is a tool for action. It enables people to find, make and take up roles, and it liberates people to use interpersonal dynamics as a resource, not a focus (see, for example, Reed, 2000). It authorises them both to give and take leadership. In the absence of a shared understanding of purpose, a team is likely to remain a fragmented group of people locked in interpersonal struggles and unable to 'make a difference'.

Finding purpose is an iterative process. As members of the team start to come together, they will bring with them experience of their agency and discipline, its understanding of child-centred work, its priorities and practices. As team members are enabled to share and reflect on that experience and begin to work with the realities of providing a service, purpose can be built. As teams begin to analyse the new context within which they are operating, and to understand more fully the needs of children in that context, a shared and robust sense of purpose will begin to grow. Reflection is key to this process; understanding the real meaning of team members' experiences in working with children and families will enable them to find, make and take up roles. Crudely, we learn how to get better at working together by working together and then reflecting on that experience.

Many multidisciplinary teams seem to reach a position where all the members of the team are taking up generic functions, as if all members of the team are the same. The desire to reduce members of multidisciplinary teams to sameness seems to be about trying to avoid conflict, but in fact produces conflict in a way that makes it difficult to manage. If a multidisciplinary team loses sight of the importance of sensitivity to difference in responding to the needs of children and families, then it no longer meets its fundamental purpose. Instead, it offers a watered-down approach that is likely to be less useful than the depth and breadth derived from creative interdisciplinary discussion and dialogue over differences in approaches to meeting children's needs.

Often teams only pay half-hearted attention to the purpose of the operation. This may be because discussion of purpose and vision is complex and difficult, and can stir up feelings of discomfort and disquiet. The desire to avoid or eliminate conflict seems to predominate, which in many ways causes some of the difficulties in thinking about the purpose and vision. And yet it can be argued that conflict is one of the most exciting, free resources that exist in any team. Conflict occurs naturally; we do not have to do anything to get it, and it is present wherever human beings interact and try to reach agreement as to how they can collectively move forward with a task.[1] Reality TV surely demonstrates this point.

This means that we need to re-frame the way we think about conflict, to stop seeing it as something to be avoided, and to embrace it as an untapped resource waiting to be harnessed. Conflict can then be understood as something that is representative of the differences in people's beliefs about the most appropriate way forward in a particular situation. It challenges individuals to remain curious, rather than becoming angry because someone holds a different view. The capacity to be

---

[1] This idea developed out of joint work between YoungMinds and the Grubb Institute. The approach of the Grubb Institute can be explored in papers available at www.grubb.org.uk.

curious about why different people hold different views opens up the potential that, through dialogue, we may discover that no single person holds the absolute truth. Through sharing our differences we may be able to move to a new understanding of the appropriate way to manage a particular issue – a complex and risky process.

Conclusion

There are excellent examples in parts of England of teams and individuals working together within a comprehensive CAMHS. The policy framework requires it, and children and families have a right to expect it. It is naïve, however, to assume that change on the scale envisaged will just happen. Integrated structures, co-location and other changes can help, but in the end the challenge is to find ways to release the energy and capacity locked up within individuals and discrete services. At the root of that challenge is clarity about vision and purpose, discovered and constructed locally through the experience of working together and learning from that experience.

References

Atkinson M, Wilkin A, Stott A, Doherty P, Kinder K (2002) *Multi-agency working: a detailed study.* LGA Research report 26. Slough: NFER.

Department for Education and Skills (2004) *Every child matters: change for children.* London: Department for Education and Skills.

Department of Health (2004) *National service framework for children, young people and maternity services.* London: Department of Health.

Leathard A (2000) *Going inter-professional: working together for health and welfare.* London: Routledge.

Rawson D (2000) Models of inter-professional work: likely theories and possibilities. In: Leathard A (ed) *Going inter-professional: working together for health and welfare.* London: Routledge.

Reed BD (2000) *An exploration of role.* London: Grubb Institute.

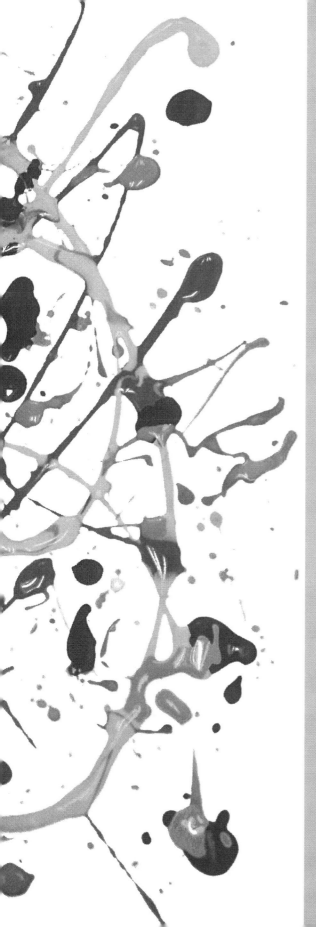

Delivering accessible and culturally competent services

Cathy Street

Key points

- Adults from black and minority ethnic communities living in the UK experience disproportionate rates of mental illness

- They also experience significant barriers to accessing services, including culturally inappropriate models of diagnosis and provision, language barriers, poor access to primary care services, and stigma

- Research suggests children from BME communities experience similar barriers to accessing services

- CAMHS need to offer accessible, non-stigmatising environments and culturally diverse staff who understand the context in which their young clients live

- CAMHS need to actively engage children and young people and their parents and carers in service design and delivery.

Key words
Cultural competence; Black and minority ethnic communities; Children and young people; Acceptability; Race equality

'Cultural competence is… the capacity to provide effective health and social care, taking into account people's cultural beliefs, behaviours and needs…' (CSIP, 2007a).

We live in an increasingly multicultural society: 7.6% of the UK population (2001 UK census data) are from minority ethnic groups – a total of 4.5 million people. Children and young people from black and minority ethnic (BME) backgrounds make up around 20% of the total population of those aged under 20 (Street *et al*, 2005). On the basis of these figures alone, it is clear that providing child and adolescent mental health services (CAMHS) that are appropriate and acceptable to children, young people and families from different cultures and backgrounds is a key challenge for services.

Unfortunately, there is limited research into the mental health needs of young people from minority ethnic groups, with much of the literature in this field concerning adults. However, this shows that people from minority ethnic groups often experience problems accessing services and, when they do, may have poorer treatment and care experiences than white people. This situation is very powerfully described in *Breaking the Circles of Fear*, a report on adult mental health services published by the Sainsbury Centre for Mental Health (2002), and is acknowledged in the National Institute for Mental Health in England (NIMHE) report *Inside Outside: Improving mental health services for black and minority ethnic communities in England* (NIMHE, 2003). Faced with these compounding factors, the challenges involved in improving service provision for children and young people in BME communities become even more apparent.

The mental health needs of different ethnic groups

Understanding the prevalence of mental illness among different ethnic groups and variations in help-seeking behaviour is widely acknowledged to be a complex issue. Authors such as O'Connor and Nazroo (2002) and Ramchandani (2004) state that caution is needed because many studies are based on very small sample sizes. There is also a lack of consistency in how ethnicity is defined, and studies often use measures of mental health developed from white populations.

An important issue also to bear in mind concerns the meanings given to 'culture' and 'ethnicity', and the crucial distinction between ethnicity as a category and ethnicity as a process through which an individual develops a sense of their identity.

As Malek explains, in a paper presented at a Royal College of Psychiatrists and FOCUS conference in 2001, the concept of ethnicity is not static; it can change over relatively short periods of time, and how it is perceived and defined is influenced by, among other things, social, political, historical and economic circumstances. Individuals can perceive themselves as having a number of different ethnic identities that may be based on sharing a common lifestyle or religion, or their ethnic identity may be informed by a geographical association with a region or country. Malek (2002) makes the important point that:

'As a category, ethnicity has been described as the process by which external categories, such as those used in the census and other ethnic monitoring for example, are created and imposed by others, and with which people so categorised may not necessarily identify. Ethnic categories do not in themselves provide information about identity...'

She also draws attention to the fact there may be differences between generations in terms of the influence of the country of origin and that it is important to think about the stages of the development of cultural identity:

'The particular stage of development an individual is at in this process could be a significant influence in the way in which feelings and emotions are expressed.'

Despite limitations and complexities in the data, however, a variety of studies do indicate that there are clear differences in mental health prevalence rates across ethnic groups, and also in referral routes and treatments offered by mental health services – factors that need to be borne in mind by all who work in or alongside CAMH services.

One of the most authoritative of these studies, the 1999 Office for National Statistics survey of the mental health of children and young people in Great Britain aged 5–16 years (Meltzer *et al*, 2000), found a prevalence of mental health disorders (as defined by ICD-10, the International Classification of Diseases, 10th edition) in nearly 10% of white children and 12% of black children. The survey also revealed important differences between different BME communities. For example, the prevalence rates of mental ill health among Asian children were eight per cent for children of Pakistani and Bangladeshi origin, but four per cent for those from India.

In other important studies, very high rates of mental health disorder have been found among young refugee and asylum seekers. Leavey and colleagues (2004) found rates as high as 40–50% in some groups. Other research has found high suicide rates in young Indian men, and in East African men and women (Raleigh, 1996); that young Asian women have higher rates of suicide compared to other young women (Aldous & Bardsley, 1999), and that rates of self-harm are also of particular concern in this group (Yazdani, 1998).

In addition to research on prevalence rates, we know from other areas of research that young people from black and minority ethnic groups are disproportionately exposed to many of the known 'risk factors' linked with mental health problems. These include being excluded from school, being looked after by the local authority, being involved in offending behaviour, and being homeless.

In Birmingham, for example, a Commission for Racial Equality investigation report found that African-Caribbean pupils were four times more likely to be excluded from school for fewer and less serious offences than white children, and were less likely to later re-enter mainstream education (Ofsted, 2001). Similarly, data on income and job prospects indicate that families from minority ethnic groups fare badly in comparison with white people from the same class, with a resulting increased risk to and adverse impact on children's health and psychological development (Dwivedi, 2002).

Barriers to accessing help

Alongside a growing awareness of the differences in the rates of mental disorders between people from minority ethnic groups and those from white backgrounds, in the last few years the issue of health inequalities – of poor access to, experiences of and outcomes from mental health treatment – has become more prominent.

As mentioned at the start of this chapter, *Breaking the Circles of Fear* (Sainsbury Centre for Mental Health, 2002) played an important role in raising awareness of this issue. As stated in its executive summary:

'Stereotypical views of Black people, racism, cultural ignorance, and the stigma and anxiety often associated with mental illness often combine to undermine the way in which mental health services access and respond to the needs of Black and African-Caribbean communities. When prejudice and the fear of violence influence risk assessment and decisions on treatment, responses are likely to be dominated by a heavy reliance on medication and restriction… Service users become reluctant to ask for help, or to comply with treatment, increasing the likelihood of a personal crisis, leading in some cases to self-harm or harm to others. In turn, prejudices are reinforced and provoke even more coercive responses…'

The report found that not only were black service users not treated with respect and their voices not heard, but services were not accessible, welcoming, relevant or well-integrated within the community for which they were meant to be providing. Likewise, primary care was seen to be limited, service user, family and carer involvement was lacking, and black-led community initiatives were not valued; nor, crucially, were they provided with secure funding on which to build capacity in the longer term.

Similar concerns are expressed in *Inside Outside* (NIMHE, 2003), which famously found the NHS mental health services to be 'institutionally racist', and that to change this required:

'… progressive community-based mental health at the centre of service development and delivery. Those who use mental health services are identified, first and foremost, as citizens with mental health needs, which are understood as located in a social and cultural context.'

Inside Outside sets out a range of proposals for addressing these issues that, it notes, will need to be linked up with initiatives aimed at combating discrimination and social exclusion of BME communities in other areas of their lives. While the Department of Health has refused to accept the criticism of institutional racism, its

Delivering Race Equality strategy and action plan, published in 2005 (Department of Health, 2005), adopts many of the *Inside Outside* proposals, as well as some of those put forward in the report of the Inquiry into the death of David (Rocky) Bennett (Blofeld, 2003). In particular, it calls for:

- more appropriate and responsive services
- community engagement of BME communities in the design and delivery of appropriate and accessible mental health services, and
- better information about the needs of BME communities.

Barriers facing children and young people

For children and young people from BME groups, we do know from the smaller research field that does exist that some of the barriers that have been identified for adults hold true for children and young people too – not least, the lack of service user involvement, the sense of services not being appropriate or accessible to them, and the fear of the stigma surrounding mental health that can make young people very wary of approaching mental health services. A tendency to only seek help when at crisis point is also apparent.

These were all prominent themes in the *Minority Voices* study undertaken by YoungMinds in 2005 (Street *et al*, 2005). This explored the experiences of young people and their families from a range of different ethnic groups, and also found that many young people:

- had little or no understanding of formal mental health services and how to get themselves referred to them (once they had realised they needed help)
- were very reluctant to talk about their concerns unless it was to someone they knew and trusted
- were deterred by long wait times for appointments, the need to often travel some distance to a service and the inflexibility of service provision in terms of only being open at times that were difficult for young people – for example, at times that clashed with school or college commitments
- encountered difficulties with a lack of interpreting support and a lack of cultural understanding among many staff when they did successfully access a service.

The study also found discontinuity and poor co-ordination of provision: many of the young interviewees described a sense of being 'passed around' between workers and agencies, with no explanation as to why they were being referred on, who they would see, and what would happen. For some, it was apparent that these difficulties, combined with worries about confidentiality, were significant deterrents to their being able to find timely and appropriate help. Some of those aged 16 and above also reported some uncomfortable and disturbing experiences of adult mental health services, and the report highlighted the lack of services for this 'transition' age group as a major concern.

Many of the findings from *Minority Voices* echo those in other studies of young people's perspectives on mental health, including work by the Mental Health Foundation (Smith & Leon, 2001), and an earlier study by YoungMinds, the *Where Next?* study (Street & Svanberg, 2003), which looked at Tier 4 inpatient CAMHS. However, while similar to those reported by young people in general, the *Minority Voices* findings add a specific cultural dimension, in particular in relation to the influence of the local community and of parents (Kurtz & Street, 2006):

'For many young people from BME communities, there are pressures related to inclusion in, and support from, their local community. If they seek help, they may be regarded as "going outside the family". It was suggested by a number of the participants that the stigma of being in contact with mental health services may be particularly marked amongst parents from some minority ethnic backgrounds...'

In addition, several of the interviewees suggested that, in many CAMHS and other mental health services, the limited understanding of the different family dynamics in minority ethnic families can make it hard for professionals to engage with them. As one of the young interviewees told the researchers:

'Asian parents don't understand eating disorder. So white professionals need to be aware of this and the fact that young Asians can't always talk to their parents in the same way that young white people might be able to.'

Interviews with staff working in CAMHS and a range of voluntary sector projects providing support to young people with mental health needs provided further understanding of some of the barriers young people from BME groups may face, not least that:

'... choice in their care, and in who they see, may affect young people from BME groups differently because it is not currently possible for many mental health services to offer a choice of staff from different cultural backgrounds.' (Kurtz & Street, 2006)

Other service gaps and pressures included services already operating at full capacity and thus being unable to target or promote readier access for young people from BME groups. A significant number reported an inability to offer interventions in any language other than English, and a widespread lack of funds with which to develop and deliver services appropriate to the needs of local BME communities was noted. It was also apparent that staff skills, experience and training in working with young people from BME backgrounds varied considerably, which impacted on staff confidence.

Additionally, some staff and workers highlighted limitations in existing training: in particular, they said that professional mental health training remains very Eurocentric and does not sufficiently address cross-cultural contexts. As one staff interviewee noted:

'More multi-agency working to address the needs of minority ethnic groups needs to be developed. This needs to ensure that there is consistency across agencies so that interventions provided by different agencies are not contradictory, replicated or otherwise inconsistent.'
(Kurtz & Street, 2006)

Assessing cultural competence

To help CAMHS to develop culturally competent provision, in 2007 the National CAMHS Support Services (NCSS) and the Centre for Transcultural Studies at Middlesex University produced a tool for service providers to review their performance in this respect (CSIP, 2007b). The organisational cultural competence self-assessment (OCCA) tool is underpinned by the relevant national initiatives and frameworks, and covers 10 key elements. These include ethnicity monitoring, information and communication, addressing spiritual and religious needs, complaints procedures, service user involvement, and collaboration with other agencies.

Under each element, a number of recommendations draw on best practice in providing culturally competent services, and suggestions are given of the kinds of evidence that might be gathered when reviewing service performance. These include, for example, that all clients are able to communicate with staff in a language they feel comfortable with; that providers of services can respond knowledgeably and appropriately to the individual, social, cultural, religious and other needs of black and minority ethnic users; that there is a commitment to the ongoing development of staff to meet the needs of a diverse local community, and that there are links with organisations representing minority ethnic communities.

While focused on CAMHS, the OCCA tool is a resource on which all who work in mental health and/or children's services can draw when considering how to ensure that the services they provide are based on what we know works for children and young people from the many different minority ethnic groups that make up our current population. Further information about the OCCA tool is available from www.csip.org.uk/~cypf/camhs.html

---

Local good practice

Alongside the interviews with young people and the staff working with them, the *Minority Voices* study mapped current specialist service provision and produced a guide to good practice (Kurtz *et al*, 2005). This showcases 19 services that aim to provide appropriate and accessible services for young people from BME groups.

The service examples given in the guide are all very different and span the different tiers of CAMHS. What they have in common is their focus on being accessible, (many accept self-referrals), their non-stigmatising environments, that the services are provided by a culturally diverse staff group, and that they have the capability and understanding to work within the context in which their young clients live. This latter point is especially important when thinking about what we mean by services that are 'culturally competent', as Malek (2002) explains:

'A lack of understanding about the cultural context within which individuals operate can lead to a number of difficulties. What is seen as normal in one context can come to be seen as abnormal in another. The presenting difficulties may not be recognised unless there is clarity about the cultural context. There may be an unhelpful impact on referral routes, accessibility and appropriateness in the type of service provided.'

Other common attributes of the service examples in the guide include their commitment to actively engage children, young people and their parents and carers, the range of tailored interventions they offer, and their close working with other agencies. The projects used many ways to reach out to young people, including employing bilingual community workers, providing outreach support via local faith groups, and involving young people themselves as advocates and peer supporters.

In terms of developing and providing these services, the *Minority Voices* guide to good practice also emphasises the importance of statutory agencies working closely with BME communities to share knowledge and expertise, that there is a need to develop the cultural competence of the CAMHS workforce, and that expert help needs to be made available in a variety of settings – all themes that reinforce the central message of the Department of Health *Delivering Race Equality* action plan.

Conclusion

Although this is a complex topic and there are significant deficits in current data, recent research gives some useful pointers for how CAMHS might be developed in the future to ensure they are more culturally competent. For commissioners of services, this might include forging new partnerships with voluntary sector organisations that are well-embedded within minority ethnic populations, and supporting the development of new community-based service models. For staff, there are new tools and resources, plus an imperative and support to develop practice that is flexible, works within a young person's context and, perhaps most crucially, promotes the active participation of the young person in the treatment process.

References

Aldous J, Bardsley M (1999) *Refugee health in London: key issues for public health.* London: London Directorate of Public Health and East London/City Health Authority.

Blofeld J (chair) (2003) *Independent inquiry into the death of David Bennett.* Cambridge: Norfolk, Suffolk and Cambridgeshire Strategic Health Authority.

Care Services Improvement Partnership (CSIP) (2007a) *The Papadopoulos, Tilki and Taylor model for developing cultural competence/CAMHS Cultural Competence Tool.* London: Department of Health/CSIP.

Care Services Improvement Partnership (CSIP) (2007b) *CAMHS cultural competence resource tool.* CD-rom of materials including the OCCA tool available from www.csip.org.uk

Department of Health (2005) *Delivering race equality in mental health care: an action plan for reform inside and outside services and the Government's response to the independent inquiry into the death of David Bennett.* London: Department of Health.

Dwivedi K (2002) *Meeting the needs of ethnic minority children.* London: Jessica Kingsley Publishers.

Kurtz Z, Stapelkamp C, Taylor E, Malek M, Street C (2005) *Minority voices: a guide to good practice in planning and providing services for the mental health of black and minority ethnic groups.* London: YoungMinds.

Kurtz Z, Street C (2006) Mental health services for young people from black and minority ethnic backgrounds: the current challenge. *Journal of Children's Services* **1** (3) 40–49.

Leavey G, Hollins K, King M, Barnes J, Papadopoulos C, Grayson K (2004) Psychological disorder amongst refugee and migrant school children in London. *Social Psychiatry and Psychiatric Epidemiology* **39** 191–195.

Malek M (2002) Developing culturally appropriate services. In: FOCUS. *Bridging the gap between policy and practice in child and adolescent mental health services. Conference proceedings.* London: Royal College of Psychiatrists' Research Unit. www.rcpsych.ac.uk/crtu

Meltzer H, Gatward R, Goodman R, Ford T (2000) *The mental health needs of children and adolescents in Great Britain.* London: The Stationery Office.

National Institute for Mental Health in England (NIMHE) (2003) *Inside outside: improving mental health services for black and minority ethnic communities in England.* London: Department of Health.

O'Connor W, Nazroo J (2002) *Ethnic differences in the context and experience of psychiatric illness: a qualitative study.* London: National Centre for Social Research/Department of Epidemiology and Public Health, Royal Free and University College Medical School.

Ofsted (2001) *Improving behaviour and attendance in schools.* London: Ofsted.

Raleigh V (1996) Suicide patterns and trends in people of Indian subcontinent and Caribbean origin in England and Wales. *Ethnicity and Health* **1** (1) 55–63.

Ramchandani P (2004) The epidemiology of mental health problems in children and adolescents from minority ethnic groups in the UK. In: Malek M, Joughin C (eds) *Mental health services for minority ethnic children and adolescents.* London: Jessica Kingsley Publishers.

Sainsbury Centre for Mental Health (2002) *Breaking the circles of fear: a review of the relationship between mental health services and African and Caribbean communities.* London: Sainsbury Centre for Mental Health.

Smith K, Leon L (2001) *Turned upside down: developing community based crisis services for 16–25 year olds experiencing a mental health crisis.* London: Mental Health Foundation.

Street C, Svanberg J (2003) *Where next? New directions in the provision of in-patient mental health services for young people.* London: YoungMinds.

Street C, Stapelkamp C, Taylor E, Malek M, Kurtz Z (2005) *Minority voices: research into the access and acceptability of services for the mental health of young people from black and minority ethnic groups.* London: YoungMinds.

Yazdani A (1998) *Young Asian women and self harm: a mental health needs assessment of young Asian women in Newham, East London.* London: Newham Innercity Multifund/Newham Asian Women's Project.

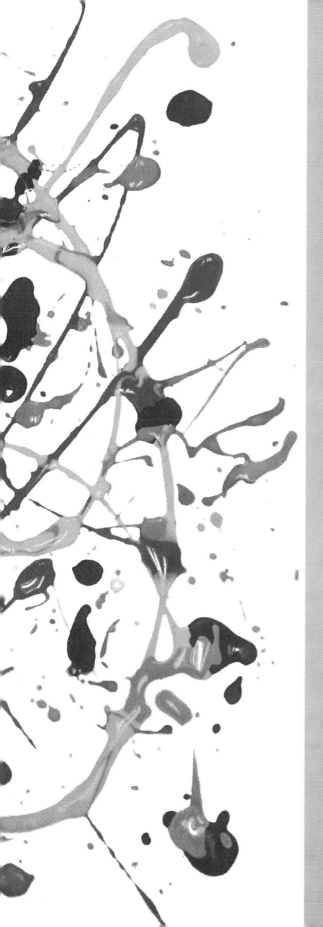

Part II

Infant and maternal mental health

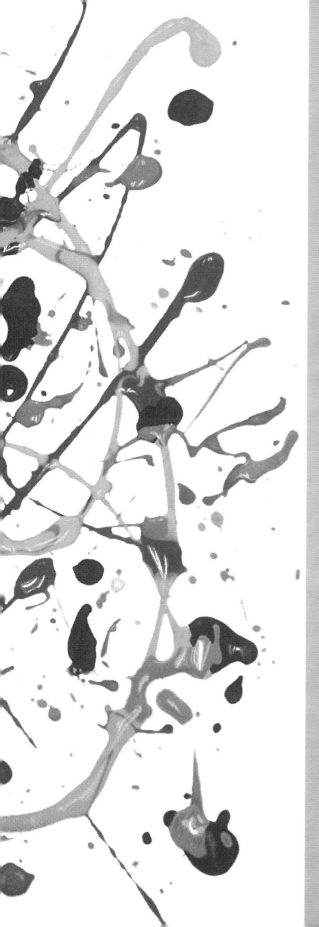

Attachment and infant development

Jane Barlow and Angela Underdown

Key points

- Attachment is essential to the emotional and neurological development of the infant

- The parent(s) or primary caregiver(s) are the most important aspect of the infant's early environment

- Securely attached infants develop the confidence to use the main caregiver as a secure base from which to explore the world

- Insecurely attached infants may limit their explorations of the wider world, or deploy defensive strategies to cope with aroused or disorganised emotional states

- Mothers who are anxious, angry or depressed may not be able to help their baby manage difficult feelings, so they overwhelm the infant.

Key words
Attachment; Containment; Emotional development; Mother–baby interaction; Neglect

If infants are to experience the warm, sensitive relationships that research indicates are necessary for healthy emotional development, we must ensure that parents' roles are acknowledged, understood and properly supported. Although it was once thought that development was a biological unfolding of inherited characteristics, it is now well accepted that environmental experience plays a major part in influencing the way in which the brain develops. The explosion of research into infant mental health has occurred at a time of increasing awareness about the challenges men and women face as they negotiate the transition to parenthood, each influenced both by their own histories and by the dynamic cultural rituals that surround birth and influence the amount of support that can be expected.

The parents or primary caregivers are the most important aspect of the baby's initial environment, and their capacity to support the infant's development is seminal. Less than optimal parenting during this period can have a significant effect on the baby's immediate and long-term development. Supporting parents to provide infants with the best start in life is therefore particularly important. This chapter will describe the infant's neurological and emotional development, the emotional and environmental factors that support this development, and the ways in which their absence can harm the growing infant in these critical early years. The next chapter will look in detail at the range of ways in which services can support successful parenting, so as to ensure children are enabled to reach their full potential.

Early brain development

Although the structural development of the brain is practically complete before birth (Nelson & Bosquet, 2000) much functional development takes place during the brain's growth spurt during the first and second years of life, with a proliferation of nerve pathways conducting electrical messages across fluid filled synapses that rapidly increase (synaptogenesis) in response to interpersonal and intrapersonal experiences. The infant brain over-produces synapses in response to sensory experiences and then 'prunes' away those that are unused, leaving neurons intact and eliminating unused synapses (Kolb & Whishaw, 2001). In addition to the hardwiring of the brain, the early interactions between mother and baby play a significant role in influencing the chemical neurotransmitters that have a direct affect on the brain (eg. neuropeptides such as dopamine), thereby setting the thermostat for later control of the stress response. Excessive stress during infancy results in the baby's brain being flooded by cortisol for prolonged periods, and an eventual lowering of the threshold for activation of fear/anxiety, resulting in the child experiencing more fear/anxiety and difficulty dampening this response (for an overview see Schore, 1994 or Gerhardt, 2004).

The social infant

From the beginning, infants are unique individuals. Close observations (Beebe & Lachman, 2004; Murray & Andrews, 2000) have revealed the many ways in which they influence and respond to their changing environments as they seek interaction with others. It is now accepted that the earliest years of life are a crucial period when infants are making emotional attachments and forming the first relationships that lay many of the foundations for future mental health (Bowlby, 1969; 1988; Stern, 1985; Sroufe, 2005; Steele *et al*, 1996; Fonagy *et al*, 2004). Infants need opportunities to attune to others, to learn to regulate or manage their emotions and behaviour, and to attach to their main carers, who in turn reflect and respond to them as an individual.

The importance of early relationships

The infant experiences a range of states of arousal, and one of the key tasks during the first year of life is learning to manage or regulate his or her own emotions (Sroufe, 1995) and behaviour. Parents play a crucial role in supporting the baby to 'co-regulate' emotional states by responding appropriately so that the infant does not become overwhelmed (Stern, 1985; Sroufe, 1995). Stern (1985) argues that attuned parents are able to act as sensitive moderators or accelerators of infant emotion. Through day-to-day interactions infants usually begin to build a sense of security and trust that gradually helps them to develop the confidence to use the caregiver as a 'secure base' (Bowlby, 1969) from which to start exploring the environment. The baby's success in negotiating these developmental hurdles depends not only on their genetic constitution (nature), but on their relationship with their primary caregiver (nurture). This relationship is important because it is now thought that the day-to-day interactions that take place between the caregiver and baby 'indelibly influence the evolution of brain structures responsible for the individual's socio-emotional functioning for the rest of the lifespan' (Schore, 1994). Indeed, it is the unique wiring of a baby's brain that determines how that particular baby behaves, thinks, feels, their memories, and what, at the end of the day, determines his or her sense of 'self'.

Thus, the development of a baby's brain occurs at the interface of relationships with key 'attachment' figures. Attachment is an affective or emotional bond between infant and caregiver (Bowlby, 1969), the role of which is the co-regulation of infant emotion and arousal (Sroufe, 1995). Babies who receive sensitive, emotionally responsive care during their first year are more likely to become securely attached; babies receiving insensitive, inconsistent or unresponsive care are more likely to become insecurely attached.

Securely attached infants develop the confidence to use the main caregiver as a 'secure base' from which to explore the world. Insecurely attached infants lack this base, and so may limit their explorations of the wider world, or deploy defensive strategies to cope with aroused or disorganised emotional states. Attachment relationships are also recognised to be a prototype for later relations, because the attachment relationship is internalised (ie. becomes what is known as an 'internal working model' or IWM), which is effectively a 'representational model' of self and self with other. This provides the child with a set of expectations in terms of what to expect from others. Physically and emotionally neglected children, for example, may expect others to be unresponsive, unavailable and unwilling to meet their needs. As Barrett (2006) describes:

'For some children who have been rejected, abused, humiliated or treated in ways that have left them feeling confused about what to expect from other people… such children will not be able to use their attachment figures as a secure base and will be more likely to be pessimistic both about the chances of people liking them and about the way people will treat them.'

Overall, insecure attachments predict a range of poorer long-term outcomes (Sroufe, 2005), while children with secure attachment relationships are more able to be independent, relate to their peers and engage in more complex and creative play (Lewis *et al*, 1984).

Adult attachment

One of the strongest predictors of a child's attachment relationships is the parents' internal working models (IWM), which psychologists can assess using the Adult Attachment Interview (Fonagy *et al*, 1995), to indicate how a parent perceives and reflects on their own early care. Insecurely attached adults may be more likely to produce insecurely attached babies, most probably because the parent's IWM influences their parenting behaviours. However, parents who have faced adversity in their own childhood, and who are able to reflect and make sense of their own care histories, may well have securely attached infants of their own.

Infants may have different attachment styles with different caregivers and a range of other factors are now recognised to be strongly associated with a child's attachment security. These include the parents' capacity to 'tune in' to infant interaction, and their capacity for reflective thought about the infant as an individual with his or her own likes, dislikes and personality traits. Reflective function and mentalisation have been the subject of much recent research and the next section describes this.

Mentalisation

Mentalisation refers to 'the capacity of the parents to experience the baby as an "intentional" being rather than simply viewing him or her in terms of physical characteristics or behaviour. This supports the infant's developing sense of self and lays the foundations for the child's understanding of mental states in other people and their capacity to regulate their own internal experiences' (Fonagy *et al*, 2004). Findings from a recent study (Meins *et al*, 2002) show that a mother's capacity to interpret her baby's moods or feelings is a good predictor of her child's development at two years of age.

Although the child's perception of mental states in him or herself and others initially depends on representations from attachment figures, as the infant grows, other adults and older siblings increasingly play a role:

'If the child's perception of mental states in himself and others depends on his observation of the mental world of the care-giver, then this sets a target for optimizing the facilitative power of early experience. Clearly, children require a number of adults with whom an attachment bond exists – who can be trusted and have an interest in their mental state – to support the development of their subjectivity from a pre-mentalizing to a fully mentalizing model.' (Allen & Fonagy, 2006)

Some adults may have less capacity for reflective function than others, particularly if they themselves have not experienced sensitive, warm relationships or if they are experiencing severe difficulties such as mental health problems, addiction to alcohol or drugs, or domestic violence.

Depression

Some mothers may experience postnatal depression, and Murray and colleagues (1996) have found that this affects the sensitivity of her interactions with the infant. It is more likely that mothers with postnatal depression will either be remote and distant with the infant or be intrusive. Interaction is two-way, and babies who become used to having unresponsive, joyless interchanges may begin to behave in that way themselves. A study by Sharpe *et al* (1995) found that there were significant delays in development in the children, particularly boys, of depressed mothers. This effect may be 'buffered', however, by other relationships that the baby has – with, for example, the father (Hossain *et al*, 1994) or grandparents – and for infants raised in cultures where there are extended social networks and there is more opportunity to find quality interaction. Research also shows that early experiences of persistent neglect and trauma result in overdevelopment of the neurophysiology of brainstem and mid-brain, resulting in increased anxiety, impulsivity, poor affect regulation, and hyperactivity, and also to deficits in cortical functions such as problem-solving, and limbic function such as empathy (see, for example, Schore, 1994, or Gerhardt, 2004).

In order to support parenting during infancy, early years professionals need to bear in mind the sort of parenting that is required to assist the baby in achieving these developmental goals.

Early parenting tasks

While babies do not show a preference for particular attachment figures until around seven months of age, the sensitive, day-by-day meeting of needs, the containing of infants' anxieties, and the proto-conversational turn-taking that forms the basis of much interaction between caregiver and baby are an important precursor to it. By two months, the face is the primary source of visual-affective communication; face-to-face interactions at this age are highly arousing and affect-laden, and expose infants to high levels of cognitive and social information and stimulation (Schore, 1994). Infant and main caregivers regulate the intensity of these interactions, 'repairing' them when the infant becomes unsettled or overwhelmed. In fact, being intensely 'tuned in' is not an ideal state, and Hopkins (1996) argues that 'it is the experience of frustration and conflict in concert with their successful repair and resolution which are optimal for development'. However, extended or extensive periods of negative affect between caregiver and baby are now thought to have negative effects on the development of the baby's brain. Adults who have difficulty 'tuning in' and are either consistently too passive or too intrusive are also likely to raise infants who are unable to co-regulate their emotional and physical arousal.

Other important parenting tasks in the first few months of life have also been identified. Mirroring occurs, for example, when a baby is aroused or upset, and a mother unconsciously provides a signal (verbal or facial) that resonates with what the baby is feeling. The child then internalises what has been reflected back to him. By mirroring the infant's emotional state the caregiver shows empathy, but also subtly ensures that the baby knows whose feelings are being registered (Fonagy *et al*, 1995). The caregiver may do this by using exaggerated voice tones, or by opening his or her eyes wide so that the infant knows the emotion is understood but also manageable, because the parent is not overwhelmed by the feeling (Gergely & Watson, 1996). The term 'markedness' (Fonagy *et al*, 2004) specifies a response that is congruent with infant feelings and allows the infant to feel 'contained' by the parental response, not overwhelmed. For example, in one study eight-month-old infants were soothed after immunisation most effectively when their mothers rapidly reflected the upset but also added some other emotional display, such as smiling or questioning to 'contaminate' the upset feeling (Fonagy *et al*, 1995). From this, infants learn about what they are experiencing, and that such experiences are not overwhelming. This process results in the infant building up what we call second or higher order representations of interactions that come to represent both him or herself and him or herself in interaction with other people.

Containment (Bion, 1962) refers to the way in which a mother takes on the powerful or overwhelming feelings of her baby and, by communicating with touch, gesture or speech, 'returns them' in a more manageable form. Winnicott (1960) described how parents 'hold in mind' the needs of the baby so the infant actually experiences a sense of security with someone who understands her needs, responds to her distress signals, and contains her difficult feelings. Mothers who are anxious, angry or preoccupied with their own emotional state may not be able to help the baby manage difficult feelings, leaving the infant overwhelmed.

Conclusion

The above aspects of parenting are particularly important because, where they are functioning well, they enable the baby to successfully negotiate important developmental tasks. These, then, are the aspects of parenting that we should be aiming to support. The next chapter examines some of the ways in which this might be done.

References

Allen JG, Fonagy P (2006) *Handbook of mentalization-based treatment.* Chichester: John Wiley.

Barrett H (2006) *Attachment and the perils of parenting: a commentary and critique.* London: NFPI.

Beebe B, Lachman F (2004) Co-constructing mother–infant distress in face-to-face interactions: contributions of microanalysis. *Zero to Three* **May** 40–48.

Bion W (1962) *Learning from experience.* London: Heinemann.

Bowlby J (1969) *Attachment.* Attachment and loss series vol I. New York: Basic Books.

Bowlby J (1988) *A secure base: parent-child attachment and healthy human development.* London: Routledge.

Fonagy P, Gergely G, Jurist E, Target M (2004) *Affect regulation, mentalization and the development of the self.* London: Karnac.

Fonagy P, Steele M, Steele H, Leigh T, Kennedy R, Mattoon G, Target M (1995) Attachment, the reflective self, and borderline states: the predictive specificity of the Adult Attachment Interview and pathological emotional development. In: Goldberg S, Muir R, Kerr J (eds) *Attachment theory: social, developmental and clinical perspectives.* New York: Analytic Press.

Gergely G, Watson J (1996) The social biofeedback model of parent-affect mirroring. *International Journal of Psycho-Analysis* **77** 1181–1212.

Gerhardt S (2004) *Why love matters: how affection shapes a baby's brain.* Hove and New York: Brunner-Routledge.

Hopkins J (1996) The dangers and deprivations of too-good mothering. *Journal of Child Psychotherapy* **22** (3) 407–422.

Hossain Z, Field T, Gonzalez J, Malphurs J (1994) Infants of 'depressed' mothers interact better with their non-depressed fathers. *Infant Mental Health Journal* **15** (4) 348–357.

Kolb B, Whishaw I (2001) *An introduction to brain and behavior.* New York: Worth.

Lewis M, Feiring C, McGuffoy C, Jaskir J (1984) Predicting psychopathology in six year olds from early social relations. *Child Development* **55** 123–136.

Meins E, Fernyhough C, Wainwright R, das Gupta M, Fradley E, Tuckey M (2002) Maternal mind-mindedness and attachment security as predictors of theory of mind understanding. *Child Development* **73** (6) 1715–1726.

Murray L, Andrews L (2000) *The social baby.* London: The Children's Project.

Murray L, Fiori-Cowley A, Hooper R (1996) The impact of post-natal depression and associated adversity on early mother–infant interactions and later infant outcomes. *Child Development* **67** 2512–2526.

Nelson C, Bosquet M (2000) Neurobiology of fetal and infant development: implications for infant mental health. Cited in: Zeanah, CH Jr (ed) (2000) *Handbook of infant mental health* (2nd edition). New York: Guilford Press.

Schore AN (1994) *After regulation and the origin of the self: the neurobiology of emotional development.* New Jersey: Erlbaum.

Sharpe D, Hay D, Pawlby S, Schumucher G (1995) The impact of post-natal depression on boys' intellectual development. *Journal of Child Psychology and Psychiatry* **36** 1315–1337.

Sroufe LA, Egeland B, Carlson E, Collins AW (2005) *The development of the person: the Minnesota study of risk and adaptation from birth to adulthood.* New York: Guilford Press.

Sroufe LA (1995) *Emotional development: the organization of emotional life in the early years.* Cambridge: Cambridge University Press.

Sroufe LA (2005) Attachment and development: a prospective, longitudinal study from birth to adulthood. *Attachment & Human Development* **7** (4) 349–367.

Steele H, Steele M, Fonagy P (1996) Associations among attachment classifications of mothers, fathers and their infants. *Child Development* **67** 541–555.

Stern D (1985) *The interpersonal world of the infant: a view from psychoanalysis and developmental psychology.* New York: Basic Books.

Winnicott D (1960) The theory of the parent-child relationship. *International Journal of Psychoanalysis* **41** 585–595.

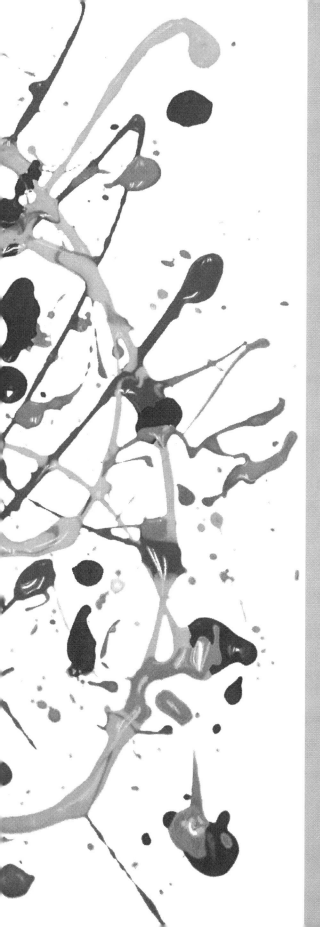

Supporting parenting during infancy

Jane Barlow and Angela Underdown

Key points

- A number of models of intervention have been developed to support positive parenting

- The universal model comprises support for all parents, regardless of identified need or risk

- The selective model comprises services targeted at parents perceived to be at risk of poor parenting

- Indicated models target parent–infant dyads where attachment difficulties are already apparent

- Such support has been shown to have benefits both for the individual parent and child and in terms of savings in later lifetime demands on health, social and criminal justice services.

Key words
Parenting support; Universal interventions; Selective interventions; Indicated interventions; Attachment

The preceding chapter showed that warm, sensitive relationships are prerequisite for the infant's healthy emotional development. How then do we ensure that parents' roles are acknowledged, understood and properly supported?

The tasks that are central to infancy (eg. impulse control, trust and attachment, and intellectual development) are each dependent on the infant having achieved a specific level of development in another domain. For example, changes in memory capacity beginning at three months (ie. cognition) allow changes in attachment (ie. emotion) at seven months. Developmental changes are, as such, taking place simultaneously across a range of developmental domains, and are interdependent. In the same way, the different sorts of support that can be provided to parents of infants seldom have implications solely for one developmental domain, and supporting the development of parenting that will help infants regulate their emotional development and behaviour may also facilitate progress across other developmental domains (eg. social and emotional development).

This chapter starts by examining the different levels of support that can be provided to parents of infants, and goes on to examine the ways in which the early years and primary care workforce need to be 'skilled up' in terms both of observational and intervention skills, to work effectively with this group of parents. It will be suggested that this work involves a range of professionals recognising the importance of early relationships, understanding how current stresses and the 'ghosts from the nursery' may impact on caregiving, and having the skills to support parents to celebrate their infant's unique personality and characteristics.

Intervening to support parenting

There are three ways in which it is possible to intervene to support parenting during infancy. A universal model consists of the provision of support for all parents, irrespective of need; the health visiting service has to date been provided on a universal basis.

A selective model of provision consists of services that are provided to parents who are at increased risk as a result, for example, of the fact that they live in socio-economically deprived parts of the country. Sure Start is possibly one of the best examples of this form of provision in the UK.

Indicated models of provision consist of interventions or services that are provided to parent–infant dyads who are experiencing attachment difficulties, severe postnatal depression or other mental health problems, or where there are child protection concerns. Possibly one of the best examples of this kind of intervention is parent–infant psychotherapy.

In order to be able to offer early appropriate support, it is necessary to identify when parents and infants are experiencing difficulties. It has been suggested that 'during postnatal periods, standardized psychobiological protocols need to be used to identify maternal and infant social-emotional risk factors and dyads that experience intense and prolonged negative affective states' (Schore, 2003). The concept of progressive universalism (HM Treasury, 2007) has been developed recently in the UK to define a model in which some level of support is available to all families, but more support is provided to those who need it most. One of the key features of progressive universalism, in addition to its recognition of the importance of prevention and of early intervention, is the possibility of using the universal service component to identify families that are in need of more intensive support. Indeed, this may be one of the most effective and acceptable ways of identifying families in need of further support, given the inadequacies and problems associated with more formal screening procedures (Peters & Barlow, 2004).

Skilling up the workforce

If we are to achieve the goal of helping parents to promote the type of care during the early years that will help the baby to develop regulatory capacities that we now recognise to be central to effective later functioning (including the management of anger and stress) (Schore, 2003), we need to provide core groups of professionals with the expertise to work in partnership with families. Working alongside families to support mental health and well-being involves sensitivity and special skills, and will involve changing aspects of the training programmes of core groups of professionals who work with young children (including midwives, health visitors and doctors), in addition to providing the existing workforce with new skills. It will also involve a wider provision of the type of formalised parenting support programme that is now widely available for the parents of older children, and, very possibly, the training of a new group of professionals whose specific remit is the promotion of infant mental health. This will require a distinct model of working with parents of infants and the development of new observational and intervention skills.

A model of working with parents of infants

Professionals working with parents of infants model the approach that the parent should take with their baby, 'hearing the cries of the parent in order that the parent can hear the cries of their baby'. Effective listening skills are particularly important, and are embodied in training programmes such as the Solihull Approach (Douglas & Ginty, 2001). This model is underpinned by three theoretical approaches: containment, reciprocity, and social learning theory. It teaches a range of groups of professionals the necessary skills to be able to work with parents of babies more effectively to address many of the common difficulties they experience, including feeding, sleeping and toileting. While many professionals already know how to teach parents behavioural techniques to address such problems, the Solihull approach teaches professionals how to identify some of the anxieties that may be underlying such problems, thereby helping parents to contain such anxieties, and also how to work reciprocally with parents in order to support them to engage reciprocally with their infants. These approaches are all embedded in respectful, warm, trusting relationships.

Supporting routine parenting during routine exchanges provides professionals with a wide range of opportunities to intervene to promote optimal outcomes for infants. What sort of skills and knowledge should professionals have to enable them to do this? First of all is the capacity to support parenting through routine provision of advice and guidance in everyday interactions. Helping parents to see their baby as a social baby, ready to interact with them from the beginning, and to recognise the language of their baby (ie. his or her behaviour) can be key in helping them provide the sort of parenting that their particular baby needs (Rauh *et al*, 1988). Training in the use of the Brazelton Neonatal Behavioural Scales gives professionals the skills to help parents to recognise their baby's cues and signals, whether they are very subtle behavioural cues such as avoidance of eye contact or more obvious cues such as arching of the back and screaming. This approach is also aimed at helping parents to recognise their baby's areas of strength and recognise and support the areas in which he or she is less strong (Brazelton & Nugent, 1995).

Parenting programmes are now widely used to support positive parenting and have been shown to be effective with parents of toddlers (Barlow *et al*, 2005). There are, however, a number of more specialist parenting programmes being developed that are specifically aimed at supporting parenting during infancy. PIPPIN was one of the first parenting programmes that was specifically directed at first-time parents to support them during the transition to parenthood, with sessions provided during pregnancy and the first postnatal year. These groups worked with women and their partners in the transition to parenthood, offering active support as men and women negotiated their new roles and relationships as parents. The postnatal sessions included the infants in the group and facilitators encouraged parents to celebrate their infants as individuals with their own likes, dislikes and specific characteristics (Parr, 1997).

Since then, a variety of other programmes have been developed based on research about the importance of the mother's capacity for mentalisation. 'Minding the Baby' is a US interdisciplinary community-based programme that uses highly trained nurses and social workers to visit high-risk pregnant women over a two-year period. While intensive support is offered in all areas, such as relationship difficulties, domestic violence, budgeting etc, the focus is on the development of mentalisation (Sadler *et al*, 2006). The nurses and social workers who visit the families are trained at postgraduate level and receive skilled supervision.

Where families are experiencing multiple difficulties, a holistic approach such as this has been found to be the most effective (Olds *et al*, 1998; 2004; Olds, 2005; Sadler *et al*, 2006). There are other evidence-based approaches that can be easily applied during routine exchanges between professional and parent, such as encouraging the use of infant carriers (Anisfeld *et al*, 1990) and helping parents to introduce books, songs and music (PEEP) (Street, 2006). Teaching parents how to use infant massage may help an intrusive mother to become more sensitive, or may help an irritable baby to relax and sleep (Underdown *et al*, 2006), thereby facilitating more relaxed and sensitive parenting.

Observational skills

Professionals should have the observational skills necessary to recognise when things are not going well between a mother and baby. This means being able to observe interactions between a mother and her baby and assess from them how well the relationship is developing. Training in the use of the CARE Index (Crittenden, 2001), a method of coding a brief period of mother–infant interaction (three minutes of normal play), could, for example, provide professionals with the skills to identify when mothers are 'intrusive' in their interactions with their baby, or when they are 'passive'. Watching a video of the three-minute interaction with a skilled helper can provide a forum for discussion, and parents can often identify how they would like things to be different (Svanberg, forthcoming). Where parents and infants are experiencing greater difficulties in establishing healthy interactions – for example, where the passivity is bordering on neglect or where the intrusiveness has elements of aggression directed at the baby – the skills of specialist mental health professionals, such as parent-infant psychotherapists (see below), and sometimes child protection services, may be required.

Intervention skills

Some groups of professionals need the skills to be able to undertake preliminary work with parents experiencing minor difficulties, and to know when to refer on to more specialist services. All professionals planning to work in this field need training to develop observational skills, and this can be approached through a number of methods: for example, longitudinal observations carried out in the home, following a baby's development during the first two years (Rustin, 1989), where the focus of the observation is the actual interaction between mother and baby, not the infant or carer, and methods such as the CARE-Index (Crittenden, 2001), where infant as well as parental interaction is assessed.

This training underpins approaches such as interaction guidance, which makes use of videos to help parents recognise aspects of their relationship with their baby that are going well, in order to reinforce them (eg. McDonough, 1995). Such an approach has recently been used as part of the Sunderland Infant Programme. Here parents, who had been identified, using the CARE Index, as having moderate problems, watched a video recording of them playing with their baby, while a specially trained health visitor explored with them what was going on and pointed out positive aspects of the interaction. This method of working with parents was also used to refer parent–infant dyads experiencing more severe problems on to more specialist services (Svanberg, forthcoming).

Parent–infant psychotherapy is now being used to support a wide range of parent–infant problems, ranging from attachment difficulties to infant feeding problems and faltering growth, to hostility toward the infant. It is also being used to support the parenting of infants on the child protection register. The earliest approaches to parent–infant psychotherapy focused primarily on the mother's 'representational' world, or the way in which the mother's current view of her infant is affected by interfering representations from her own history. This approach was developed by Fraiberg (1980), who referred to the phenomenon as 'the Ghosts in the Nursery' (Fraiberg *et al*, 2004). It is underpinned by the belief that, once the mother has been helped to recognise the ghosts and to link them to her own history and present, changes to the mother's representational world can take place, facilitating new paths for growth and development for both mother and infant. Much more recently this representational approach has been combined with a more behavioural approach. 'Watch, Wait and Wonder' is an 'infant-led' parent–infant psychotherapy that involves the mother spending time observing her infant's self-initiated activity, accepting the infant's spontaneous and undirected behaviour, and being physically accessible to the infant. The mother then discusses her experiences of the infant-led play with the therapist with a view to examining the mother's internal working models of herself in relation to her infant (Cohen *et al*, 1999).

Conclusion

Babies undertake a number of key developmental tasks during the first few years of their lives that provide them with the necessary foundation to achieve later developmental goals. Supporting parenting during infancy involves recognising that the first few years of life are particularly important if a baby is to develop their true potential. Infants who have not been provided with the opportunity to develop trust and secure attachment with at least one primary caregiver during infancy are less likely to show signs of empathy during toddlerhood, or to develop social relationships during childhood or supportive social networks during adolescence and adulthood. Similarly, babies who have not been helped to begin to manage their emotions and behaviour will have poorly developed self-management skills during toddlerhood, and will be ill-equipped to behave in socially responsible ways during adolescence and later life. Babies whose early alertness and curiosity have not been stimulated will be less likely to achieve optimal later development in terms of reasoning and problem-solving, or to optimise their learning ability.

Key professionals working across a range of early years settings should be alert to the opportunities to support positive parenting that will enable infants to achieve key developmental tasks across the three core developmental domains. There is a range of informal ways in which early years and primary care professionals can do this as part of their daily interactions with parents by developing their professional skills in ways that will better enable them to support parenting during infancy. This may involve learning how to share with parents that their baby is a social individual with his or her own likes and dislikes, or to promote greater closeness by helping a mother to massage her baby. It may also mean developing the observational skills to be able to identify the 'intrusive' parenting that may result in a baby developing later behaviour problems, or the passive parenting that may result in a baby being insufficiently stimulated. Some groups of professionals should be offered opportunities to develop the skills to be able to provide remedial intervention to families in need of additional support, and to know when to refer families facing severe difficulties to more specialist services. Supporting parenting during infancy should also involve linking parents into support that is appropriate for their individual family needs.

References

Anisfeld E, Casper V, Nozyce M (1990) Does infant carrying promote attachment? An experimental study of the effects of increased physical contact on the development of attachment. *Child Development* **61** 1617–1627.

Barlow J, Parsons J, Stewart-Brown S (2005) Systematic review of the effectiveness of group based parenting programmes for infants and toddlers. *Child: Care, Health and Development* **31** (1) 33–42.

Brazelton TB, Nugent JK (1995) *Neonatal behavioral assessment scale.* Cambridge: Cambridge University Press.

Cohen NJ, Muir E, Lojkasek M, Muir R, Parker CJ, Barwick M, Brown M (1999) Watch, wait and wonder: testing the effectiveness of a new approach to mother–infant psychotherapy. *Infant Mental Health Journal* **20** 429–451.

Crittenden P (2001) *CARE-Index infant and toddlers. Coding manual.* Miami, Florida: Family Relations Institute.

Douglas H, Ginty M (2001) The Solihull approach: evaluation of changes in the practice of health visitors. *Community Practitioner* **74** 222–224.

Fraiberg S (1980) *Clinical studies in infant mental health.* New York: Basic Books.

Fraiberg S, Adelson E, Shapiro V (2004) Ghosts in the nursery: a psychoanalytic approach to the problems of impaired infant–mother relationships. Cited in: Raphael-Leff J (ed) *Parent–infant psychodynamics.* London: Whurr.

HM Treasury (2007) *Aiming high for children: supporting families.* London: HM Treasury.

McDonough S (1995) Promoting positive early parent child relationships through interaction guidance. *Child and Adolescent Psychiatric Clinics of North America* **4** 661–672.

Olds D (2005) The nurse-family partnership: foundations in attachment theory and epidemiology. Cited in: Berlin L, Ziv Y, Amaya-Jackson L, Greenberg M (eds) *Enhancing early attachments: theory, research, intervention and policy.* New York: Guilford Press.

Olds D, Eckenrode J, Henderson C Jr, Kitzman H, Luckey D, Pettitt L, Sidora K, Morris P, Powers J (1998) Long-term effects of nurse home visitations on children's criminal and anti-social behaviour: 15 year follow-up of randomised trial. *Journal of the American Medical Association* **280** 1238–1244.

Olds D, Robinson J, Pettit L, Luckey D, Holmberg J, Ng R, Isacks K, Sheff K, Henderson C Jr (2004) Effects of home visits by paraprofessionals and nurses: age 4 follow-up results of randomised trial. *Pediatrics* **114** 1560–1568.

Parr M (1997) A new approach to parent education. *British Journal of Midwifery* **6** 160–165.

Peters R, Barlow J (2004) Systematic review of screening instruments to identify child abuse during the perinatal period. *Child Abuse Review* **12** 416–435.

Rauh VA, Achenbach TM, Nurcombe B, Howell CT, Teti DM (1988) Minimizing adverse effects of low birthweight: four-year results of an intervention program. *Child Development* **59** 544–553.

Rustin M (1989) Observing infants: reflections on methods. In: Miller L, Rustin M, Rustin M, Shuttleworth J (eds) *Closely observed infants.* London: Duckworth.

Sadler LS, Slade A, Mayes LC (2006) Minding the baby: a mentalization based parenting program. In: Fonagy P, Allen J (eds) *Handbook of mentalization-based treatment.* Chichester: Wiley.

Schore AN (2003) *Affect dysregulation and disorders of the self.* New York: WW Norton.

Street A (2006) *The role of singing within mother–infant interactions.* Unpublished PhD thesis. London: Roehampton University.

Svanberg PO (forthcoming) Promoting a secure attachment through early screening and interventions: a partnership approach. In: Svanberg PO, Barlow J (eds) *Keeping the baby in mind: prevention in practice.* London: Routledge.

Underdown A, Barlow J, Chung V, Stewart-Brown S (2006) Massage intervention for promoting mental and physical health in infants aged under six months. *Cochrane Database of Systematic Reviews* 4. CD005038. DOI:10.1002/14651858.CD005038.pub2

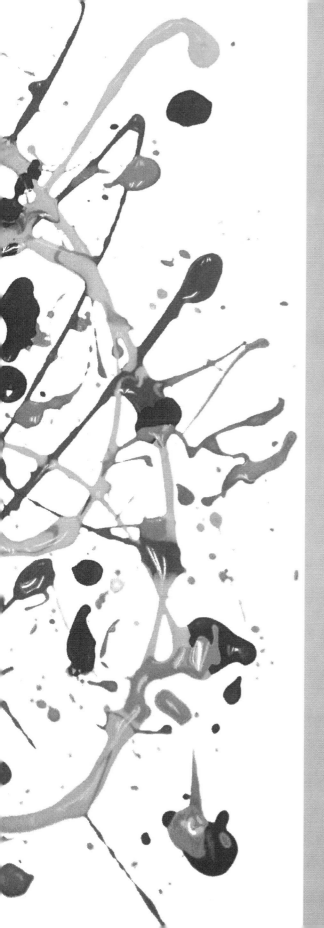

Part III

Children's mental health

Risk and resilience in childhood

Carly Raby and Sam Raby

Key points

- Risks are more likely to have long-term serious impacts if they are ongoing problems rather than one-off traumatic events

- Risks can have a domino effect, where one problem can lead to the development of a series of other problems

- Protective factors that are linked to resilience may be individual (ie. a sense of autonomy and mastery), family (ie. having a close bond with at least one other person), and community (good experiences at school, links within their neighbourhood)

- Research shows that effective interventions can prevent the potentially life-lasting damage of exposure to trauma or abuse in childhood

- It is only through listening and responding to children that services can target their work to address the real risks that concern them, and find solutions that work for them.

Key words
Risk; Resilience; Interventions; Protective factors; Participation

This chapter will seek to explain the findings of research into risk and resilience in child development. It will do this first by setting out a clear definition of risk and resilience as understood in the literature, and second by reviewing the key issues that have emerged from research in this area.

Researching risk and resilience is about understanding what can be done to make a difference to the lives of children and young people. It is essentially an optimistic field, as it is based on the principle that something can be done to improve the lives of children who have had unhappy or traumatic childhoods. This chapter will show that the research suggests that there is good reason to be hopeful, because there is clear evidence that the right interventions can make a real difference. The chapter will also highlight good, evidence-based practice, and draw out the lessons that have been learnt from research. It is hoped that by the end of the chapter readers will have gained both the knowledge and the inspiration to do the things that can make a real difference to the lives of children.

Defining risk and resilience

What do risk and resilience mean? Risk in this context refers to factors in a child's life that may have a negative impact on their development and later life. These can be unhappy or unsettling normal life events, such as moving house or school, illness of a parent or sibling, or the death of a close relative such as a grandparent, or they can be more extreme: abuse, abandonment, imprisonment of a parent, fleeing war, witnessing domestic violence, and other stressful or traumatic events. The study of risk is important because it enables those who want to improve the lives of children to understand the factors that are most likely to cause long-term problems for the young people who experience them.

Studying risk alone would be rather depressing as it largely entails trawling through study after study of the terrible impact that children's experiences can have on their later life. Studying resilience restores hope, as well as providing the knowledge needed to make a difference. Resilience looks at the factors that help some children avoid the problems that befall many others who have had comparable experiences or grow up under similar circumstances. How is it that some children from high crime estates do not themselves take up a life of crime but go on to gain a university degree and a successful career, when so many of their peers don't? How do some children survive sexual abuse and go on to avoid the later mental health problems that mar the lives of so many others? The study of risk and resilience seeks to answer questions like these. Although there are many questions still unanswered, we attempt to summarise below what we know so far.

What we know about risk

The available evidence suggests that the risks for children are more likely to have long-term serious impacts if they are ongoing problems rather than one-off traumatic events. Adults tend to focus on major traumatic events as risk factors, but research by Sandberg *et al* (1993) and Rutter (1994) suggests that more minor but distressing ongoing problems are bigger risks for children's future. When children have been asked, they tend to highlight these everyday problems that research shows are correlated more closely with negative outcomes. YoungMinds held a series of children's meetings and conferences during 2007. The children and young people who took part were really clear about the problems (risks) that they felt children (aged five to 24) would like help with (table 1) (YoungMinds, in press).

Table 1: Problems that concern children

- Bullying
- Siblings being mean
- Parents getting divorced
- Family problems
- Living with parents who don't look after you
- Fears about being taken away from your parents
- Worries about money
- Someone hurting your body
- Mum and Dad always arguing
- Missing friends
- Relationship problems
- Drugs and alcohol
- Isolation
- Boredom
- Things that we see in the news that no one talks to us about properly.

The list highlights the importance of ensuring participation in services that work with children, because it is only through listening and responding to children that services can target their work to address the real risks that concern them, and find solutions that work for them.

The evidence also suggests that risks can have a domino effect, where one problem can lead to the development of a series of other problems. For example, if a child is abused she or he is more likely to be removed from their family and put in care, but children in care are less likely to do well at school, and poor academic qualifications often lead to problems getting a job.

In addition to this domino effect, one of the key factors for children is how risks interact with each other. Rather than simply accumulating, they often appear to increase each other's impact, and multiply the chances of negative outcomes for the child.

Poverty, homelessness, alcoholism or substance abuse, domestic violence and imprisonment of a parent are all likely on their own to have a negative impact on a child who has to grow up with them, but the research suggests that when they are combined they are much more likely to cause profound problems for children's development.

What we know about resilience

A good summary of the factors associated with resilience in children has been produced by Daniel and Wassell (2002). These are divided into individual factors, family factors and the wider community. Looking first at the child-centred factors, factors associated with greater resilience include:

- being female
- having hobbies
- being sociable
- being independent
- having a sense of humour
- being reflective rather than impulsive
- having a willingness and a capacity to plan
- having good communication skills
- having empathy with others
- having a sense of competence and being able to do things for themselves
- having problem solving skills
- having autonomy (for girls)
- being able to express emotions (for boys).

Family factors that augment resilience include:

- having a close bond with at least one person
- nurturance and trust
- lack of separation
- required helpfulness
- encouragement for autonomy for girls
- close grandparents
- sibling attachments
- four or fewer children
- enough money and other material things
- absence of parental mental health problems or substance abuse.

Last, protective factors provided by the wider community include neighbour and wider family support, friendships, good experiences at school, and having good adult role models.

Developing interventions

What do these factors mean and how can we use them to develop interventions to improve the life chances of unhappy and troubled children? Common sense tells us that a bright, sociable girl who is good at problem solving and has a good time at school is less likely to get in trouble with the police than a lonely, impulsive boy who hates school and finds it hard to sort out problems. However, things become more complicated when we try to understand which of these elements are acting most protectively and how they combine to give children resilience.

Childhood is an ongoing process of physical and psychological development. On top of this, the environment in which the child is growing up is also constantly changing and developing. Researchers now focus more on interactive models of risk and resilience in order to gain a better understanding of the processes that take place. This is leading to models that go beyond simply explaining why bright children and happy families have acquired the resilience to avoid or recover from risk to look at how services can intervene to improve the future trajectory of unhappy children whose lives have not so far contained these saving graces.

What we know about making a difference

There have been considerable efforts to improve the lives and futures of children in the UK over the last 10 years. These have included the *Every Child Matters* agenda (Department for Education and Skills, 2004), with its focus on the five key areas of children's well-being, and on services to improve the life chances and outcomes of the children with whom they work. In addition, there has been the creation of Sure Start, which was aimed at improving the physical and mental well-being of 0–5-year-old children in deprived communities. Funding was also made available across England for preventative services for five to 11 year olds through the Children's Fund. Extra funding has also been made available to primary schools through initiatives such as the SEAL (social and emotional aspects of learning) programme. However, the UK was rated last of the 24 industrialised nations in terms of children's well-being in the recent UNICEF report (2007). Whether or not the report was an up-to-date and fair picture of the situation for children in the UK today, two things are clear: first, we are not meeting the needs of the children in this country well enough, and second, it is crucially important that efforts are focused on what has been found to make a difference. With this in mind, let us turn to what research has found about managing the risks in children's lives and promoting their resilience to life's setbacks and traumas.

NCH has compiled an excellent review of the research into risk and resilience children (NCH, 2007). Newman (2004), cited in the review, has identified the key factors that have been found to promote resilience in children. These are:

- the creation of strong social networks
- the presence of at least one unconditionally supportive parent or parent substitute
- a committed mentor or other person outside the family

- positive school experiences
- a sense of mastery and a belief that one's efforts can make a difference
- participation in a range of extra-curricular activities
- the capacity to reframe adversities so that the beneficial as well as the damaging effects are recognised
- the ability or opportunity to make a difference by helping others
- not to be excessively sheltered from challenging situations that provide opportunities to develop coping skills.

Ways forward and conclusion

The study of risk and resilience is crucial if services want to find ways to improve the lives of unhappy children and help those who have suffered trauma or abuse to survive these experiences and enjoy a better future. Equipped with this information, services can stand back from the front line and analyse local circumstances in the light of what they know of the bigger picture, and target their resources on the elements that are known to make a real difference to children. When we know that ongoing minor unhappiness in children's lives can have long-term and profound negative effects on their emotional well-being, we can seek to do something about it. For example, schools can make a massive difference by introducing effective and robust anti-bullying policies and procedures that protect the children in their care; professionals working with families in crisis can focus their efforts on reducing parental conflict and supporting positive parenting. These kinds of interventions can make a huge difference to children who would otherwise avoid school and miss out on their education, or have to live in hostile and unhappy homes.

Another crucial lesson is the importance of listening to children when designing and delivering services. Participation is now a central component in the delivery and planning of children's services, and the evidence strongly suggests that it is an essential element.

Finally, it is crucial for services to understand that they can only ever be a part of the solution. They can make a big difference, but it is only by working with children and parents, and collectively with the wider community that they can most effectively protect children from risk and promote resilience.

References

Daniel B, Wassell S (2002) *Assessing and promoting resilience in vulnerable children.* London: Jessica Kingsley.

Department for Education and Skills (2004) *Every child matters: change for children.* London: Department for Education and Skills.

NCH (2007) *Literature review: risk and resilience in children.* London: NCH.

Newman T (2004) *What works in building resilience?* Ilford: Barnardos.

Rutter M (1994) Stress research: accomplishments and tasks ahead. In: Haggerty R, Sherrod L, Garmezy N, Rutter M (eds) *Stress, risk, and resilience in children and adolescents.* Cambridge: Cambridge University Press.

Sandberg S, Rutter M, Giles S, Owen A, Champion L, Nicholls J, Prior V, McGuiness D, Drinnan D (1993) Assessment of psychosocial experiences in childhood: methodological issues and some illustrative findings. *Journal of Child Psychology and Psychiatry* **34** 879–897.

UNICEF (2007) *Child poverty in perspective: an overview of child well-being in rich countries.* Innocenti Research Centre report card 7. New York: UNICEF.

YoungMinds (in press) *Children's conferences 2007: emerging findings.* London: YoungMinds.

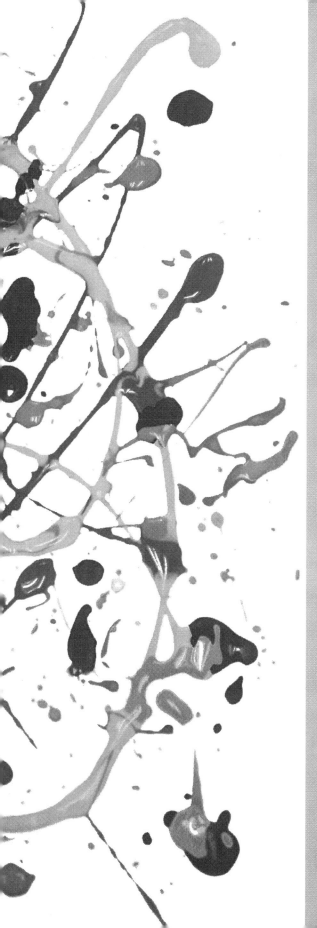

Mental health promotion in primary schools

Peter Wilson

Key points

- The primary school offers an important opportunity for interventions both to work with children with emotional and behavioural problems and to promote the mental health of the whole school community

- Research shows that mental health is important to learning, and learning is important to mental health

- Some primary schools have launched or are hosting programmes to provide counselling and preventative interventions for children, families and school staff

- A growing body of evidence suggests such interventions do make a difference, to the individual children concerned and their families, and to the whole school

- Education and health departments and agencies need to work together to maximise the potential for reaching vulnerable children.

Key words

Primary school; Emotional and social development; Interventions; Education; Behavioural problems

The local primary school plays a central role in the lives of the children and families it serves. It sits in the midst of their communities, and is often valued as much for its general support and guidance as for its educational provision. For many parents, it is a source of primary care, a place of relative safety and reliability. It is also the setting in which children make their way into the world beyond the domain of their childhood homes. It is where they encounter new friends and experiences, where they can find out more about themselves and about the world into which they are growing up. It is the arena in which much of their cognitive, emotional and social development takes place.

Primary school aged children have a great deal to learn in terms of literacy, numeracy and a wide range of creative and physical activities. How well children progress in their learning depends on many factors, some innate and some environmental. There is a growing body of evidence to suggest that the emotional development of children is of primary importance in the process of learning (Greenhalgh, 1994; Weare, 2004). Children who feel confident and free enough to be receptive to new knowledge and to pursue their curiosities are more likely to achieve mastery of what they are learning.

Recent advances in brain research and attachment theory and practice have thrown light on the impact of early experience on the child's sense of well-being and capacity to learn. Children enter the primary school in different states of readiness to participate in the learning process. Some are eager to find out things and enjoy friendships and relationships with teachers. Others are more cautious, wary, defensive and closed to what is being offered. Children who are fearful, mistrustful or preoccupied with troubling feelings and experiences in their lives are more likely to have difficulty concentrating and being responsive to their teachers. The fundamental tasks of the primary school are to maximise the potential of the former and to redress the difficulties of the latter. The primary school builds on what children have achieved in their early childhood and lays the foundation for their future growth and development.

In many respects, it is in a privileged position. The children are at a stage of life when the maturation of cognitive abilities and the reduction in the intensity of childhood feelings enables them in general to be more focused and organised in their learning. Most are more biddable, more 'innocent' than in later life. In the development of their concrete operational thought, they become increasingly interested in naming and putting things into order, reasoning things out, and establishing rules in their games and relationships. The majority of primary schools, moreover, are relatively small in comparison with secondary schools. This helps to create a family atmosphere, in which children and teachers come to know each other quite well. It also makes more possible than in a larger secondary school the establishment of a coherent school management system and ethos.

Child mental health

There has been much discussion in recent years about the definition of mental health. It is a difficult concept to grasp, but there is general agreement that it is more than the absence of mental illness. Child mental health can be seen as the strength and capacity of a child's mind to grow and develop with confidence and enjoyment. It consists of the capacity to learn from experience and to overcome difficulty and adversity. It is about physical and emotional well-being, the ability to live a full and creative life, and the flexibility to give and take in friendships and relationships. Children who have good mental health are not saints or models of perfection – they are ordinary children who are able to make the most of their abilities and opportunities.

Children who do not have good mental health are those who struggle to develop in ways that enable them to take in what is being offered to them. Many are overwhelmed by their feelings and the experiences to which they have been subjected in their homes and communities. Some may withdraw within themselves and isolate themselves from other children. They may feel unhappy and become depressed at school; they may find it difficult to concentrate or refuse to attend. Others may be more outgoing, or may be irritable, aggressive and disruptive in class.

It is difficult to be precise about the prevalence of such disturbance; similar emotional and behavioural phenomena may be interpreted very differently by different cultures with different moral standards. The Office for National Statistics' (Green *et al*, 2005) epidemiological study of child and adolescent mental disorders showed that 10% of children aged 5–15 have a mental disorder, 5.8% have clinically significant conduct disorders, 3.8% have emotional disorders – anxiety and depression – and 1.8% are rated as having hyperkinetic disorders. The figures are likely to be lower for children of primary school age, as the prevalence of mental health problems increases during adolescence. However, it is generally calculated that, at any given time, a large proportion of children – approximately 20%–30% – experience psychological problems of varying severity. There is convincing evidence, moreover, to indicate that child mental health problems that are not attended to in childhood continue on into adolescence and adulthood (Scott, 2003; Sainsbury Centre For Mental Health, 2007).

National policy

From a historical point of view, there has existed a longstanding friction between the interests of educationalists and medical professionals in relation to children showing difficulties in their behaviour and attitude to learning. Different terminologies have both led to and added to this tension. Educational staff use terms such as 'maladjusted' and 'EBD' (emotional and behavioural difficulties, more recently referred to as EBSD – emotional, behavioural and social difficulties) and seek to find solutions in classroom management and teaching techniques. Psychiatrists prefer to describe such behaviours as symptomatic of 'mental illness' and 'mental disorder', and see 'treatment' in clinical settings as the most appropriate response. Within each domain, too, there have been wide differences: in education, between those who emphasise academic achievement and those who stress social and emotional learning; in psychiatry, between those who favour medical, pharmacological treatments and those who lean towards psychotherapeutic and systemic approaches.

However, particularly in the last 20 years or so, great strides have been made towards bringing 'Health' and 'Education' together, not only in the interests of understanding and helping children in difficulty, but also to create conditions in schools and communities that foster greater well-being in all children. A broad holistic approach, drawing on the many aspects of a child's experience, is now being increasingly promoted. So, for example, in the government's most recent Comprehensive Spending Review (October 2007), health and local authorities are required, inter alia, 'to identify co-ordinated action to promote mental health and early intervention in universal and mainstream services' and to ensure that 'increasing numbers of schools' are 'delivering school-based mental health support'.

Considerable effort has been made in parts of the health sector to broaden the definition of mental health and to see the mental health of children as 'everybody's business' (not just the province of psychiatry). This idea has been particularly promoted by the YoungMinds (Wilson, 2003), the national children's mental health charity. Its implications in terms of service delivery have been spelt out in a number of significant reports, most notably *Together We Stand* (Williams & Richardson, 1995). This conceptualises a comprehensive child and adolescent mental health service (CAMHS) as operating at different tiers involving a wide range of professionals and practitioners engaged in the promotion of mental health and the prevention and treatment of mental health problems. In this model, school staff are clearly seen as an intrinsic part of CAMHS, contributing to children's mental health at Tier 1. Specialist mental health professionals working at Tiers 2 and 3 are required to provide consultation in primary settings such as schools. All of this thinking has culminated in the government's recent guidance in the National Service Framework for Children, Young People and Maternity Services (Department of Health, 2004).

In the education sector, seemingly in a separate stream of policy development, greater attention has been paid to mental health in schools (Department for Education and Skills, 2001; 2004). Of particular relevance in this field has been the acknowledgement of the importance of emotions in the learning process. Daniel Goleman's book *Emotional Intelligence* (Goleman, 1996) has made a substantial impact in many quarters of the educational establishment. School-based programmes such as PHSE and Circle Time have taken on a much more significant role in school life, attending as they do to the general emotional well-being, confidence and positive behaviour of children. National education strategies have sought to promote excellence and enjoyment in learning, parental involvement and behavioural improvement.

A most significant development that has emerged from all these initiatives has been the National Healthy Schools Standard (Department for Education and Skills, 1999). This was sponsored by what is now the Department for Children, Schools and Families (DCSF) and the Department of Health in 1999 to provide a national framework for local education and health partnerships. It consists of eight themes, all of which have a bearing on the mental health of children and one that is particularly specific: emotional health and well-being (EHWB). Since 2003, the National Curriculum and the Ofsted Framework for Inspecting Schools have placed clear requirements on schools to take account of and promote EHWB.

Major developments in approach

An increasing amount of attention is now paid to the structure, environment and attitude of the whole school in the overall promotion of the mental health of all children in a school (Atkinson & Hornby, 2002). A positive school ethos that values the contribution of children, teachers and school staff alike and provides for continuity of teacher–child relationships is one essential ingredient of such an approach. So too is the quality of pastoral care, classroom management and teaching, and relationships with children's families and communities. One of the key aims of the government's recent development of extended schools is to build environments that facilitate learning at all levels: social, cognitive and emotional. Much depends on effective leadership that generates clear direction and social cohesion and that ensures the implementation of whole school policies: for example, in relation to children's behaviour and bullying.

SEAL (Social and Emotional Aspects of Learning – www.seal.org.uk) is a whole school approach funded and developed by the government that is now being provided in 70% of primary schools across the country. The government intends that all primary schools should embrace it. SEAL is a set of theme-based curriculum materials that reflect Goleman's areas of emotional literacy – self-awareness, management of feelings, and recognition of and respect for others' emotions. It is a resource that is built into the routine of the school and the various curricula and designed to be delivered through a combination of school assemblies and classroom teaching for all children.

More specifically, a wide range of in-school initiatives and activities have been developed to promote the mental health of children. Some have focused on enabling children to think and reason more clearly in order for them to gain confidence in their learning and thus in their sense of well-being (for example, Philosophy for Children (www.p4c.org.nz), and Assessment for Learning (www.qca.org.uk). The Penn Resiliency Programme (www.sas.upenn.edu/prpsum.htm) is an example of a manualised intervention for schools that was developed in the US and has been applied in some schools in this country. The emphasis here is on enabling children to cope more constructively with the challenges of daily life in schools and to develop an overall optimistic way of thinking. Other interventions have focused on building self-esteem and resilience in different ways: some through after school clubs for vulnerable children (for example, the National Pyramid Trust (www.nptrust.org.uk)); some through small groups for children not ready developmentally to engage in normal classroom activity (eg. nurture groups (Bennathan & Boxall, 1996) held within the school during the school day).

ThePlace2Be (www.theplacetobe.org.uk; Wilson & Refson, 2007) has developed an innovative model of emotional and therapeutic support predominantly in primary schools through the provision of a comprehensive counselling service. This service is based in the school and is readily available to children, teachers, school staff and parents. CAMHS teams in various parts of the country have developed their Tier 2 work through providing consultation and support to schools and assisting with appropriate referrals for specialist help. Multi-Agency Locality Teams (MALTS) in Nottingham and Family Solutions in Norfolk are two examples of such a service. Behaviour and Education Support Teams (BESTs) (www.dfes.gov.uk/best) have also taken an active role in mobilising multidisciplinary teams to work with clusters of schools. Some interventions have focused on work with children's families, primarily to promote positive behavioural and emotional improvements, for example, the Incredible Years (www.incredibleyears.com) and Family Links (www.familylinks.org.uk) programmes. Finally, the employment of learning mentors in most parts of the country, of school nurses in some schools, and the development of peer mentoring, counselling and mediation, as well as the setting up of school councils in many schools, have added to an extraordinarily lively picture of mental health support and promotion.

Does it work?

There can be no doubt that over the last 20 years or so there has occurred a quite remarkable surge of interest in the emotional well-being and mental health of children in primary schools. This has largely arisen as a consequence of a convergence of thinking between the domains of education and health. Whatever terms may have been used – mental health, emotional well-being, emotional literacy and intelligence, resilience – the common concern has been to promote the readiness and motivation of children to enjoy their learning and to build their confidence in themselves and their abilities.

Four major lines of development have taken precedence in policy thinking. The first has been the increasing emphasis placed by government on the safety and well-being of children. This is most comprehensively expressed in the document *Every Child Matters* (Department for Education and Skills, 2004). The second has been the growing acknowledgement of the interdependence of health and education in the upbringing of children. It is clearly recognised now that physical and mental health are enhanced in the very process of education. Equally, it is out of physical and mental health that the learning potential of the child is increased. The third has been the increasing importance attached to mental health promotion, particularly in terms of preventable suffering and cost saving. There are differences of view about the meaning of mental health promotion – whether it refers to specific interventions to anticipate psychiatric disorders or to the proactive building of strengths and resources. It is clear, however, that for the most part preventative and promotional interventions closely overlap and that their development falls very much within a public health agenda. The fourth has been the recognition of the fundamental importance of the structure and morale of the whole school in setting the context in which children can grow and learn and in which school-based mental health projects can be encouraged. Various measures and checklists are being devised to construct a practical framework to gauge the emotional literacy of a school (Sharp & Faupel, 2002; Cowie, 2004; Antidote, 2003).

The major question that now needs to be answered is whether or not these many interventions are making the difference that they claim. Most interventions today are subject to evaluation, some quite rigorous (as in the case currently of SEAL), although few to the standard of controlled and randomised controlled trials (mostly conducted in the US). For example, The Place2Be uses a range of measures to evaluate its impact. Individual and group counselling is evaluated using the Goodman's Strengths and Difficulties Questionnaires (SDQ) with child, teacher and parent ratings. The Clinical Outcomes in Routine Evaluation – Outcome Measure (CORE-OM) is used to evaluate its support work with parents. It also evaluates the impact of its service on the whole school, through a needs analysis and longitudinal study and a systematic recording of the head teacher's concerns. The findings are encouraging. For example, clinical audits report that its individual and group counselling is effective at dealing with a broad range of difficulties experienced by primary school-aged children and, importantly, the improvements are noticeable to teachers, parents and the children themselves. These changes involve not only a reduction in unwanted behaviour such as conduct problems, emotional difficulties, hyperactivity and peer problems, but also an increase in desired behaviour indicative of positive social and emotional well-being in the child.

There are comparable studies being conducted in other organisations, and in most cases the results are impressive, with benefits being shown in reduced anxiety, raised self-esteem and improved behaviour. However, further examination is needed in two main areas. The first concerns the nature of the actual therapeutic work undertaken with individuals or groups of children. Therapists and counsellors vary a great deal in how they approach their work, and there is still a great deal of uncertainty about what approaches and orientations are most appropriate with which children and under what circumstances. A thorough critical review of treatments for children and adolescents has been written by Fonagy *et al* (2003). As important as these publications are, the evidence on which they rely is derived largely from the more structured and prescriptive, and so more readily measurable, therapeutic approaches such as behaviour therapy or cognitive behavioural therapy. Relatively less attention is paid to therapies that are less easy to measure. A useful publication providing a thematic review of process and outcome research in child, adolescent and parent–infant psychotherapy goes some way to provide a counterbalance (Kennedy & Midgley, 2007); so too does a review of what works for children and adolescents in preventive work (Carr, 2002). There is, however, much more to do to create a body of knowledge based on systematic studies, evaluations and clinical experience in the broad field of counselling and psychotherapy in prevention as well as treatment.

The second area is the examination of the many variables that impact in different ways on children and parents in the course of their lives in their communities, and on the teachers and school staff in their changing schools. It may be the case that many interventions succeed or fail depending on the attitude of the school towards them in the first place. Equally, it may be that their positive effect is seen not just in individual children but more widely in the morale of the whole school. The current pressure on primary schools to meet performance targets also needs to be taken into account. Tests, such as the Standardised Assessment Tests (SATs), create inevitable tension in both children and teachers as to whether they will succeed or fail; this may well conflict with the ethos of many of the interventions highlighted above.

The pivotal position of the primary school in the community and the greater potential for development and change in primary school aged children (than in children at a later age) open up all kinds of possibilities for the promotion of mental health. These possibilities need to be pursued in the service of improved mental health not only in all children but also in those children who are struggling – children whose prospects of a creative and productive life in adolescence and adulthood are less favourable without early preventative intervention in early childhood and in the primary school.

References

Antidote (2003) *The emotional literacy handbook: promoting whole-school strategies.* London: David Fulton Publishers.

Atkinson M, Hornby G (2002) *Mental health handbook for schools.* London: Routledge.

Bennathan M, Boxall M (1996) *Effective intervention in primary schools: nurture groups.* London: David Fulton Publishers.

Carr A (ed) (2002) *Prevention: what works with children and adolescents?* London: Taylor and Francis.

Cowie H (2004) *Mental health handbook for schools.* London: Routledge.

Department for Education and Skills (1999) *National healthy school standard.* London: Department for Children, Schools and Families. www.standards.dfes.gov.uk

Department for Education and Skills (2001) *Promoting children's mental health within early years and school settings.* London: Department for Education and Skills. www.dfes.gov.uk/mentalhealth/index.shtml

Department for Education and Skills (2004) *Every child matters: change for children.* London: Department for Education and Skills.

Department of Health (2004) *The national service framework for children, young people and maternity services.* London: Department of Health.

Fonagy P, Target M, Cottrell D, Phillips J, Kurtz Z (2003) *What works for whom: a critical review of treatments for children and adolescents.* London: Guilford Press.

Goleman D (1996) *Emotional intelligence.* London: Bloomsbury.

Green H, McGinnity A, Meltzer H, Ford T, Goodman R (2005) *Mental health of children and young people in Britain 2004.* London: Office for National Statistics.

Greenhalgh P (1994) *Emotional growth and learning.* London: Routledge.

Kennedy E, Midgley N (2007) *Process and outcome research in child, adolescent and parent–infant psychotherapy: a thematic review.* London: North Central London Strategic Health Authority.

Sainsbury Centre For Mental Health (2007) *Supporting young people's mental health.* London: Sainsbury Centre for Mental Health.

Scott S (2003) Childhood antecedents of juvenile delinquency. In: Bailey S, Doolan M (eds) *Adolescent forensic psychotherapy.* Oxford: Butterworth Heinemann.

Sharp P, Faupel A (eds) (2002) *Promoting emotional literacy: guidelines for schools, local authorities and the health service.* Southampton: Emotional Literacy Group/Southampton City Council Local Education Authority.

Weare K (2004) *Developing the emotionally literate school.* London: Paul Chapman.

Williams R, Richardson G (eds) (1995) *Together we stand: the commissioning, role and management of child and adolescent mental health services: an NHS Health Advisory Service (HAS) thematic review.* London: HMSO, 1995.

Wilson P (2003) *Young minds in our schools.* London: YoungMinds.

Wilson P, Refson B (2007) The hard to reach and the Place2Be. In: Baruch G, Fonagy P, Robins D (eds) *Reaching the hard to reach.* Chichester: John Wiley & Sons.

The mental health needs of looked after children

Mary Bunting

Key points

- Looked after children experience much higher rates of mental health problems than children in the general population

- This can be explained by their poor parenting experiences and frequent disruption in their home life and fostering placements

- They may also experience problems at school, either because of disruption to their education and/or because they struggle to get on with other children and school staff

- Recent policy changes aim to improve the life chances of looked after children and young people

- Good practice suggests interventions should be holistic, multi-agency, and offer long-term work if they are to meet the needs of this very vulnerable group.

Key words
Looked after children; Mental health; Life chances; Attachment; Foster care

The statistics tell a sad story. In many aspect of their lives, children and young people in the looked after system fare worse than those who live with their birth families.

A Social Exclusion Unit report, *A Better Education for Children in Care* (Social Exclusion Unit, 2003), found that eight per cent of looked after children gained five or more A–C grades at GCSE, compared with 50% of children in the general population. Only one per cent went on to university, compared with 43% of the general population.

The same report found that:

- between a quarter and a third of children leaving care end up homeless and sleeping rough
- young people who have been in care are two-and-a-half times more likely to be teenage parents
- around a quarter of adults in prison spent some time in care as children.

Numerous researchers have found that looked after children have significantly higher rates of mental health problems than their peers, both as children and continuing into their adult lives. For example, McCann and colleagues (1996) found that 56% of children in foster care and 96% of children in residential care have a formal diagnosis of mental health disorders. The Office for National Statistics (2005) has produced figures that suggest rates of mental health disorder are between four and five times higher for children in care than for children in the general population. Phillips (1997) found that 80% of looked after children were identified by their social workers as being in need of input from specialist mental health services.

When we consider the factors that help children to develop good mental health, the reasons for this become clear.

In order to develop in emotionally healthy ways, young children need to have a secure attachment to at least one consistent figure. To develop this, their physical and emotional needs from babyhood onwards need to have been met in a timely, caring and consistent way, so that they develop a feeling of security, trust and safety. They require clear boundaries and guidance as to what is expected of them, and the consequences of not complying, and these need to be consistent. Children do best when their parents are able to be responsive to their needs and sensitive to their feelings and growing sense of identity. In this way, they begin to develop a sense of themselves, and a positive inner working model of how their world operates (YoungMinds, 2003; 2004).

Many children and young people in the looked after system have either never experienced a secure attachment or, if they once had a secure attachment, it subsequently suffered interruptions or disruption. The experience of trauma, abuse and neglect is common among many children entering care today, and this has a major impact on a child's thinking, feeling and behaviour, and on the way their brain develops (Balbernie, 2001). 'The factors which lead to a child entering the care system tend to be the same factors which can lead to mental health problems' (Department of Health, 2006).

The stories of twins Toby and Louise (not their real names) demonstrates the complex interplay of external experience and how the child makes sense of this and internalises it in ways that impact on his or her life.

Toby and Louise are twins. They have two older siblings. Their early years were not happy. Their father was often unemployed, and spent much of his time in the pub, returning home to bully his wife and children. The children quickly learned to stay quiet, and duck when their father returned home drunk, but often they weren't fast enough, as the bruises showed. They often saw their mother being hit, and listened to the verbal abuse heaped on her by their Dad.

Their mother had the spark beaten out of her. She was depressed, and often sat gazing into space while the children played, got themselves food, and did what they could to survive.

Toby had no adult figure to whom he was securely attached. He cared about his mother, but knew she could not be relied on to care for him. His father ruled the household with his fist. Sometimes he would play with the children, but Toby learned to live in fear – always watching for signs of his father's abrupt changes of mood.

He saw himself (his inner working model) as bad, unlovable, unloved, and worthless. He viewed his parents as unreliable, uncaring, and sometimes a direct threat to his safety and well-being.

Louise, however, saw her home situation differently. She saw it as her responsibility to care for her mother, so when her father hit out at her mother, or at any of the children, Louise blamed herself for failing in her self-appointed role. She believed (her inner working model) that her world would be safe if she worked hard enough and was good enough. In her mind, adults needed care from her; they could not be relied on to provide safety and nurture for her.

The experience of poor parenting and trauma was similar for Toby and Louise, but its impact was different. This was in part because in this family there were different expectations of boys and girls, but it was mainly because they made sense of their experiences differently.

Some children come into care as a result of a single serious incident or event that means that it is no longer possible for them to live with their family. But for the majority, there is a period during which many professionals are involved with the family to try to improve the quality of care the children receive so they can stay in their parents' care. Only if this fails to keep the children safe, or their development is significantly impaired and the parents are assessed as unable to offer effective care to their children, does the local authority step in.

Toby and Louise were three years old when the children first came into care, after Toby was found wandering in the streets at 11pm. Neither parent was at home.

After some intensive input from social services, the children were returned home, and for a time things improved. Their mother made more effort to keep the house tidy and prepare meals. There was some routine to the days. Their dad's behaviour was still erratic, but he spent more time with the children and hit them less often. Social workers came to the house regularly.

Toby liked having regular meals – but he wasn't used to being told what to do. He rebelled when his mother tried to bring in routines – he couldn't trust that she could care for him, so he often hit out at her – mirroring his Dad's behaviour.

The children had several short periods in care following repeated family crises. Each time they returned home to parental protestations of love, and promises that things would change. They did not.

Eventually, when the twins were six years old, the children were placed permanently in care. Their eldest brother was placed in a residential school for children with behavioural and emotional difficulties. Toby and Louise were fostered together.

For many looked after children, their early experiences of family disruption and breakdown that led to them coming into care have caused them to be more vulnerable to mental health problems than their peers. Their experiences in the care system have often compounded the problems. Children who have suffered trauma and abuse in their early years take their experiences and their survival strategies into their new families. The very strategies that helped them to survive their past experiences now have the potential to destroy the new relationships (see Levy & Orlans, 1998).

Toby brought to the placement his low self-esteem, and his inability to trust adults to nurture and care for him. When feeling threatened or insecure, he lashed out with his fists, at home and at school. Louise worked very hard at being good and trying to care for the new adults in her life, and felt rejected when they encouraged her to play instead.

Five months into the placement, the exhausted and dispirited foster carers asked for the twins' removal.

For some children this sets up a cycle of regular moves, an increasing inability to trust others, and a confirmation of their unworthiness. They feel in control of the situation while they are initiating the problems, and this is much less scary than learning to trust adults. However, this learning does not teach positive life skills, and can lead to much unhappiness, and often to mental health problems.

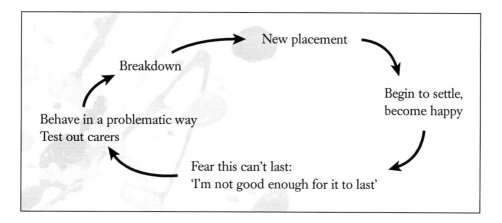

Until the last decade, looked after children have been significantly under-represented in the numbers of children and young people being seen by child and adolescent mental health (CAMHS) professionals. Sadly, this was not a reflection of lack of need, but that many looked after children did not fit easily into the CAMHS referral systems and structures.

The reasons for this are complex, and include:

- some children in care move from one placement to another and are not in one place long enough to access services and receive the help they need
- waiting lists may mean a child has moved on before their name reaches the top of the list
- many have learnt coping strategies that exclude adults, whom they view as untrustworthy and ineffective, and so are difficult to engage
- a lack of hope that life can be better, or that they deserve any better.

Resilience

The experience of each looked after child is unique. Their early history and reasons for coming into care often tell a story of pain and suffering, abandonment, and a struggle to make sense of what is happening to them and to adjust their view of self and the world around them.

In spite of the difficulties outlined above, many children in care have developed strong coping mechanisms that enable then to overcome difficulties, and demonstrate a resilience unusual for their age and experience. This is most likely to happen where there has been continuity of caregivers and key adults in their lives, who have worked through problems with them and not been intimidated by their fears and behaviours.

Developing resilience is a key feature of those with positive mental health. It requires that there are individuals around the child to:

- help build their self-esteem
- give positive messages about their abilities and achievements
- encourage positive aspirations and hope for a positive future.

All who work with looked after children have a part to play in reinforcing these positive messages, whether their role be foster carer, residential social worker, looked after children's nurse, teacher or classroom assistant, or someone who comes into contact with the child on a less regular basis, such as a doctor.

In addition to these positive one-to-one encounters, the systems and services for children need to work in ways that enhance the self-respect and dignity of each individual child.

Education

Having experience of success is an important aspect of developing resilience and positive self-esteem. When it comes to achieving academic potential, stability is again a key factor. Children and young people who experience frequent moves of home and school are unlikely to succeed academically.

The Social Exclusion Unit report (2003) identifies five barriers to their success:

- instability of placement (home and school)
- time out of school (truanting or excluded or waiting to be placed in a new school)
- lack of help with schoolwork
- lack of support and encouragement from home
- poor health and well-being.

Children in care are now a priority group in term of school admissions policies, so fewer are missing education while waiting for a school placement. However, a significant minority remain hard to place because their behavioural or educational needs make it hard for them to succeed in mainstream classrooms.

Children who have coped with their experiences by a 'fight or flight' response, either hitting out at whoever is in their way, or running away from perceived conflicts, or who fail to attend school regularly because they find it too difficult or not relevant to their needs, need special consideration: how can they be helped to realise their potential?

At school, Toby was under-achieving, although of average ability. His behaviour was erratic. Most of the time he tried hard to 'be good', but when faced with a difficult situation in the classroom, such as work he found challenging, or being asked to do something he didn't want to do, he would often get angry and would hit out at anyone and anything nearby. Later, he would calm down, apologise, and try very hard to 'be good' again. He saw these outbursts as confirmation of his innate wickedness, and it validated his low sense of self-esteem.

Hard though criticism was for Toby to cope with, praise was even harder, and after receiving positive attention Toby would often spoil his good work – or hit a child nearby. His behaviour was very hard to manage in the classroom.

Louise was assessed as having special educational needs and required additional support in her work. She found it hard to concentrate or to learn new skills. She believed she was 'stupid' and her low grades at school confirmed this to her. Only when placed in a supportive foster home where she received much encouragement to persevere and appropriate praise for each step of her learning did this belief begin to alter, and progress was made. This required very close co-operation between home and school, with daily communication, and the clear message to Louise that all the adults in her life were now working together to help her.

Where the educational needs of looked after children remain unmet, this has a severe impact on their achievements and expectations, and this is one reason for the high number of adults who spent time in care and now have severe problems as adults, often at great cost to society, as well as to the individuals concerned.

Policy

Policies are the backbone of professional action. Using policies to enhance the experience of children in care in an imaginative way is the key to developing services that are responsive to their needs and really make a difference in their lives.

The *Every Child Matters* agenda (Department for Education and Skills, 2003), which underpins all children's policy, has a dual emphasis on providing services that encourage good outcomes for all children, and specialist services for those with specific and complex needs, including children and young people who are looked after. Through the *Quality Protects* programme (Department of Health, 1998) and *Care Matters* (Department for Children, Schools and Families, 2007), the government has targeted the needs of these children in a series of initiatives aimed at improving their life chances, including their emotional well-being, and ensuring that their general health needs are met and they have improved access to specialist mental health services.

Local authorities are now encouraged to take the role of 'corporate parents': ie. the services they provide and the way in which they are delivered must be of a standard that would be expected for children not in their care. The quality of care provided needs to be that of a good parent. This has encouraged a holistic approach to meeting the needs of looked after children in terms of health provision, dental care, and individual plans to encourage young people to meet their full potential, through education and the constructive use of leisure time.

Examples of good practice

Improving the mental health and emotional well-being of children in care has been given a higher priority in recent years, and the need for dedicated services for looked after children and their carers has been recognised. There are now many innovative specialist services up and down the country. Some focus on supporting the foster carers of children whose complex problems have led to repeated placement breakdowns; some address specialist education provision; others work directly with the children and young people, either on a one-to-one basis or in groups, to build self-esteem and help them devise new strategies for coping with their problems.

In 2007 YoungMinds published a report on emerging good practice in mental health services for looked after children (Bunting, 2007). The following features characterised successful services:

- **flexible** in order to be accessible and acceptable
- **jointly commissioned and jointly managed**, ensuring mental health services incorporate health, education and social care elements
- managed and staffed by individuals with **vision and passion**
- take **time to engage** with children and young people
- are able to offer **long-term work**
- have a **holistic** approach that supports the whole child
- use **systemic thinking** when engaging with all of those in contact with the child and family
- are **participative**, with formal and informal mechanisms for consulting with young people

- use **evidence-based** practice, evaluating services to ensure they are being effective
- are **reflective and responsive** to feedback from all stakeholders.

Conclusion

For too long the emotional needs of looked after children have not been addressed holistically. This, coupled with the complex and difficult circumstances that necessitated their coming into care in the first place, meant that many of them developed mental health problems, which also were not adequately addressed.

In recent years, the very marked change of focus in policy is leading to improvements in this situation. Service developments in many areas of the country have shown that imagination and a flexible approach, combined with the traditional specialist knowledge and skills of CAMHS professionals, can result in services that really make a difference to the lives of these children and young people, helping them to work through the difficulties of their past experiences, and empowering them to achieve the goals that are important to them.

We all have a role to play. Improving the mental health of looked after children is everybody's business.

References

Balbernie R (2001) Circuits and circumstances: the neurological consequences of early relationship experiences and how they shape later behaviour. *Journal of Child Psychotherapy* **27** (3) 237–255.

Bunting M (2007) *Looking after the mental health needs of looked after children: sharing emerging practice.* London: YoungMinds.

Department for Education and Skills (2003) *Every child matters* (green paper). London: Department for Education and Skills.

Department for Children, Schools and Families (2007) *Care matters: transforming the lives of children and young people in care.* London: Department for Children, Schools and Families.

Department of Health (1998) *Quality protects.* London: Department of Health.

Department of Health (2006) *Report on the implementation of standard 9 of the national service framework for children, young people and maternity services: promoting the mental health and psychological well-being of children and young people.* London: Department of Health.

Levy T, Orlans M (1998) *Attachment trauma and healing: understanding and treating attachment disorder in children and families.* Washington, DC: Child Welfare League of America Press.

McCann JB, James A, Wilson S, Dunn G (1996) Prevalence of psychiatric disorders in young people in the care system. *British Medical Journal* **313** 1529–1530.

Office for National Statistics (2005) *Mental health and young people looked after by local authorities in Great Britain (2001–2003).* London: Office for National Statistics.

Phillips J (1997) Meeting the psychiatric needs of children in foster care: social workers' views. *Psychiatric Bulletin* **21** 609–611.

Social Exclusion Unit (2003) *A better education for children in care.* London: Office of the Deputy Prime Minister.

YoungMinds (2003) *Tuning into our babies: the importance of the relationship between parents and their babies and toddlers.* London: YoungMinds.

YoungMinds (2004) *Mental health in infancy.* London: YoungMinds.

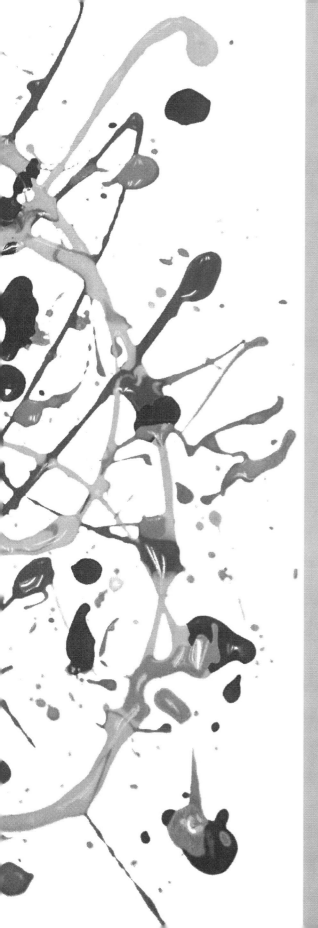

The mental health of children with learning disabilities

Jill Davies and Alison Giraud-Saunders

Key points

- more than one in three children and young people with a learning disability also have mental health problems

- accessing help and specialist services may be difficult for a number of reasons, including problems identifying the mental health problem and its causes, and communication difficulties

- children and young people with learning disabilities may be at greater risk of mental health problems because of socio-economic circumstances and physical ill health

- government policy stresses the need for joined-up, multi-agency provision and equal access to mainstream CAMHS

- young people with learning disabilities should also have access to specialist care where their needs are more complex or challenging.

Key words
Learning disabilities; Mental health; Risk factors; Access to services; Specialist services

'Children with learning disabilities are everyone's business. They are children first and should have access to the range of services that other children are entitled to.'

This quote is from a clinical lead in child and adolescent mental health services (CAMHS). Although it may sound like common sense, not all CAMHS have had such an inclusive approach. It is hard to believe that, until recently, many children with learning disabilities were excluded from their local service. During the past few years there has been a raft of policy initiatives to ensure that 'all means all' and that children and young people with learning disabilities are entitled to access their local CAMHS. This chapter will address the mental health needs of this group of children, along with an outline of the current policy and practice perspectives.

Who are we talking about?

Let us start by defining the group we are talking about: that is, what do we mean by a learning disability?

A learning disability includes the presence of:

- a significantly reduced ability to understand new or complex information, or to learn new skills (impaired intelligence), with
- a reduced ability to cope independently (impaired social functioning), which started before adulthood (Department of Health, 2001).

It has been estimated that 985,000 people in England (two per cent of the population) have a learning disability, of whom 189,000 are aged under 20. The numbers known to learning disability services are much smaller: an estimated 224,000 people in England, of whom 55,000 are aged under 20 (Emerson & Hatton, 2004).

Incidence and prevalence

Emerson and Hatton (2007) recently analysed the latest Office for National Statistics data to estimate how many children in the UK have a learning disability and mental health problem. They found that over one in three children and adolescents with a learning disability in Britain (36%) has a diagnosable psychiatric disorder, compared with eight per cent of children who do not have a learning disability. These figures are in line with previous analyses, including Emerson (2003) and the original study by Michael Rutter over 30 years ago in his Isle of Wight studies, in which it was reported that 30% of 10–12 year olds with learning disabilities had mental health problems (Rutter *et al*, 1976).

Emerson and Hatton (2007) state that the increased risk of having a mental health problem cuts across all types of psychiatric disorders. Children with learning disabilities are:

- 33 times more likely to have an autistic spectrum disorder
- eight times more likely to have ADHD
- six times more likely to have a conduct disorder
- four times more likely to have an emotional disorder
- 0.7 times more likely to have a depressive disorder.

They are also significantly more likely to have multiple psychiatric disorders.

The social situation for children with learning disabilities can create further problems: it costs three times as much to raise a child with a disability (Dobson & Middleton, 1998); they often live in more challenging family circumstances, and they are likely to have fewer friends. All of these factors are known to be associated with an increased risk of mental health problems. Another major contributing factor is physical health. People with learning disabilities are far more likely than non-disabled people to have secondary health problems such as epilepsy, sensory deficits or other disabilities, and these conditions are also associated with long-standing depression and anxiety if not identified. The following quote is from a parent of a son with high support needs:

'The times he was running about screaming with his wisdom tooth and I didn't have a clue what it was, I could have done with somebody then – somebody to come in, professional, unprofessional, whatever, just to help me fathom out what it was. I just didn't know what it was and that's torment, more torment on Aiden. That was the hard bit about it, because he was trying to tell me what was wrong, but how did I know? It's probably that it had got Aiden down but he hadn't shown it.'

The policy context

There have been a number of policy initiatives that aim to improve the quality of life and access to services for this group of children. There are too many to address comprehensively here, but some of the recent key policies that have shaped services are listed below:

- *Valuing People: A new strategy for learning disability for the 21st century* (Department of Health, 2001) is the government's plan for making the lives of people with learning disabilities better. It is based on their rights as citizens; inclusion in local communities; choice in daily life, and real chances to be independent

- *Every Child Matters* (Department for Education and Skills, 2004) sets out five outcomes, based on consultations with children and young people, that should be the aim for all. They are: being healthy, staying safe, enjoying and achieving, making a positive contribution, and economic well-being

- The National Service Framework for Children, Young People and Maternity Services (Department for Health/Department for Education and Skills, 2004) sets out detailed standards for children's and young people's health and social care. The standards that most directly concern children with learning disabilities are:

- standard 8 – disabled children and those with complex health needs. The standard calls for disabled children to have equal access to child and adolescent services; for assessments to be provided by professionals with expertise, and for local services to include plans to improve mental health services across all four tiers of provision

- standard 9 – promoting mental health and psychological well-being. The standard states that all children with learning disabilities and a mental health problem should have access to appropriate child and adolescent mental health services.

- The Disability Discrimination Act 1995 and the Disability Equality Duty for the public sector should improve access to health and other public sector services for disabled people.

In addition to the above policies, the 2005 public service agreement (PSA) (Department of Health, 2005) between the Treasury and the Department of Health set a target for all areas to have a comprehensive CAMHS by late 2006, and specifically a complete range of services for children with learning disabilities.

Service delivery framework

Service delivery varies across the UK, as there is no one model to suit all local areas. The *Count Us In* (Foundation for People with Learning Disabilities, 2002) inquiry, conducted in 2002 by the Foundation for People with Learning Disabilities, heard evidence that some children were excluded from their local CAMHS because they had a learning disability. However, the inquiry also heard that children and young people were referred to a lottery of different services – CAMHS, specialist learning disability CAMHS, community learning disability teams and community paediatricians. For example, a 16-year-old boy presenting with depression could be referred to the local CAMHS, the community team for learning disability (CTLD), or adult mental health services, depending on where he lived.

This finding was reinforced by further work by the Foundation (2005a) looking at the configuration of CAMHS. In a sample of 20 services, nearly 40% were specialist learning disability services that included a psychiatrist who worked with children, but only a small number were fully integrated services. Other services had a learning disability service set within a mainstream CAMHS, and some had no provision at all. A positive finding was the growing number of specialist learning disability teams based within a mainstream CAMHS. This format means learning disabled children have access to their local CAMHS and the range of interventions available to other children, but also ensures access to learning disability expertise for those with more complex problems.

Future developments in CAMHS

In response to the policy initiatives and the PSA target, the Department of Health funded the development of a mental health care pathway (Pote & Goodban, 2007) to address concerns about how to best support children with learning disabilities and mental health problems. At the heart of every care pathway should be transparency about referral procedures and the range of support available, as young people and their families often do not know where to turn if they experience mental health problems.

While there is no magic wand to show which configuration is the best, services providing good care to the child and the family will be following the 10 guiding principles set out in the mental health care pathway (Pote & Goodban, 2007). Chief of these is that the service will:

- be holistic and child-centred
- see the child within a developmental framework
- be inclusive and offer equal access
- involve multi-agency commissioning.

Future developments in CAMHS should also reflect what children and young people want from such a service. The Foundation recently produced guidelines called *This is What We Want* (Foundation for People with Learning Disabilities, 2007) for CAMHS, based on consultations with young people and their families. They want appointments at convenient times and in non-stigmatising locations. Having a child with a learning disability often means that parents are required to attend numerous appointments, so flexibility around appointments can make a huge difference to their lives. They also want to know more about the service they have been referred to, and want professionals to use language they understand.

Identification of mental health problems

Findings from our research programme *Making Us Count* (Foundation for People with Learning Disabilities, 2005b) indicated that few young people with learning disabilities and mental health problems had received a formal psychiatric diagnosis. This is a significant concern, because it means that young people often do not receive the appropriate mental health support. A number of factors could account for this, one being that young people and their parents were told that the mental health problem was part of the disability.

'The doctor saw the disability first and the person second.' (Evidence from a parent, *Count Us In* inquiry)

The terminology used by services was found to be a barrier to identifying mental health problems because it tends to be rather abstract. Many people with learning disabilities, due to their cognitive deficits, need help to identify the feelings they are experiencing and the triggers behind those feelings. The quote below is from a young person who had difficulty in recognising his emotional distress as a mental health need:

'I don't talk to anyone – I just bottle it in. If I get angry, I just bottle it in, and then it explodes.'

Help can be in the form of using easy English, together with photographs, graphics, symbols or sign language. The use of photography and video diaries can provide alternative means for young people to express their views: photographs taken by the young person can help the therapist probe more fully into what is contributing to the person's poor mental health.

Where the young person has multiple and high support needs, and especially if they are unable to communicate verbally, services may be reliant on family carers to identify mental health problems. Research undertaken for the Foundation for People with Learning Disabilities (2005b) has shown that people with profound and multiple learning disabilities do experience a wide range of emotional problems. These tend to be demonstrated by their behaviours, such as changes in facial expression, posture, appetite and in sleep patterns, frequent crying, repetitive hand movements, unusual sexual behaviour, seizures, self-injury, and social withdrawal.

Further evidence from the *Making Us Count* programme demonstrated that young people had varying insights into their mental health problems. They did not discuss their understanding of mental health issues in abstract terms, but tended to use descriptive terms. For example, they described the physical effects of anxiety and depression as 'sweaty palms' or 'heavy breathing', and used words like 'panic', 'bored', 'frightened' or 'temper'. The following quote is from a teenager with an anxiety disorder:

'Nervous, I get sweaty palms, I feel sick a bit, you know what I mean, and it's just one of those things and it really annoys me it does.'

The factors behind the mental health problems identified included physical health problems, feelings of worthlessness, coping with everyday life, having nothing to do, and emotional difficulties. Some young people with epilepsy were extremely anxious about going out alone in case they had a seizure.

A key issue was that young people, their families and staff were not used to discussing mental health or the young person's needs for mental health support. Some people did not like the words 'mental health' because this term was viewed negatively and seen as stigmatising. Parents in particular were unhappy about adding another 'label' to their son or daughter. We also noted from our work that most young people turned to their teacher, parents or youth worker for advice about their mental health problems, and these are the people who should be targeted to improve identification and referral rates.

An important factor to take into consideration when working with young people with learning disabilities is that assessments tend to be time-consuming. It can take longer to find out what is causing the problems, particularly if the child is unable to articulate what is upsetting them. It may involve a period of assessment in the home, or at school or other residential or support service they are attending to get a better picture of what is happening. Children with learning disabilities are more likely than other children to be receiving support from numerous services, and some may have a key worker who acts as a liaison between the child and the various services with which he or she is in contact. Traditionally, CAMHS have tended to be clinic-based and offer time-limited interventions. This approach is beginning to change, with some services trying to be more creative in their responses to these young people.

The quality standards set by the mental health care pathway (Pote & Goodban, 2007) for CAMHS state that assessments should:

- be holistic (consider the mental health needs in the context of the learning disability and the family's needs)
- follow established protocols and good practice, such as the NICE (National Institute for Clinical Excellence) depression and self-harm guidelines (2004; 2005).

Interventions

There is little research at present using standardised measures to evidence successful mental health interventions for children with learning disabilities. However, the learning disability subgroup of the Children's NSF external working group on child and adolescent mental health and psychological well-being (2002) stated that 'there are no prima facie reasons to suppose that [children and adolescents with learning disabilities] respond differently [to other children]', so the evidence of effectiveness of interventions should be assumed to apply to them. This is backed up by a discussion paper written for the group (Gale, 2002).

Practitioners are advised, therefore, to follow the current evidence base for all children, and adapt the methodology when and if necessary (Pote & Goodbann, 2007). The quality standards for intervention in the mental health care pathway for children with learning disabilities state:

1   interventions should be individually tailored to meet the mental health needs of the child and their family, taking into account their age, developmental level, and culture

2   emotional and behavioural interventions should be available at all levels of service delivery (Tiers 1-4), from a variety of psychological models (behavioural, systemic, cognitive, psychodynamic and humanistic), in a variety of formats (individual, group or family therapy, and consultation)

3   interventions targeted at mental health issues need to be considered within the context of other interventions (social, educational, physical) that the child is receiving. Services should develop effective inter-agency co-ordination to achieve this.

Adaptation of interventions to suit children with varying cognitive levels will require the use of a range of verbal and non-verbal communication methods. Consultation with key people involved in the child's life is necessary to ensure the intervention has a positive outcome. Below are two case studies that reflect the range of mental health problems experienced by children and young people with learning disabilities.

Thomas

Thomas is 15 and has mild learning disabilities, epilepsy and an autistic spectrum disorder. He attends his local secondary school (with support), but has recently become withdrawn and is reluctant to go to school. On most mornings Thomas and his mother end up arguing and he has been known to hit and push her when she is telling him to get dressed for school. He lives with his mum and two younger sisters in a housing association two-bedded flat.

Suggested interventions

- Assessments should be multi-agency and involve the school, his paediatrician and any other professionals involved in his care and support, as well as Thomas and his mother. This could involve visiting him in his home and at school.

- Assessment tools or rating scales should be adapted to ensure Thomas can understand them.

- Consider the use of photography or other visual images to help him discuss his problems, as people with autism tend to process information and understand the world in more concrete and visual ways.

- Interventions should be discussed with Thomas and his family and the school to ensure consistency. If the cause of his mental health problems is bullying, interventions should include strategies to tackle and help him deal with it, and ways to increase self-esteem.

- Any interventions should be adapted to suit his level of understanding.

- Consider a referral for more suitable housing, and identify other sources of support for the whole family.

- Identify any activities, clubs or short-term break providers for Thomas and his family.

Jessica

Jessica is 11 years old. She has a severe learning disability, poor expressive language and attends a special school. Her mother and father have noticed an increase in her self-injurious behaviour – she bangs her head against people and objects, slaps her face and bites her hands.

Suggested interventions

- With self-injurious behaviour it is very important to consider pain as a factor. For example, does she have tooth decay or an ear infection that is causing distress?

- Identify the cause – is there a biological factor contributing to this; has it become a learned behaviour, or are there other causes – is she tired, bored, hungry, ill, anxious or depressed?

- Are there any triggers in the environment – such as under- or over-stimulation; is she not getting enough attention, or is she finding demands difficult to cope with?

- Devise a strategy with her parents to keep her safe during these episodes, and make sure it is being used consistently by different people in different environments. Make sure the school staff and other people in contact with her know what to do.

- If the cause is not pain, teach Jessica a more functional way to express her needs, to replace the self-injurious behaviour. For example, if she finds demands hard to cope with, teach her to sign or say a short phrase such as 'stop'. It would be extremely useful to involve Jessica's speech and language therapist, or make a referral to one for help with communication.

- Encourage the family and school to keep records of her behaviour to evaluate the intervention.

- Consider putting the family in touch with any local support groups or voluntary organisations that support parents whose child has a challenging behaviour – for example, the Challenging Behaviour Foundation (www.thecbf.org.uk).

Conclusion

Children and young people with learning disabilities have historically experienced a double disadvantage: an increased risk of developing mental health problems, and poor access to mental health services. Evidence collected by the Foundation for People with Learning Disabilities indicates that they face delays in receiving help and support, due to fragmented service provision. This issue has now been recognised by the Department of Health and the Department for Children, Schools and Families. It is encouraging that both the policy framework and some of the current service developments explicitly address the needs of children and young people who have learning disabilities and mental health problems. Let's hope that, within the next few years, all children and young people with learning disabilities will have equal and speedy access to the whole range of mental health services to which they are entitled, both mainstream and more specialist, and that these services are provided in ways and environments that they find acceptable and helpful.

References

CAMHS learning disability subgroup for the Children's NSF CAMHS external working group (2002) *Summary statement*. London: Department of Health.

Department for Education and Skills (2004) *Every child matters: change for children*. London: the Stationery Office.

Department of Health (2001) *Valuing people: a new strategy for learning disability for the 21st century*. London: Department of Health.

Department of Health (2005) *Public Service Agreement 2005–2008*. London: Department of Health.

Department of Health/Department for Education and Skills (2004) *National service framework for children, young people and maternity services*. London: Department of Health.

Dobson B, Middleton S (1998) *Paying to care: the cost of childhood disability*. York: YPS.

Emerson E (2003) The prevalence of psychiatric disorders in children and adolescents with and without intellectual disabilities. *Journal of Intellectual Disability Research* **47** 51–58.

Emerson E, Hatton C (2004) *Estimating the current need/demand for supports for people with learning disabilities in England*. Lancaster: Institute for Health Research, Lancaster University.

Emerson E, Hatton C (2007) *The mental health of children and adolescents with learning disabilities in Britain*. Lancaster: Institute for Health Research, Lancaster University.

Foundation for People with Learning Disabilities (2002) *Count us in*. London: Mental Health Foundation.

Foundation for People with Learning Disabilities (2005a) *Services for children and adolescents with learning disabilities and mental health problems: a managed care approach*. Internal report by Tina Jackson. London: Mental Health Foundation. (Summary available at www.learningdisabilities.org.uk)

Foundation for People with Learning Disabilities (2005b) *Making us count.* London: Mental Health Foundation.

Foundation for People with Learning Disabilities (2007) *This is what we want.* London: Mental Health Foundation. (Available at www.learningdisabilities.org.uk)

Gale I (2002, updated 2003) *Is the general evidence base for child and adolescent mental health problems applicable to children and young people with learning disabilities?* Unpublished discussion paper for the learning disability subgroup of the Children's NSF external working group on child and adolescent mental health and psychological well-being.

NICE (2004) *Self-harm: the short-term physical and psychological management and secondary prevention of self-harm in primary and secondary care.* London: NICE.

NICE (2005) *Depression in children and young people: identification and management in primary, community and secondary care.* London: NICE.

Pote H, Goodban D (2007) *A mental health care pathway for children and young people with learning disabilities.* London: CAMHS Publications.

Rutter M, Tizard J, Yule W, Graham P, Whitmore K (1976) Research report: Isle of Wight studies 1964–1974. *Psychological Medicine* **6** 313–332.

Part IV

Adolescent mental health

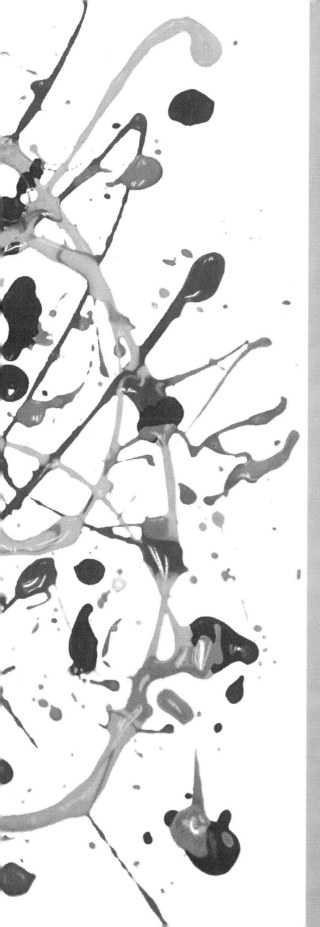

Resilience and risk in children and young people

Richard Williams

Key points

- Human beings are generally highly resilient to trauma and adversity

- Resilience is dependent on a number of factors – personal, environmental, social and experiential

- Ensuring access to relationships with and social support from families, schools and society is one of the key factors in promoting resilience in childhood and adolescence

- Young people who are resilient and have access to external support and continued positive, close relationships have the capacity to recover and learn from temporary adversity

- Interventions to promote young people's resilience should aim to enable them build their own hardiness and personal skills in relating well to others, assist them to recognise and protect themselves from risk, protect them from risk when they are unable to do so for themselves, and provide effective social support following any inevitable exposure to risk.

Key words
Resilience; Risk; Resistance; Protective factors; Developmental psychology

This chapter explores the meaning of resilience and the implications of current knowledge for strategies and interventions to assist children and young people to face well and learn from the challenges that everyone experiences while they are growing up and throughout life. Some of those challenges are sudden and/or extreme; other children and young people grow up in circumstances of sustained adversity or recurrent abuse or trauma. Yet humans are surprisingly resilient. In the words of Masten (2001), resilience is 'ordinary magic'. Nonetheless, there is much that we could and should do to maximise the resilience of our children and young people.

Masten and colleagues (1990) describe resilience as 'the process of or opportunity for successful adaptation despite difficult or threatening circumstances'. Masten (2001) also defines it as 'a class of phenomena characterized by good outcomes in spite of serious threats to adaptation or development'.

Condly (2006) states: 'Resilience can be thought of as an enduring characteristic of the person, a situational or temporal interaction between the person and the context, or a unitary or multifaceted construct [which] can be applied to social, academic or other settings.'

These definitions begin to identify some of the key phenomena that, together, constitute resilience. They include the personal characteristics and capabilities of children and young people, the nature of their family, peer, school and employment situations, the life events that they experience, and the nature of their attachments and relationships.

There are at least two broad uses of the concept of resilience. The first derives from developmental psychology and relates to how children develop psychosocially in the face of common challenges and stressors of variable duration and intensity. The second concerns recovery from abuse, disaster, conflict and terrorism: ie. recovery from extreme stressors and experiences.

Resilience may be applied to how particular people respond to the challenges they face, which depends, in turn, on their personal characteristics, repertoire of knowledge, skills and capabilities (inherent and acquired), the qualities of their relationships and their life experiences and circumstances. This is known as personal resilience.

The term is also used increasingly with reference to how groups of people, communities, organisations and countries respond to, cope with and recover from disasters and catastrophes. This is termed collective resilience. This chapter focuses on personal resilience, defined by Williams (2007) as: 'A person's capacity for adapting psychologically, emotionally and physically reasonably well and without lasting detriment to self, relationships or personal development in the face of adversity, threat or challenge.'

Core features of resilience

In technology, resilience describes the capacity of a material to return to its original shape after an applied force is removed. This happens provided the material is not pushed past its elastic limit. Thus, resilience in adolescents may be described as their capacity for returning to a positive, purposeful and adaptive path of development following challenge, sudden threat, or chronic stressors such as adversity.

Certain core features of resilience emerge repeatedly from research and practical experience. Genetic and acquired personal characteristics are known to be related to people being more likely to being resilient or more vulnerable. Resilience also describes a dynamic, interactional and systemic quality, in which personal factors interact with experience and changing circumstances. These multifaceted and interactive characteristics are the second core feature of resilience.

Another core feature is that resilience is a very common quality. Masten (2001) refers to the 'ordinariness of resilience', appreciation of which enables us to take 'a more positive outlook on human development and adaptation' than if we focused solely on people's deficits. Resilience also provides a 'direction for policy and practice aimed at enhancing the development of children at risk for problems and psychopathology'.

In the words of Hoge and colleagues (2007): '… the notion of resilience encompasses psychological and biological characteristics… that might be modifiable and that confer protection against the development of psychopathology in the face of stress.'

Resilience and allied concepts

The concept of resilience recognises that all children and adolescents are affected by challenging events or circumstances. However, if they are resilient, and are provided with appropriate external support and continued positive, close relationships, most of them have the capacity to recover and learn from temporary setbacks on their progress and development that may result in a regression to less mature forms of behaviour.

Resistance

Resistance is a concept that describes the ability of people to respond to stressors with only very minor or no change. It is related to resilience, but the two are not identical, and should not be used interchangeably (Layne et al, 2007). An example of the difference is provided by research showing that people who have greater capacities for empathy are also more likely to be distressed or temporarily upset when others confide worries in them (Firth-Cozens, 1987; Alexander & Klein, 2001). That is to say, people who are empathic and who experience temporary upset after engaging with others who are in difficulties may not appear to be as resistant as people who do not get upset, but most of them are just as likely to be resilient.

Hardiness and sense of coherence

Resistance and resilience are related to the concept of hardiness. Hardiness describes the capacity of plants to survive adverse growing conditions. There is a clear analogy here with children who grow up in adverse circumstances. Some children appear tougher or hardier than others. As defined by Maddi and Kobasa (1984), hardiness has three characteristics: control, commitment, and challenge. Control describes the belief that a person can control or influence events, commitment describes the ability of people to feel deeply involved in the activities in their lives, and challenge means seeing change as normal and providing opportunities. Commitment has been shown to be the component of hardiness that moderates the relationship between stress and depression in adults (Pengilly & Dowd, 2000).

These concepts are similar to and overlap with the notion of 'sense of coherence' (SOC). SOC describes a perception that events are comprehensible, manageable and meaningful. A strong SOC in adults has been shown to be a stable protective factor for health that is independent of known risk factors and inversely related to distress (Breslin *et al*, 2006). It is also a potential marker of people's capacity to adapt to social stress (Surtees *et al*, 2006). There is support from research for SOC having a role both in mediating and buffering the impact of adverse experiences on psychological well-being in adulthood. There is also evidence that adversity and stress might not affect well-being directly (Gana, 2001).

A sense of coherence, the capacity for feeling involved in activities around us, and belief that we are able to influence other people and events are some of the features of our personal and unique identities that emerge more clearly during adolescence, as young people develop the capacity for introspection and understanding themselves and their feelings, desires and motives. Indeed, adolescence is a most important time of development. Positive experiences, learning how to cope with challenges, and, as this chapter describes, achieving self-efficacy and learning to receive and use support from relationships are important parts of growing up that can shape people's later resilience.

Risk and resilience

The risk factors that affect children and young people fall into three categories: genetic, related to personal attributes, and environmental. They interact with protective factors in complex ways (Fairbank *et al*, 2007; Layne *et al*, 2007). Too many children and young people grow up in the face of series of challenges and seriously adverse circumstances with which they cannot deal alone.

There is evidence from research that suggests there may be a two-way interaction between social exclusion, for example, and the risks of developing many problems and disorders in adolescence (Social Exclusion Unit, 2004). Social exclusion is not a single concept; it describes an array of factors that may raise substantially the profile of risks faced by children and young people. Figure 1, for example, depicts the relationships between social exclusion and the risks of young people developing behaviour problems, psychiatric disorders and substance misuse.

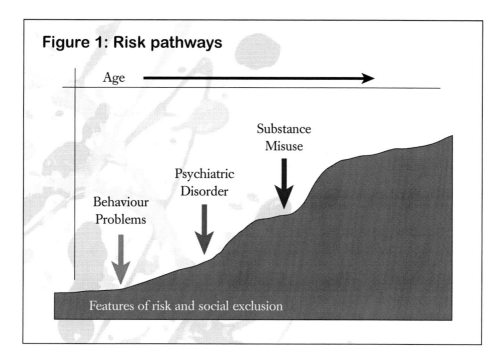

Figure 1: Risk pathways

Age

Substance Misuse

Psychiatric Disorder

Behaviour Problems

Features of risk and social exclusion

Thus, a young person who develops behaviour problems is also at a higher than average risk of becoming socially excluded, and this, in turn, increases the risk of that same young person becoming socially alienated and moving into substance misuse, or of developing a mental health problem or disorder. Each of these conditions may, in turn, result in greater exclusion and higher risk.

Resilience and protective factors are those circumstances, personal attributes or events that ward against such progressions to developing problems. Some young people appear to be either more resistant or resilient than others to developing problems, despite experiencing unfavourable events, challenges or circumstances. Also, there is some research showing that young people can derive benefits from experiences of adversity: one Israeli study, for example, found that, while around 40% of adolescents who had experienced terrorist incidents reported post-traumatic symptoms, 75% also reported emotional growth (Laufer & Solomon, 2006). This raises the possibility that, if challenges are well handled, they may be associated with positive as well as negative outcomes.

However, other young people are much more vulnerable and, in coming to a view about how best to intervene, research has shown that it is important to understand a little more about risk factors and how resilience operates and can be bolstered. For example, some factors may initially appear to convey risk but may actually be part of a larger risk factor and have no separate effect. These are sometimes called risk markers. Other factors may have a direct effect, and others still may mediate or moderate risk. It is important to recognise that risk and resilience interact in complex ways that are still being researched.

Developmental psychology

Many research projects in the last 40 years have examined the elements that contribute to good resilience. Bonanno (2004) describes the ways in which resilience can be achieved after loss and trauma, through:

- achieving hardiness
- self-enhancement (because people with higher opinions of themselves appear to be more resilient to stressful events) (Bonanno *et al*, 2002)
- repressive coping, and
- positive emotion and humour.

The first two of these are thinking processes; the second two relate more to how people handle their emotions. Thus, Bonanno's approach indicates that resilience has cognitive and emotional aspects as well as those that relate to relationships and the nature of external events.

Schaap *et al* (2006) have reviewed the literature on a number of different theories to identify the characteristics of resilience to the effects of trauma. Table 1 (which has been developed from Schaap *et al*, 2006) presents an overview. Schaap *et al* group their factors under two headings; social support and self-efficacy. Again, a mix of cognitive skills, emotional and personal attitudes and the nature of relationships emerge as core features.

Table 1: Resilience factors (developed from Schaap *et al*, 2006)

Personal skills:
- the capacity to receive social support
- good cognitive skills
- good communication skills
- active problem-solving skills
- flexibility – the ability to adapt to change
- ability to cope with stress (seeing stress as a challenge).

Personal beliefs and attitudes:
- self-efficacy (general expectation of competence)
- self-esteem
- hope
- a sense of purpose
- religion or the feeling of belonging somewhere
- positive emotion and humour
- the belief that stress can have a strengthening affect
- acceptance of negative feelings.

Table 1 continued ⇨

Interaction skills, relationships and achievements:

- good relationships with other people
- contributions to community life
- talents or accomplishments that one values oneself or that are appreciated by others
- access to and use of protective processes
- adaptive ways of coping that suit the situation and the person
- growth through negative experiences.

In parallel, Condly (2006) has drawn together the characteristic attributes of resilience in his review of the literature on children's development in the face of chronic, and often repeated, challenges (table 2 summarises and adds to Condly's findings).

Table 2: The nature of resilience (developed from Condly, 2006)

Resilience is:

Dynamic		Resilience changes over time and may be of differing strength in differing situations
Developmental		Resilience is affected profoundly by each person's experience in childhood and beyond
Interactive	Passive – increasing a person's ability to withstand trauma	Resilience may be thought of as related to each person's ability to withstand trauma. So, one approach is to help people to develop their ability to cope well when faced with trauma
	Active – shaping the environment to minimise trauma	A second approach to developing resilience is based on the observation that more resilient people express agency in doing what they can to organise the world around them to minimise the risks of being exposed to situations that are traumatic

Table 2 continued ⇨

		At the same time, most people also wish to experience some risks and each one of us has our own setting on our 'risk thermostat'. Actively coping well may, therefore, be related to knowing our own comfort with risk and adjusting the risks we face when this is an option
Related to attachment capabilities		Research has shown strong relationships between people's capacities for secure attachments and their resilience
Gender related		Generally, women are more resilient than men, although they are also more likely to develop longer-term psychiatric disorders after exposure to adversity

In the same paper, Condly reviewed Garmezy's work (1991), and the following factors emerged as most affecting the resilience of children and young people.

1 Intelligence and temperament

There is research evidence showing that resilient children 'tend to possess an above average intelligence and a temperament that endears them to others'. In Condly's opinion, the combination of these two features is particularly important.

2 Family relationships and level of support available from family

There is support for the notion that the roles of families in the development of resilience are most important early in life and decline as children grow older.

3 External support from other persons and institutions

Support of specific types for families is a major factor in promoting resilience in urban children who have experienced life stresses. These positive social supports must actively include the children at risk and work best when whole families are supported.

Hoge *et al* (2007) have reviewed research on the resilience factors that distinguish children who face high risk to their development and mental health from abuse, poverty and adversity, family discord, mental disorder, chronic stress and institutional care. Feelings of control, self-esteem, positive attitudes to self, higher IQ and socioeconomic status, close relationships with an adult, and external support systems emerge repeatedly as conveying resilience.

In a recent book chapter, Layne and colleagues (2007) recommend that, if we are to understand resilience and risk and how they relate to each other, we should pay attention to people who have resistant and resilient outcomes after traumatic events. Children of divorced parents, children whose parents misuse substances, and children who have been abused are at risk of poor outcomes, yet many of them fare much better than we might expect. While we still know little about how protective mechanisms and processes operate, there are strong suggestions that certain factors may intervene in risk-producing mechanisms to moderate or reduce the risk of an unfavourable outcome. Masten (2001), for example, summarises research that shows that 'children with competent parents are exposed to fewer adverse life events' because their parents avert possible risks. She also draws on her own research showing how the quality of parenting predicts child competence over time.

Layne and colleagues (2007) cite research by Brewin, Andrews and Valentine (2000) that shows that absence of social support is one of three factors that has greater impact on risk for adults of them developing post-traumatic stress disorder after their exposure to trauma. Apparently, the presence or absence of social support has greater influence than abuse in childhood, intelligence, socioeconomic status and education. This supports the contention that understanding resilience is important in understanding risk, and that risk and resilience factors should be considered together when assessing young people. There is a high risk of under- or over-estimating the risks faced by children if one or the other concept is assessed alone.

Hopefully, further research into the risk and resilience factors experienced by children and young people will throw more light on the pathways of influence by which resilience and risk have their effects. This could have potent messages for designing the services that we should offer.

Interventions to strengthen resilience

Our knowledge of risk and resilience is far from complete and, as yet, we know too little about how resilience factors operate as mechanisms and processes in children and young people, and how some features of resilience act to nullify or moderate risk.

Nonetheless, what we do know about resilience does allow us to produce an approach to intervening to assist children and young people to develop resilience generally, and to assist young people who are more at risk or more vulnerable than their peers to avoid the worst effects of the risks that they face. Briefly put, and following Schaap *et al* (2006), the approach consists of two main streams of work: those actions that enable young people to develop self-efficacy, and activities to ensure that young people receive and are enabled to use adequate family and social support. Indeed, effective parenting and high quality social and educational support in schools stand out as important components of the approach described here. In parallel, it is particularly important to intervene to assist young people who have impairments in their intellectual achievements to achieve to their potential.

Schaap *et al* (2006) cite Masten's recommendations for intervention (Masten, 2000). They highlight her argument for promoting universal healthy development as a strategy for strengthening resilience, and quote her three basic strategies for intervention. These can be summarised as:

- risk-oriented strategies that are intended to reduce the exposure of children to hazards

- quality-orientated strategies that are intended to increase the quantity, accessibility and quality of resources that children need in order to develop competence

- process-orientated strategies that aim to activate children's own, fundamental protective systems by making children aware of them, thereby increasing their self-confidence when they learn something, and their feelings of control.

This means that we should design and implement universal programmes that are available to all children and their families and that are multifaceted and involve all relevant agencies. The objectives of those programmes should be to promote children's and young people's emotional well-being and good mental health and enhance their cognitive, personal and interpersonal skills within strongly supportive relationships provided both by parents and by society working through schools and the third sector, in particular.

Children and young people who are at high risk or who have existing problems require similar planned, holistic, targeted and indicated programmes of intervention through which the various sectors work together in networks, rather than passing children and young people between them. This is because no one sector in the UK's distribution of services is able to provide all the necessary modalities of intervention to support and bolster young people's inherent resilience.

Conclusion

The research shows that, while we have a great deal more to learn, what is known now about resilience does allow us to offer advice about designing services to assist children, young people and their families. In summary, services should work together to ensure that all children and young people are enabled to:

- develop their cognitive skills in order to:
  - achieve the potential of their intelligence and temperament
  - achieve good communication skills (in reading, writing and conversation)
  - become effective solvers of problems

- be assured of receiving good enough parenting and adequate support from family relationships

- receive external support from other people and institutions that is sensitive and appropriate to the challenges they face

- achieve positive attitudes to themselves and their attainments, and a positive sense of purpose and commitment

- be encouraged to express their feelings and, thereby, learn from negative as well as positive experiences.

References

Alexander DA, Klein S (2001) Impact of accident and emergency work on emotional health and well-being. *British Journal of Psychiatry* **178** 76–81.

Bonanno GA (2004) Loss, trauma and human resilience: have we underestimated the human capacity to thrive after extremely aversive events? *American Psychologist* **59** (1) 20–28.

Bonanno GA, Field NP, Kovacevic A, Kaltman S (2002) Self-enhancement as a buffer against extreme adversity: civil war in Bosnia and traumatic loss in the United States. *Personality and Social Psychology Bulletin* **28** 184–196.

Breslin FC, Hepburn CG, Ibrahim S, Cole D (2006) Understanding stability and change in psychological distress and sense of coherence: a four year prospective study. *Journal of Applied Social Psychology* **36** (1) 1–21.

Brewin C, Andrews B, Valentine J (2000) Meta-analysis of risk factors for post-traumatic stress disorder in trauma-exposed adults. *Journal of Consulting and Clinical Psychology* **68** 748–766.

Condly SJ (2006) Resilience in children: a review of the literature with implications for education. *Urban Education* **41** (3) 211–236.

Fairbank JA, Putnam FW, Harris WH (2007) The prevalence and impact of child traumatic stress. In: Friedman MJ, Kean TM, Resick PA (eds) *PTSD: science and practice – a comprehensive textbook*. New York: Guilford.

Firth-Cozens J (1987) Emotional distress in junior house officers. *British Medical Journal* **295** 533–536.

Gana K (2001) Is sense of coherence a mediator between adversity and psychological well-being in adults? *Stress and Health* **17** 77–83.

Garmezy N (1991) Resilience in children's adaptation to negative life events and stressed environments. *Pediatric Annals* **20** (9) 459–466.

Hoge EA, Austin ED, Pollack MH (2007) Resilience: research evidence and conceptual considerations for post-traumatic stress disorder. *Depression and Anxiety* **24** (2) 139–152.

Laufer A, Solomon Z (2006) Post-traumatic symptoms and post-traumatic growth among Israeli youth exposed to terror incidents. *Journal of Social and Clinical Psychology* **25** 429–447.

Layne CM, Warren J, Shalev A, Watson P (2007) Risk vulnerability, resistance and resilience: towards an integrative conceptualization of post-traumatic adaptation. In: Friedman MJ, Kean TM, Resick PA (eds) *PTSD: science and practice – a comprehensive textbook.* New York: Guilford.

Maddi SR, Kobasa SC (1984) *The hardy executive: health under stress.* Homewood, Illinois: Dow Jones-Irwin.

Masten AS (2000) *Children who overcome adversity to succeed in life.* University of Minnesota Extension Service, Communication and Technology Services.

Masten AS (2001) Ordinary magic: resilience processes in development. *American Psychologist* **56** (3) 227–238.

Masten AS, Best KM, Garmezy N (1990) Resilience and development: contributions from the study of children who overcome adversity. *Development and Psychopathology* **2** 425–444.

Pengilly JW, Dowd ET (2000) Hardiness and social support as moderators of stress. *Journal of Clinical Psychology* **56** (6) 813–820.

Schaap IA, de Ruijter AM, van Galen FM, Smeets EC (2006) *Resilience: the article.* Amsterdam: Impact. www.impact-kenniscentrum.nl (accessed 20 December, 2007).

Social Exclusion Unit (2004) *The impact of government policy on social exclusion among young people: a review of the literature for the Social Exclusion Unit in the Breaking the Cycle series.* London: Office of the Deputy Prime Minister. www.cabinetoffice.gov.uk/upload/assets/ www.cabinetoffice.gov.uk/social_exclusion_task_force/publications_1997_to_2006/impact_ young_people.pdf (accessed 20 December, 2007).

Surtees PG, Wainwright NWJ, Khaw K-T (2006) Resilience, misfortune and mortality: evidence that sense of coherence is a marker of social stress adaptive capacity. *Journal of Psychosomatic Research* **61** 221–227.

Williams R (2007) The psychosocial consequences for children of mass violence, terrorism and disasters. *International Review of Psychiatry* **19** (3) 263–277.

Stressed out and struggling: making the transition from child to adult

Kathryn Pugh

Key points

- Young people aged 16–17 are at a key transitional point in their lives, where they are vulnerable to considerable pressures and stress

- Often they fall into a gap between children's and adult services – mentally (if not chronologically) too old for children's services, but adult services do not understand or are not structured to meet their needs

- They are often reluctant to access statutory mental health services because they say what is on offer is not age-appropriate, or accessible to them

- Commissioners need to ensure services are multidisciplinary and multi-agency, age-appropriate, and open at times when young people say they can access and need them. Providers should take a holistic approach to address a wide range of needs, and be knowledgeable of other services on offer, referring on when appropriate

- Statutory services will need to work in partnership with the voluntary sector, as young people tend to find non-statutory sector agencies and venues less intimidating and stigmatising.

Key words

Adolescence; Transition; Age-appropriate services; Cultural needs; Access

This chapter is about what it is like to be a 16 or 17 year old today, and what they want from mental health services. Is it a time when young people feel ready to stretch their wings, when they have and make choices, or is it a confusing, challenging and difficult two years? How can mental health services encourage young people to access them when they need help? YoungMinds conducted a piece of qualitative research to ask young people aged 16–25 about the transition years (Pugh *et al*, 2006), as part of its Stressed Out and Struggling project (see details at end of the chapter). We held focus groups in England and Northern Ireland in 2005–2006. This chapter draws on the views of the young people interviewed for the project.

Although many young people negotiate the transition from childhood to adulthood successfully, others struggle and find the process more difficult. Young adults can see a series of endings and beginnings before them: the end of statutory education, the beginning of a life in employment or moving to further education; for some it means leaving home, the end of being closely parented and taking up new and complex responsibilities for their own lives. Whatever the social circumstances, for all young people it is a time of change and, consequentially, stress and anxiety to varying degrees.

Young people at 16 and 17 years are still growing and changing physically and mentally. New studies (Sowell *et al*, 1999; Blakemore & Choudhury, 2006) have changed our previous belief that the structure and make-up of the brain is largely fixed from early childhood onwards. The human brain undergoes significant changes through adolescence and young adulthood, with a mismatch between the powerful emotional urges experienced by the young person for sexual behaviour, independence and to form new social bonds, and their ability to assess and weigh up risk.

We know that adolescent mental health is getting worse: emotional and conduct problems have increased over the past 25 years (Collishaw *et al*, 2004). The research suggests that these increases may not be caused by changes in family make-up, such as the greater number of single parent families, but may be the outcome of a complex interplay of a wide range of factors.

On one hand, young people are faced with what seems like a wide range of opportunities to experiment: for example, sex, drugs and drink are readily available to them if they choose. They also face high levels of academic pressure – the average young person has undergone at least four periods of assessment and testing by the time they emerge from the state school system, and there is an expectation that at least half will go on to university or further education. Yet for many, their real choices and opportunities seem to be diminishing in a world in which jobs for life are no longer guaranteed, where buying a home may be beyond their earning capacity, and where they may face up to seven years of financial dependence on their parents after leaving school. In a recent UNICEF report (2007) the UK's children and young people were the most unhappy in Europe, and reported having the least sympathetic peers.

The SOS Project conducted a series of focus groups with young adults from a wide range of backgrounds. The young people were asked to identify issues that were particularly important to them. Young people aged over 18 were asked what advice they would give 16 and 17-year-olds about the choices they might make. The young people were generally quite optimistic about the future, even those who had had the most challenging start in life. Their ambitions were focused on having enough money, an interesting career and a happy personal life. Their wishes were mainly for personal success, but some also raised more political issues, such as ending poverty, war or Aids.

The key themes that emerged were as follows (all quotes are from focus group participants).

The importance of having friends

'Young people feel they have to live up to their friends' expectations, because they will get picked on if they don't.'

'If I didn't have friends I would just bottle up my emotions.'

Friends and peers had replaced the family in importance to many young people. Friends were a major source of advice but also could be a source of stress. There was enormous pressure to fit in, to be part of a group, even if that meant making choices (good or bad) about behaviour such as drug taking or crime, or choosing academic courses that were not necessarily what the young person really wanted to do. The level of pressure in some cases amounted to bullying, particularly during the school years when there were limited opportunities for individuals to form new peer groups unless they changed schools to a sixth form college or further education college. Pressure to become sexually active was very high for 16 and 17-year-olds. Being seen to be sexually experienced was particularly important for young men, but the age-old double standard still applied to young women, who were still viewed by the majority as 'slags' if they were highly sexually active, whereas boys were 'studs'.

Money

'I have to get a job because I don't have anywhere to live once I'm 18.'

The 16 and 17-year-olds in our research reported being trapped by a lack of money. Part-time jobs were hard to find. In rural areas with poor public transport, it was difficult for young people to get to work unless they had a car – but without a job, they could not afford a car. Some had worked illegally, without proper pay or protection, for cash in hand. If they complained about conditions, hours or pay, they were sacked.

Money was a source of tension with parents, particularly for those in receipt of Education Maintenance Allowance, which young recipients regarded as 'their' money, whereas some parents required it as a contribution to household expenses.

There were very limited opportunities for young people to meet up and socialise outside the home for free or minimal cost. For young people on a budget, activities such as the cinema, bowling alley or swimming pool were too expensive, especially when transport had to be paid for. Young people resented the negative attention given to them if they just 'hung out' together in town centres or in parks. They felt that if the community did not like them gathering in public places, then it should provide low cost, safe places where they could meet.

Education

'In school there are special kids, naughty kids and invisible kids – no one would notice if I wasn't there.'

The consensus among all the focus groups was that there was an unfair concentration of effort and attention by schools on those who might go to university, whether or not the young people interviewed had been or intended to go, with the other young people feeling second rate. Those who had dropped out of school regretted it, and found it difficult to return to learning. Some reported 'waking up' at 16 to the importance of getting qualifications, only to find that the school had given up on them because of their persistent bad behaviour or truanting. Many wished that they had been better prepared for life while in school, and that they had been given, for example, financial planning advice, or more advice about drugs and alcohol.

These 16 and 17-year-olds were very worried that the choices they made now would affect their future, and felt these choices were made in a vacuum. Those who were in training schemes resented being given 'fake' jobs that were short-term; they were more interested in finding a 'real' job that had prospects. Those who went into work felt isolated unless the companies they worked for had arranged a 'buddying' scheme with an older colleague, which many found very helpful in understanding the difference between complying with workplace rules and obeying school rules. There was a lack of consistent transitional support: some had received a very good service from Connexions (the national careers advice service for young people aged 13–19); others had not.

Some young people were very focused about their plans for the future, and had mapped out their lives from A levels to university and beyond. First generation university students had very high expectations of the kind of job they would get if they took a university degree; those whose parents had been to university were more realistic. For some, taking out a student loan was a major worry, and several talked of friends who had chosen not to go to university because of the cost.

The family

'When you are younger you just see your parents as there to give you lifts and money, but as you get older you spend time with them because you want to, not because you have to.'

Young people who had a relatively stable family background agreed that the family still played a significant role in their lives. The family was important to those from a black or minority ethnic community, and particularly to young asylum seekers, who regarded any member of their family, even if not from their immediate family, as a very important influence. Those who had had troubled childhoods and had left the family under difficult circumstances found this subject too challenging to discuss in detail, but were able to reflect in the abstract about the importance of good parenting. The young people who had been looked after (in foster care or local authority care) had all formed close bonds with their key workers. We saw many examples of how good key workers could provide positive support to young people by setting appropriate boundaries and helping them to understand and cope with the difficulties they had experienced. The young people who had been in care were in the main the most optimistic about the future and convinced that their future was theirs to make.

Some of the interviewees were experiencing more conflict than ever before, because their parents had high expectations of them; they felt their parents were living through them, and were asking for achievements that were not realistic.

Drugs and alcohol
'Just go and get wasted then sleep so you don't have to think or worry about things and can block them out.'

'I started drinking at 15 as there was nothing else to do, so was bored of going to the pub and drinking by the time I was 18.'

Alcohol played a significant role in many of the young people's social lives, with a few reporting using illegal drugs. All the young people knew how to obtain illegal drugs, but cannabis was viewed as much less harmful than heroin. Many used alcohol and drugs as a part of a good night out, but there were also young people who self-medicated to shut out issues that bothered them. Reports of binge drinking and excessive use of alcohol were much more common among those who said they were bored and had no access to leisure facilities. Most felt that education about drugs and alcohol for 16 and 17-year-olds came too late, and that children in school years six and seven should be targeted. Many of the older interviewees felt that their social binge drinking had peaked when they were 16 and 17, but that they had now moved on. Many of the young people were amused by the level of interest in the media and from older people about binge drinking; they saw it as phase that people grow out of.

Respect
'Why do they go on about "young people" as if we were something different? We are society.'

The young people who attended the focus groups did not feel that society respected or even liked them. They were very media aware, and not taken in by the cult of celebrity. They resented the way they were blamed for so many of society's ills when little or nothing was done to give them safe places where they could meet their friends. They felt let down that this wasn't a new issue, that it was a well-known problem but nothing had been done to change it.

However, although the young people interviewed included a higher ratio of young people from black and ethnic minority cultures than is found in the UK population as a whole, most young people from ethnic backgrounds had experienced very little racism. Some of the white interviewees were baffled by racism towards black or Asian groups, but were hostile to 'new' migrant groups, such as eastern Europeans. Faith was a particularly important part of life for young people from minority backgrounds.

Young people from rural areas

'You can sit on a wall and hold someone else's cigarette and within half an hour your parents will be on the mobile asking why are you smoking. But you can sit on the same wall and cry for two hours, but no one will see it or do anything.'

Most of the groups showed remarkable levels of consensus, but the one area in which there was a divergence of views was between those from rural and urban communities. Young people from rural communities reported feeling simultaneously isolated within, yet suffocated by the weight of parental and community attention. They were more likely to report high levels of boredom and difficulty in accessing, for example, even basic health services in confidence in communities where there was only one doctor or one chemist. Transport was most difficult for them: public transport was expensive and irregular, and going into town for a night out could mean either leaving very early to catch the last bus or taking the risk of hitch-hiking.

Accessing mental health services

'There's no point having a service available between nine and three on a Monday, Wednesday and Thursday. I need to know where to go for help when it's just me and four walls on a Sunday night.'

There has been considerable research into what young people want from health services in general. The Department of Health's *You're Welcome* programme (Department of Health, 2007) sets out guidance and practical advice to services and commissioners on how to make services more accessible and acceptable to young people. Mental health specific information for commissioners has been produced by YoungMinds, in its *Call to Action* (YoungMinds, 2006a) and *Emerging Practice* (YoungMinds, 2006b) guidance, and also by the HASCAS transitions project (HASCAS, 2006), by Youth Access (Street, 2007), which has published guidance on commissioning counselling services for young people, and by the Mental Health Foundation, which has published reports on crisis services for young people, and 'what works' in voluntary sector services (Mental Health Foundation, 2004; Garcia *et al*, 2007).

Broadly, mental health services that want to be young person-friendly need to consider the following.

- Make sure that young people are involved in service evaluation and development, and that changes are made as a result. Young people repeatedly tell us that they are tired of being asked what they want, and then nothing is done (Street & Herts, 2005). Young people find voluntary sector drop-in services less intimidating and more acceptable than services that are clearly labelled 'medical' or 'mental health', probably because these are seen to be less stigmatising (Macleod & Parker, 1986; Department for Education and Skills, 2005). The best way to find out if your service is accessible, and what would make it more so, is to ask your users – and also those who do not use it – what they do or do not like about it.

- Think about your environment. No 16 or 17-year-old is going to feel comfortable in a child development clinic full of baby toys.

- Young people need their peer group and need their family (if there) to support them. Services that offer young people psychosocial support within their community, and those that involve and work with parents and carers, can help young people to maintain or create good social relationships.

- Services need to be clear about how they can be accessed. Is your service open to self-referrals or drop-in, or do young people have to be referred by other agencies? This information needs to be publicised widely, in leaflets and posters as well as on the internet, and in areas where young people meet, such as schools, colleges, leisure centres and cinemas. Not all young people have access to the internet. Young people particularly like telephone helplines staffed by skilled counsellors who know what services are available locally out of hours (Mental Health Foundation, 2004).

- Services need to think about how they will respond to a young person in crisis – telling a young person that their particular type of crisis does not fit the team's criterion for intervention will drive young people away. Young people who feel they are in crisis are more likely to act on impulse, and services need to be able to signpost young people to services where they can get help.

- Young people rarely have one problem, so multi-problem, multidisciplinary services that can offer practical advice about a wide range of issues are more likely to meet a young person's needs.

- Services need to work constantly to maintain and improve pathways to other agencies. Services need to know about agencies for young people who do not meet the threshold for adult mental health services but still require support (HASCAS, 2006; Street, 2007). Some young people may need support beyond the age at which they would normally be referred to adult services. Many young peoples' services enable this by extending their age range, from 16 to 25 for example; others operate a flexible age policy, depending on the individual's needs (YoungMinds, 2006b). Services need to know how to refer quickly to other service providers. They need to have a good understanding of what specialist services, such as early intervention psychosis teams, offer – repeated inappropriate referrals will not help relationships with these services.

- Services need to develop a thorough understanding of the cultural needs of young people – notably, the needs of young people from specific faith groups (Street *et al*, 2005; Department of Health, 2005).

- Mental health services need to offer a range of evidence-based treatments. Young people are sophisticated consumers. They and their families will want choices other than just medication (Street *et al*, 2005; Anna Freud Centre, 2007).

- Services need to be age-appropriate. Young people with a mental health problem can recover; they can still pursue their dreams, even if their dream may have to change (11 Million, 2007).

Conclusion

Young people are facing an increasingly complex world. The choices open to young people aged between 16 and 17 can be bewildering; in some areas the choices seem endless; in others it can feel as though one set of doors is closing and that any new doors are opening into a world where they do not feel they belong, or through which they see no escape. Reaching out to services and asking for help can be difficult; there is still considerable stigma about mental ill health. Youth services that provide a flexible, accessible service, with a range of interventions, and, above all, that listen to young people without judging or labeling them, are more likely to succeed and support their young clients through this difficult and challenging period.

For the range of publications on services for young people aged 16–25 published by the YoungMinds Stressed Out and Struggling project, visit www.youngminds.org.uk/ publications/all-publications/publications-by-audience-1/professionals/

References

Anna Freud Centre (2007) *Choosing what's best for you: what scientists have found helps children and young people who are sad, worried or troubled*. London: Anna Freud Centre.

Blakemore S-J, Choudhury S (2006) Development of the adolescent brain: implications for executive function and social cognition. *Journal of Child Psychology and Psychiatry and Allied Disciplines* **47** (3–4) 296–312.

Collishaw S, Maughan B, Goodman R, Pickles A (2004) Time trends in adolescent mental health. *Journal of Child Psychology and Psychiatry* **45** (8) 1350–1362.

Department for Education and Skills (2005) *Youth matters.* London: Department for Education and Skills.

Department of Health (2005) *Delivering race equality in mental health care: an action plan for reform inside and outside services and the government's response to the independent inquiry into the death of David Bennett.* London: Department of Health.

Department of Health (2007) *You're welcome quality criteria: making health services young people friendly.* London: Department of Health.

11 Million (2007) *Pushed into the shadows: young people's experiences of adult mental health facilities.* London: Office of the Children's Commissioner.

Garcia I, Vasiliou C, Penketh K (2007) *Listen up! Person-centred approaches to help young people experiencing mental health and emotional problems.* London: Mental Health Foundation.

HASCAS (2006) *CAMHS to adult transition.* London: HASCAS.

Macleod RJ, Parker Z (1986) Considerations in community mental health programming for youth. *Canadian Journal of Psychiatry* **31** (6) 568–574.

Mental Health Foundation (2004) *No help in a crisis: developing mental health services to meet young people's needs.* London: Mental Health Foundation.

Pugh K, McHugh A, McKinstrie F (2006) *Two steps forward, one step back? 16–25 year-olds on their journey to adulthood.* London: YoungMinds, 2006.

Sowell ER, Thompson PM, Holmes CJ, Jernigan TL, Toga AW (1999) In vivo evidence for the post adolescent brain maturation in frontal and striatal regions. *Nature Neuroscience* **2** (10) 859–861.

Street C, Herts B (2005) *Putting participation into practice.* London: YoungMinds.

Street C, Stapelkamp C, Taylor E, Malek M, Kurtz Z (2005) *Minority voices: research into the access and acceptability of services for the mental health of young people from black and minority ethnic groups.* London: YoungMinds.

Street C (2007) *Commissioning counselling services for young people: a guide for commissioners.* London: Youth Access.

UNICEF (2007) *Child poverty in perspective: an overview of child well-being in rich countries.* Innocenti Report Card 7. Florence: UNICEF Innocenti Research Centre.

YoungMinds (2006a) *A call to action: commissioning mental health services for 16-25 year olds.* London: YoungMinds.

YoungMinds (2006b) *Emerging practice: examples of mental health services for 16–25 year olds.* London: YoungMinds.

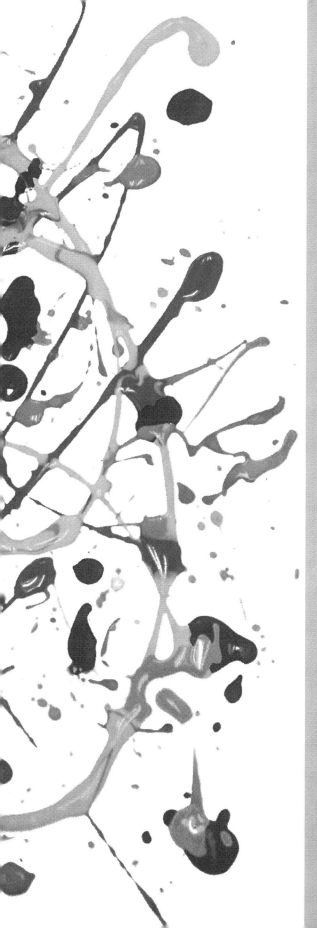

Listen Up! young people's participation in service design and delivery

Christina Vasiliou Theodore and Kim Penketh

Key points

- Young people are often reluctant to approach statutory services because they feel they are inaccessible, intimidating or unacceptable

- Encouraging the participation of young people in service design and delivery has clear benefits, for the young people and for services

- Young people's participation can ensure services are delivered in a way that meets their needs, and so ensure young people use them

- Services will find it easier to engage young people in their care and treatment and achieve better outcomes

- Participation must be genuine: young people do not want tokenistic consultations that do not result in real change.

Key words

Participation; Service design; Service delivery; Engagement; Influencing change

There are no data specifically on young people's mental health in the 16–25 age range – those making the crossing from childhood to adulthood. Yet this is an age when children can be acutely vulnerable, mentally and emotionally, and are subject to a wide array of different pressures and stresses. The Mental Health Foundation has for nearly a decade pursued a research and practice development agenda aimed at understanding how best to provide services that meet the mental health needs of this group. In 1999, the *Bright Futures* (Mental Health Foundation, 1999) report described a three-year programme of work that examined factors affecting children and young people's mental health and emotional development. In 2001 *Turned Upside Down* (Smith & Leon, 2001) reported the views of young people specifically in the 16–25 age group. One of its key findings was that neither children's nor adult services were equipped to provide adequate care for young people going through the transition from childhood to adulthood. The 45 young people involved in the project made a number of suggestions concerning this issue, and argued strongly that the involvement of service users and ex-users in developing and running services would go some way in helping to create services that are more appropriate to their specific needs.

Subsequently, in 2002, the Mental Health Foundation initiated its Youth Crisis Project. The first stage of the project, Youth Crisis I, was a two-year consultation project to find out from young people what they wanted from services when they were experiencing mental health problems. The second phase, Listen Up! (Garcia *et al*, 2007), worked with eight 'partner sites' – voluntary organisations in the UK – and focused in greater depth on exploring young people's actual experiences of using services.

All eight partner sites had adopted an overall 'person-centred' approach in their work with young people. Fundamental to taking a young person-centred approach is engaging and involving young people in service design and improvements. The research sought to demonstrate how the eight organisations achieved this, and what it meant to the young people.

'All staff within the project from grass roots upwards must share the same vision and philosophy of service user involvement.' (Project worker)

The eight partner sites (see box) were diverse in terms of their size, geographic locations and organisational structures, but all were based in the community – often placed within or offering a generic service. Seven of the eight organisations provided services directly to young people needing support and information. The eighth, Experience in Mind, was set up to involve young people who had used mental health services in the creation and delivery of training to those who came into contact with young people with mental health problems, such as staff working in child and adolescent mental health services (CAMHS) and colleges.

Focus groups were held at six of the sites, and face-to-face interviews at two. In total, 32 young people were interviewed. In addition, 31 staff were interviewed: 14 in person and 17 by telephone.

> **The Listen Up! partner sites**
> - Sorted Not Screwed Up, Aberdeen Foyer, Aberdeen
> - Experience in Mind, Mind in Brighton and Hove and Hove YMCA
> - Community Links, Canning Town
> - Caterpillar Service, Barnardo's Marlborough Road Partnership, Cardiff
> - Support @ The Junction, The Junction, Colchester
> - The Market Place, Leeds
> - Streetwise, Newcastle
> - IceBreak, The Zone, Plymouth.

The challenge of participation

Our research found that young person participation brings added value, in terms of benefits, positive outcomes and/or changes both to young people's lives and the services they access. For the services, reported benefits included improved access for young people, development of a more responsive service to meet the range of needs of all young people in the local community, and increased accountability to their funders and other organisations with which they worked. They also reported that the training on young people's mental health and emotional well-being needs that they provided to staff in other services was better informed.

Young person participation can sometimes be challenging for organisations to achieve, mainly due to lack of human or financial resources. All the organisations had striven to overcome these challenges.

'It is essential to not become blasé about the success of service user participation, but instead to look constantly for ways to improve or build upon the ways in which young people are involved in the service… Projects must adapt their manner of working to suit each new set of young people.' (Project worker)

Services need to devote sufficient staff, time and money to achieving effective and meaningful young person participation that is not tokenistic. They also need to develop structures and processes for young person participation, to ensure they respond to their views fully. This aspect of service provision can drop down the list of priorities when resources are stretched or when workloads increase. Services can ensure this does not happen by identifying what they hope to achieve from young person participation, and reviewing these objectives regularly:

'… you often involve young people at the beginning, such as in the development of the service, and people assume that this is young people involvement, but after the initial developments have been made in the service, young people involvement can slip… This process has happened to us, so we are now having to try and recapture and re-evaluate their continual involvement in service development.' (Project worker)

A dedicated youth participation project worker can help to ensure young person participation remains high on the agenda. Although only one service involved in the Listen Up! project had a dedicated member of staff working on this, others were considering seeking, or were already seeking funding for a new post.

'... a dedicated worker is essential in ensuring that service user participation retains the priority that it should be given... it requires someone who is focused entirely on developing strategies for keeping young people engaged and motivated, as well as making the process fun.' (Project worker)

Consulting with young people

The organisations involved in this project used a number of methods for consulting with young people, including:

- setting up formal youth advisory boards (see next page) for consultation on all aspects of the service
- asking young people to provide feedback through monitoring and evaluation forms and surveys
- running informal group and individual feedback sessions with key workers
- having formal panel board meetings with young people and senior management
- asking young people to provide anonymous feedback through suggestion boxes or 'post-it' note postings
- running focus groups on understanding specific identified issues
- giving young people the opportunity to provide expressive feedback through art, music, drama or poetry.

Consultation with young people at all organisations was described as a continual process. Staff recognised that successful participation was dependent on maintaining an honest dialogue with young people to ensure the organisation was delivering a service reflective of their needs. All the organisations engendered a culture whereby staff were approachable.

'Being open, honest and transparent about what we are and what we're doing [means] they will know they have no need to fear us... Some services are too closed and young people become suspicious... so having good, clear communication is important.' (Project worker)

Some organisations reported that it was not always easy to ensure young people's participation was truly representative: there tended to be a core group of young people who wanted to contribute, and the voices of other young service users, such as those using the service on an *ad hoc* basis or those less willing to give their views, were not heard.

'It is difficult when some service users have such chaotic lives... feedback is not always representative of all the young people accessing the service.' (Project worker)

Youth advisory boards

Five of the eight partner sites ran a youth advisory board to provide young people with a forum in which they had an effective voice within the organisation. Through these boards, young people can have the opportunity to influence organisational development, provision and delivery from the 'grass roots' up to strategic and operational level. They can also become powerful advocates of the organisation to the wider community and contribute to the young people's mental health agenda at a local and national level.

These boards varied in nature and size, but were all seen as an essential part of achieving meaningful and effective young person participation, and all met regularly throughout the year. All young people participating in the projects were welcome to be a member of the board. At some services, young people who had moved on from the organisation were also welcome to continue their membership for a period of time.

All boards were allocated a member of staff as co-ordinator, to provide relevant information about the organisation to the board, and to keep the board's discussions focused and purposeful.

All members of the boards were involved in decisions on the running, development and direction of the board. The boards had a small amount of annual funding for activities, events and equipment, for which the young people were responsible.

'Our advisory board enriches the project not only in promoting the project but also from the buzz created by having young people involved. It is also really positive to see the confidence of young people grow as they develop through the service from initially beginning group work and then moving on to working on the advisory board, giving them invaluable experience.' (Project worker)

Types of young person participation

Young people using these services were involved in organisational development in a number of ways. Some were facilitated through a youth advisory board, and some happened independently.

Internal activities

All organisations consulted with young people on issues relating to the organisation's internal activities and policies. These included the physical environment and design of the organisation, and marketing and promotional activities.

All the organisations also provided young people with the opportunity to plan, organise and run various events and social activities. Most organisations also held open evenings for all young people and staff to join in, including arts, music and drama productions. At some events, external professionals such as practitioners and commissioners were also invited, so they could meet young people and take part in activities.

Work experience

'Helping out as a volunteer enables me to make other young people's experiences more comfortable and better.' (Young person)

Most of the organisations involved in Listen Up! provided a range of opportunities for young people to undertake work experience within the organisation. These included helping out with administrative tasks, handing out information leaflets to young people, helping with events and activities, peer mentoring, and assisting staff in the running or delivery of drop-in or group work sessions.

The need to maintain client confidentiality can limit the type and level of work that young people can undertake as volunteers for the organisation. Staff said that personal information about a young person – their diagnosis, for example – would only be made available with prior permission to another young person doing work experience. All the organisations provided young people who were volunteering with training and had clear guidelines on confidentiality.

Community Links

Community Links in Canning Town ran a project based on the BBC TV programme *The Apprentice*. Over the course of eight weeks in the summer, young people took part in various aspects of service delivery, and one young person was 'fired' each week. In the end, there were three winners, as the judges could not decide between them.

Each of the winners received a week's paid work in the project, at junior worker rates. This type of activity helped the young people to build up valuable and transferable work-related skills. The project was so successful that there are plans to run it each year to coincide with the BBC programme.

Staff recruitment and induction

'When recruiting staff, it is crucial to be selective and ensure they are equipped with the necessary professional and interpersonal skills, experience and qualifications to successfully engage with young people. Thus, young people must be involved in the recruitment panel as a standard measure.' (Project worker)

At the majority of the organisations young people were involved in the recruitment of staff, including short-listing candidates and sitting on the interview panel as well as being involved in staff inductions. This provided young people with the opportunity to engage in group discussions or presentations highlighting key aspects of organisational delivery that they felt new staff should be made aware of. The staff felt that young people involvement in recruitment was an effective way of continuing to learn from the young people accessing the service, and of ensuring the service was responding to what young people felt they needed to meet their needs.

The Market Place

The HYPE (Helping Young People through Experience) group at The Market Place in Leeds developed a method called 'speed interviewing', based on the concept of 'speed dating', for interviewing candidates for jobs. First, the group – all young people using the service – agreed on a list of interview questions designed to make candidates reflect on and learn 'what a young person needs from a counsellor'. Each young person was then allocated one question to ask, and the interview room was set up with each young person sitting at a table with one empty chair. The candidates were invited to circulate the room until they had visited each table and answered each young person's question. The young people discussed their views of each of the candidates with one another in a series of feedback sessions, and reported back to staff. While the young people recognised that they did not have the final say in who was recruited, they knew that staff noted and took their opinions seriously.

Taking part in external events

All eight organisations encouraged and supported young people to take part in external events and consultations, and to network with other organisations and professionals. Young people from the partner sites attended, presented and ran workshops at local and national events and conferences aimed at raising awareness of mental health and emotional well-being and tackling stigma. Young people also presented their personal stories and shared their experiences, as well as participating in discussions with a range of key stakeholders.

At all times, young people's involvement in external activities was flexible, and they were able to contribute at a level they felt comfortable with. Members of staff were always on hand to provide support for young people preparing for activities, and to debrief them after participation work.

'I have gained a big boost in confidence by talking in front of adults in a big room.'
(Young person)

Training staff in other agencies

Many young people consulted as part of Youth Crisis I wanted to be involved in training staff in the services with which they had contact. This reflected the young people's need to be listened to and respected, particularly in times of potential crisis and/or powerlessness. Young people felt that psychiatrists, community psychiatric nurses, GPs, social workers, police officers and A&E staff would provide more sensitive services if they received such training and heard from young people about their experiences of mental health issues.

'Sharing their personal experience of mental health problems is a powerful tool in de-stigmatising and dispelling myths.' (Project worker, Experience in Mind)

As stated above, at Experience in Mind the young people developed and delivered a training programme for staff from outside agencies. The training covered communication, self-harm, depression and stress, and was 'experiential' – that is, based on the young people's actual experience. Young people who wanted to deliver the training had the opportunity to take a Level 2 OCN (Open College Network) accredited course, Training through Experience, to learn the necessary training skills, such as presentation and group work.

'We want to reduce the stigma… and not be seen just as people with mental health difficulties, but as people like everyone else.' (Young person)

Young people's experiences of participation

Young people were asked about their experiences of being consulted with and involved in decisions about service provision and delivery, as well as external events and consultations. Their responses reflect both the barriers to participation they had encountered, and the positive impact it had on their personal development. They also shared their views on its value and importance beyond meeting their personal needs.

'It is a positive and empowering experience and provides the opportunity to voice our opinions.' (Young person)

Barriers to participation

Young people said that they had encountered only one main barrier to meaningful participation: tokenism. Some young people reported feeling that consultations with some organisations, particularly statutory organisations, felt tokenistic, and said that they did not think their feedback would influence change. They said that, at times, external professionals did not take them seriously, which resulted in them feeling devalued. However, one young person stated:

'I think it's because they just think that we are little kids and we've got problems, but once they see that we are making a difference in what we are doing, we then prove them wrong.'

All the organisations in the project aimed to forestall tokenism by actively building relationships with external organisations and negotiating in advance with other professionals how young people would be involved in consultations and at events.

In addition, service staff informed external professionals about the benefits to them of consulting with young people.

'We try to encourage other professionals to include service users, but only when we feel a young person wants to be involved and that is appropriate… we've had conversations with the young person and considered what it would mean for them to be involved with that particular activity.' (Project worker, The Caterpillar Service)

Personal development
Feeling empowered, independent and in control
Young people said that being provided with the choice and flexibility to make decisions about the support they received, as well as the security of knowing they could change their key worker if necessary, gave them a strong sense of empowerment and control over their lives. Consequentially, they became more confident in making decisions about other aspects of their lives.

Having the opportunity to 'shape' internal service provision and delivery as well as being involved in external events and consultations enabled young people to strike a healthy balance between receiving support and enhancing their confidence to be responsible and independent adults.

Acquiring specialised knowledge and language
Young people felt that, through their involvement with the organisation at a strategic level, they had acquired a clear understanding of the direction and purpose of the organisation they attended.

Involvement in external events and consultations also provided them with a better understanding of policy and practice in other sectors of the mental health system. They felt that this specialised knowledge had enhanced their ability to navigate independently through, and access a selection of services to meet their needs. In addition, they felt they had gained a better understanding of their rights and entitlements and could pass this knowledge on to other young people who were facing similar experiences. Finally, they felt more able to contribute significantly to the ongoing mental health agenda.

The opportunity to network with professionals from other services, and in some cases with policy makers and commissioners, helped the young people to develop their communication skills. This was, in fact, a two-way process: young people educated professionals on how to use language that young people could understand, while simultaneously learning the different styles of language and terminology used by professionals.

Gaining transferable skills
Young people said that their engagement in the activities involved in service user participation – public speaking, networking, consultation activities, organising and engaging in fun events, recruitment and training of professionals, health promotion,

marketing their organisation – had helped them develop a wide range of transferable skills. These included organisation and time management skills, communication and language skills, life skills and coping strategies, and relationship development skills. Overall, participation helped young people to develop the necessary skills to make progress in other aspects of their lives.

Wider benefits of participation

Influencing change and making a difference

Young people saw their involvement as a valuable opportunity to voice their opinions, not just within their organisation but in the mental health and public arena more widely. Being in a position where their viewpoint was valued was described as empowering.

'You're not ignored… your opinion is heard.' (Young person)

Many said their participation was an excellent opportunity to play an active role in contributing to the children's and young people's mental health agenda, and helping to influence change at a local and national level. The young people were passionate about designing and using participation so that it could make a real difference to the lives of other young people experiencing similar issues.

'… not only can we make a difference to our lives, but also to the lives of others.' (Young person)

Raising awareness, and reducing stigma and discrimination

Some young people had experienced discrimination from family and friends because of their mental health problems and use of services.

Participation provides young people with the opportunity to help raise awareness of the issues encountered by young people with mental health problems. The young people we spoke to wanted to share their personal experiences with others so they could see that '… I'm a person, you're a person, whatever problems we have.'

The young people felt that raising awareness of mental health problems, combined with promoting the importance and value of emotional well-being and happiness to the general public, would help to reduce stigma and discrimination. In order to achieve this, they felt that all relevant organisations working with young people, as well as families, needed more education and training that had been developed and led by young people.

'I think what needs to happen really is that people need to be educated from a young age, just like there's sex education – do like… a mental health education in schools.' (Young person)

'It'd be good to educate family as well as professionals, because at the end of the day professionals do know a bit more than our parents, and our parents need to know, because they have to look after us and they don't get to read books about it, they only have their experience.' (Young person)

Giving something back to the service

Young people also felt that being involved in internal participation as well as external events and consultations was a way to support the service in its aim to promote best practice to meet the needs of all young people. Supporting the service in this way was seen as a way of showing their gratitude and giving something back.

'It's nice to give something back for all the help they gave us… I just feel like I owe them so much, [and] this is the only way I can do it.' (Young person)

Conclusions

The Listen Up! research (Garcia *et al*, 2007) produced a number of detailed recommendations for commissioners and providers of services to young people. First and foremost, it argues that every provider should have a strategy for young people's participation that covers operational policy and practice, strategy and the presentation of the services, and should monitor it to make sure that participation is happening. Support and training for young people must be built in to the strategy.

But, as the participating projects and the young people said, it is vital that services devote sufficient staff, time and money to achieving effective and meaningful young person participation; it must not be tokenistic. Services need to develop formal structures and processes for young person participation, and for responding to their views. This aspect of service provision can too easily drop down the list of priorities when resources are stretched or when there is an increased workload. To avoid this, services should identify what they hope to achieve from young person participation, and regularly review these objectives to ensure they continue to be worked towards.

References

Garcia I, Vasiliou C, Penketh K (2007) *Listen up! Person-centred approaches to help young people experiencing mental health and emotional problems.* London: Mental Health Foundation.

Mental Health Foundation (1999) *Bright futures: promoting children and young people's mental health.* London: Mental Health Foundation.

Smith K, Leon L (2001) *Turned upside down: developing community-based crisis services for 16–25 year olds experiencing a mental health crisis.* London: Mental Health Foundation.

Taking a whole school approach to promoting mental health

Katherine Weare

Key points

- Schools provide an important setting for mental health promotion interventions with children and young people

- In England, the SEAL primary and secondary programmes provide the framework and materials for promoting social and emotional well-being in schools

- Effective interventions adopt a whole school approach, drawing on resources within the school and in the wider school community of parents, the local community and other agencies

- Effective interventions adopt a universal approach, seeking both to promote the mental health of the whole school and also to target individuals with specific needs

- Schools need to actively teach emotional and social literacy skills, not just to pupils but also to teaching and school staff.

Key words

Mental health promotion; Whole-school approaches; Social and emotional literacy; Skills development

The last 20 years has seen a tremendous surge in research on the prevention of mental health problems and the promotion of positive mental health through school-based programmes, interventions and policies. Schools are increasingly seen as one of the most important settings for interventions that can provide children with physical, emotional and social wellness that they will carry forward into adulthood (Hosman *et al*, 2004). This is in part simply because children spend a good deal of their time in school, and so form a 'captive audience'. But there is also an expanding research base to support the usefulness of school-based programmes in achieving positive outcomes and reducing risky behaviours. It also reflects the growing recognition that emotional and behavioural problems undermine academic and social success, and that, in addition to their central role of enhancing intellectual/academic development, schools have a key role in the health, social and emotional development of students, and in creating well-rounded citizens who are able to relate to others, care about their community and their environment, and make their own, informed choices in a rapidly changing world.

To date, very few schools have sought systematically to achieve broader goals such as promoting social and emotional learning or promoting mental health. However, the picture is changing fast, and across the world a significant and growing number of programmes are emerging with promising results. Such programmes tend not to be presented under a 'mental health' heading: they are more likely to be titled 'emotional literacy', 'emotional intelligence', 'social and emotional aspects of learning', 'coping skills', 'resiliency' or 'lifeskills'. In the US there are possibly thousands of 'social and emotional learning' programmes, and a few 'major hitters' that systematic reviews using rigorous evaluation criteria have shown to be highly effective. There are also several major US research and practitioner networks, most notably perhaps Casel (the Collaborative for Academic, Social and Emotional Learning) (see www.casel.org). Such programmes are less well established elsewhere in the world, but interest has been growing very quickly, particularly in English speaking Australasia and the UK. An international network, Intercamhs (International Alliance for Child and Adolescent Mental Health and Schools) is attempting to bring the learning from this work together (www.intercamhs.org).

In England, Scotland, Wales and Northern Ireland, a wide range of specific interventions and approaches are being been tried. Some schools and local authorities have been using successful US models, such as Promoting Alternative Thinking Strategies, Second Step, Penn Resiliency, the Dino Dinosaur Curriculum and Emotional Literacy in Middle Schools. Some authorities have been using programmes they devised themselves, while others have brought in programmes from national and European agencies, such as Antidote, the School for Emotional Literacy, and Partnerships for Children.

Primary and secondary SEAL

In England, in the last seven years or so, the Department for Children, Schools and Families (DCSF, formerly the Department for Education and Skills) has developed two new programmes that are attempting to provide a basic and comprehensive entitlement for all pupils. Building on the successful whole school work of the Healthy Schools initiative on self-esteem and anti-bullying (see also chapter 8), the DCSF has devoted considerable resources to developing even more explicit mental health promotion programmes, under the umbrella title 'Social and Emotional Aspects of Learning' (SEAL).

The primary SEAL programme (ages 4–11) is now in place in about two-thirds of primary schools and is having a clear impact on social and emotional learning, on behaviour, and even on pupils' reading and science test scores (Hallam *et al*, 2005). However, SEAL and related social and emotional development programmes remain relatively rare in secondary schools. The reasons for this difference are debatable; it may be a combination of secondary schools' focus on academic subjects, rather than on children's well-being, their larger size and more impersonal nature, and perhaps reluctance by school staff to tackle social and emotional issues with adolescents, who may be seen as more resistant and challenging. The DCSF is attempting to fill this evident gap with a secondary SEAL programme (ages 11–18), which was piloted successfully in 60 schools and is now being rolled out to 10% of secondary schools, with the intention that they become lead schools and help others to introduce it.

Good intentions and a warm heart are not enough on their own – by no means do all programmes work. What follows is based on a review of the research literature conducted to underpin the SEAL programmes (Weare & Gray, 2003). It will summarise 'what works' and the key components of effective programme design as drawn from the literature and exemplified in the content of the secondary SEAL programme.

A holistic/whole school approach

The first characteristic of an effective social and emotional health programme is that it should adopt a holistic, whole-school approach. The evidence shows clearly that effective approaches are those that work on several fronts at once, in a co-ordinated and coherent way (Lister-Sharp *et al*, 2000; Wells *et al*, 2003). These are much more likely to make long-term changes to pupils' well-being, attitudes and behaviours across a wide range of issues than are programmes that only address one aspect of school life. An 'emotionally literate school' (Weare, 2006) addresses the whole school context, including its management, ethos, relationships, policies, teaching and learning, curriculum, physical environment, relations with parents, and relations with the community. It regards the total experience of school life as contributing to the emotional and social well-being of all who learn and work there. Looking even more broadly, effective programmes draw in the wider community – parents, local health services, and other agencies – to support the efforts the school itself is making to promote mental health.

Mental health for all

The research also suggests that pupils with mental health problems are helped more effectively by universal approaches aimed at everyone, rather than targeted approaches aimed only at them. The key elements in programmes that help children and young people with problems are, in fact, the same as those that promote the mental health of all; they promote warmth, empathy, positive expectations and clear boundaries; they focus on helping young people acquire the skills and competences to promote their own mental health, and they involve users and their families to encourage ownership and participation (Weare, 2006). Children with difficulties need 'more of the same', not 'different'. Taking a universal approach does not mean we should not target pupils with particular needs, and some pupils will obviously need more, and more energetic, targeting, but having a backdrop of provision for all makes it easier to provide extra help while avoiding the stigma that so often attaches to mental health interventions.

Some recent reviews (eg. Durlack, 1995; Durlack & Wells, 1997; Wells *et al*, 2003; Weare & Gray, 2003; Zins *et al*, 2006) have identified the elements of successful programmes in promoting the mental health of all and helping those with problems. Well-designed programmes need to be able to address mental health problems, such as depression and aggression; tackle risk factors often associated with mental health problems, such as impulsiveness and antisocial behaviour, and promote protective factors such as self-esteem and confidence, happiness, resilience and optimism, relationship skills, stress management and problem-solving skills.

The research also shows that children who receive effective social and emotional learning programmes are likely also to do well academically at school, in some cases achieving higher marks in subjects such as mathematics and reading, to make more effort in their school work, and to have improved attitudes to school, with fewer exclusions and absences (Zins *et al*, 2006). Programmes can also have an impact outside school, helping prevent and reduce early sexual experience, alcohol and drug use, and violence and bullying in and outside schools (Greenberg *et al*, 1995), and even sometimes reduce juvenile crime (Caplan *et al*, 1992).

The school environment

Some mental health promotion and prevention strategies focus particularly on creating a mental health promoting environment within the school. Fortunately, we have a growing evidence base on what kind of environments these might be (Weare, 2000). They turn out to be ones that achieve the right combination of four key factors.

Perhaps the most obvious feature of a school environment that promotes mental health is that it encourages warm relationships and places the emotional well-being of all school members at the heart of the educational process. In an emotionally literate school, everyone has a genuine sense of belonging, and feels that they are valued, listened to and respected. The focus is on the positive, learning is fun, and there is zero tolerance not just of bullying and violence but also of sarcasm and belittling.

Linked with this is a sense of genuine participation – a feeling of engagement and ownership by all, and the fostering of genuine partnerships between pupils, staff, parents, the community, outside agencies, and education and mental health agencies. The emphasis is on equity, diversity and inclusion, with shared, open and transparent goals and values.

The evidence also shows that sound mental health and learning are both based fundamentally on a sense of autonomy. This means the school ethos needs to encourage independence, self-determination, reflection, critical thinking and self-control. Pupils and staff are empowered to make real choices, and have appropriate levels of genuine decision-making and responsibility.

To achieve all this also demands clarity about discipline, rules and boundaries. An emotionally literate school also has clearly stated aims and strategic plans, strong boundaries, rules and roles, and high standards and expectations. Behaviour and actions have real-life, known rewards and consequences, both positive and negative.

The balance of these four key factors may well be different in different contexts. Primary schools, for example, may focus more on warmth and participation, while secondary schools may need to focus more on clarity and autonomy. Whatever the context, the need for balance between the four features remains.

Skills development

Important though the environment is, programmes that rely solely on environmental changes are less effective than those that also ensure pupils and staff develop emotional skills (Catalano *et al*, 2002). It is argued that schools that provide opportunities for students to learn and use their social and emotional skills and positively reinforce emotionally and socially literate behaviour, encourage motivation for learning, more positive beliefs, and a greater sense of attachment to the school, which leads in turn to better mental health, improved behaviour and greater academic achievement (Hawkins & Catalano, 1992).

Social and emotional skills are critical throughout life, but are especially important during the school years (Harden *et al*, 2001). They are not only important for negotiating the challenges of growing up and making transitions (Newman & Blackburn, 2002); they also act as protective factors by promoting mental health and preventing the development of risky behaviour, such as antisocial behaviour, identifying with deviant groups, drug use, and risky sexual behaviour (Greenberg & Kusche, 1994). Children who possess good social and emotional skills are aware of feelings in themselves and are empathetic towards others (Furlong, 2002). They can recognise social cues and norms, and read the intentions of others. They are able to regulate their own behaviour and emotions, to engage in short and long-term goal setting and planning, and to generate effective solutions to interpersonal problems.

There are many ways of describing and categorising these skills. The SEAL programmes make use of a simple taxonomy created by Goleman (1993), which categorises them in five domains: self-awareness, understanding and managing feelings, motivation, empathy, and social skills. These are underpinned by a comprehensive set of learning outcomes that are phrased in ways that make them accessible to young people. For example, an outcome of self-awareness skills building might be: 'I know what makes me feel good and know how to help myself have a good time (eg. to feel calm, elated, energised, focused, engaged, have fun etc) in ways that are not damaging to myself and others'. An outcome of social skills might be: 'I can evaluate and choose from a range of strategies to solve problems and know how to resolve conflicts with other people.'

Skills are not acquired by osmosis; schools need to ensure they are learned, and sometimes may need to teach them explicitly. Learning needs to go well beyond just talking about these skills; rather, extensive and specific work needs to be put in place to help pupils move through the stages of skills development – identification, modelling, coaching, feedback, practice, reflection, consolidation, internalisation, and generalisation.

The teaching of these skills must not be reductionist or behaviourist. This is not about imposing the views of one social group on another, or telling children exactly how to live their lives and be 'nice' people. The process of skills development needs to be explored with pupils, so they are enabled to select the skills they see as relevant and useful for them and which they think would work in the contexts in which they live.

Both the primary and secondary SEAL programmes have produced learning support materials to guide schools (see www.bandapilot.org.uk). The materials take full account of ethnicity, culture, disability, family group, and sexual orientation, and aim to help pupils develop the skills they need for living in a multicultural and multi-faith society. They are not prescriptive or manualised – they are necessarily very flexible, and can apply in a wide range of contexts. The intention is that schools draw on them to develop approaches that suit their specific needs and preferences.

The materials encourage schools to use existing learning opportunities to promote emotional and social development, such as subject lessons, personal, social and health education (PSHE) sessions, tutorials, assemblies, and whole school activities such as school councils, peer mentoring, clubs and societies, breaks and lunchtimes, and school visits. In addition to work in the classroom, school staff are expected to support pupils' skills development outside the school structure – by, for example, setting them structured tasks for homework, encouraging personal reflection and diary writing, and using 'golden moments' outside the classroom to help pupils consolidate and practise skills. Examples might include observing a pupil using conflict resolution skills at break and congratulating them, or praising a hitherto impulsive and impatient pupil who has waited their turn in the lunch queue.

Staff development

The final characteristic of effective programmes is that they embrace everyone who learns and works in the school, including school staff. Staff cannot be expected to promote the emotional and social well-being of their pupils if their own needs are not met. Effective programmes therefore include strong professional development opportunities for staff, where they can explore their own emotions, consider ways to promote their own well-being, and feel supported and understood (Weare & Gray, 2003). This activity needs to develop staff capacity and flexibility, link with existing professional development opportunities, such as training, coaching and mentoring, encourage self-reflection, critical reflection, and dissent, and develop the ability to model mental health promoting behaviours. It needs also to be supported by the rest of the school and conducted in a safe, co-operative and supportive atmosphere, with plenty of fun, laughter, and enjoyment.

Conclusion

In the 21st century, to become happy, healthy and effective individuals and citizens, children need social and emotional skills. The demands of a fast moving society and the changing nature of work mean that children need to know first and foremost how to relate to people. They need to have sound values, and to be able to make positive choices and moral decisions. They need to be able to work in a group and participate fully in their community and across cultures, and also be autonomous and self-reliant. To achieve all this, children need sound mental health, which comes from feeling valued and loved, from having their opinions listened to and their points of view recognised, and from the feeling of belonging in environments that promote these social and emotional skills, that have meaning for them, and with which they can identify. Such places include their schools.

References

Caplan M, Weissberg RP, Grober JS, Sivo PJ, Grady K, Jacoby C (1992) Social competence promotion with inner-city and suburban young adolescents: effects on social adjustment and alcohol use. *Journal of Consulting and Clinical Psychology* **60** 56–63.

Catalano RF, Berglund L, Ryan AM, Lonczak HS, Hawkins J (2002) Positive youth development in the United States: research finding on evaluations of positive youth development programmes. *Prevention and Treatment* **5** 15.

Durlak J (1995) *School based prevention programmes for children and adolescents.* London: Sage.

Durlak J, Wells A (1997) Primary prevention mental health programs for children and adolescents: a meta-analytic review. *American Journal of Community Psychology* **25** (2) 115–152.

Furlong A (2002) *Youth transitions and health: a literature review.* Edinburgh: Health Education Board for Scotland.

Goleman D (1993) *Emotional intelligence.* London: Bloomsbury.

Greenberg M, Kusche C (1994) *Promoting social and emotional development in deaf children: the PATHS project.* Seattle: University of Washington Press.

Greenberg M, Kusche C, Cook E, Quamma J (1995) Promoting emotional competence in school aged children – the effects of the PATHS curriculum. *Development and Psychopathology* **7** (1) 117–136.

Hallam S, Rhamie J, Shaw J (2005) *Final report: primary behaviour and attendance pilot.* London: Department for Education and Skills.

Harden A, Rees R, Shepherd J, Ginny B, Oliver S, Oakley A (2001) *Young people and mental health: a systematic review of research on barriers and facilitators.* London: EPPI-Centre.

Hawkins JD, Catalano R (1992) *Communities that care: action for drug abuse prevention.* San Francisco: Jossey-Bass.

Hosman C, Jané-Llopis E, Saxena S (2004). *Prevention of mental disorders: effective interventions and policy options. Summary report.* Geneva: World Health Organisation.

Lister-Sharp D, Chapman S, Stewart-Brown S, Sowden A (2000) Health promoting schools and health promotion in schools: two systematic reviews. *Health Technology Assessment* **3** (22).

Newman T, Blackburn S (2002) *Transitions in the lives of young people: resilience factors.* Edinburgh. Scottish Executive.

Weare K (2000) *Promoting mental, emotional and social health: a whole school approach.* London: Routledge.

Weare K (2006) *Developing the emotionally literate school.* Sage: London.

Weare K, Gray G (2003) *What works in promoting children's emotional and social competence?* London: Department for Children, Schools and Families.

Wells J, Barlow J, Stewart-Brown S (2003) A systematic review of universal approaches to mental health promotion in schools. *Health Education* **103** (4) 220.

Zins JE, Weissberg RP, Wang MC, Walberg H (2006) *Building academic success on social and emotional learning.* New York: Teachers College, Columbia University.

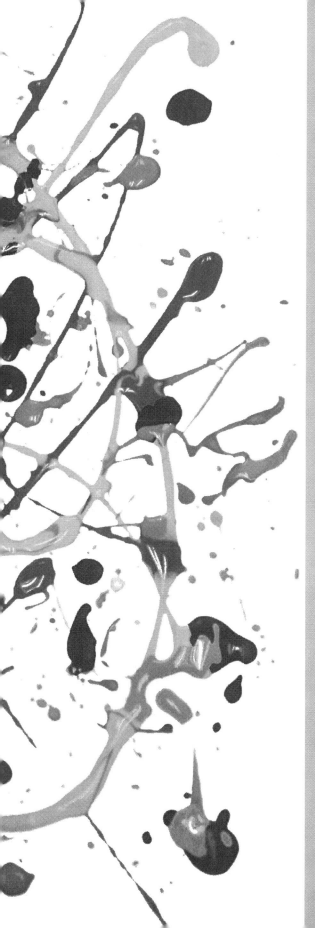

The mental health needs of young offenders

Jo Tunnard

Key points

- Some 3,000 children aged under 18 are held in prison or other secure setting

- Mental distress among children and young people in custody is common, and can be linked to their histories and family circumstances

- Research has shown that these young people need intensive support to enable them to identify and achieve their aspirations in life

- Interventions include mental health promotion activities, specific interventions for identified mental health needs, and practical support with housing, education, training and employment needs

- Continuity and consistency of care, both in custody and following release, are an important element of any intervention programme.

Key words

Young offender institute; Youth offender team; Mental health; Custody; Interventions

'Mental health problems, both in young offenders and older offenders, represent the single area of most concern in the available literature.

'The findings of an overall association between mental health problems and offending in young people are variable from different studies in different countries. However, most, especially those from the UK, conclude that the prevalence of mental health problems is increased among young offenders before, during and following incarceration.

'The most obvious and serious example of this is demonstrated by the high rates of suicide or attempted suicide amongst young offenders.' (HM Inspectorate of Prisons for England and Wales, 1997)

There are approximately 3,000 children under 18 who are held in a prison or other secure setting at any time. Almost 9,000 enter custody each year (Department of Health, 2007).

They are held in the 45 children's establishments that make up the secure estate in England and Wales. These are the 19 young offender institutions (YOIs), which are part of the prison service; four secure training centres, run by private operators; and 22 secure children's homes, almost all run by local authorities. The YOIs hold the vast majority of children and young people in custody.

Most of the children in any form of custody are boys, and over one in 10 is from a minority ethnic group. The main crimes committed by these children and young people are robbery and burglary. The average length of stay in custody is 84 days. The turnover rate is high, and so is the reconviction rate, with approximately seven in 10 re-offending within 12 months of release (Social Exclusion Unit, 2002).

Most children in custody are held on a Detention and Training Order (DTO), under the Crime and Disorder Act 1998, section 73. This involves a sentence of between four and 24 months, with half spent in custody and the other half in the community after release, under the supervision of the local Youth Offending Team (YOT).

In addition to these children, there is a much larger group of children who also have contact with the youth justice system. These are children and young people who have got into trouble with the law but remain living in the community because they have not been taken to court or given a custodial sentence.

When talking about young offenders, it is important to take account of all the children concerned and the whole of the offender pathway. There is considerable movement between and within the different parts – from community to custody, from one custodial establishment to another, and from custody back to the community or to another residential setting.

What needs are we talking about?

General needs

Children in custody have general needs that are similar to those of the children identified in government policy documents as being 'in special circumstances', meaning that they require extra attention if they are to enjoy the same life chances as other children (Department of Health, 2004). They have similar difficulties and experiences of family and peer relationships, high levels of poverty, entrenched parental needs, and histories of under-performance and exclusion from school, homelessness, and life in or on the edge of care.

Literacy and numeracy levels are low – half of the young people of school age in custody have a learning age of 11 years or under, and over a quarter have the learning age of the average seven-year-old, or below. Learning and communication difficulties are also high, some as a result of inherent disabilities and others because of the accumulated effects of missed schooling.

Mental health needs

The mental health needs of children in the youth justice system, whether in custody or in the community, are known to be considerable, severe and complex (Harrington *et al*, 2005). Harrington and colleagues conducted a study of the clients of one YOT and one custodial establishment in each of six geographical areas. One in three of the young people surveyed were found to have a mental need. Overall, girls had more mental health needs than boys, especially depression, self-harm and post-traumatic stress, while young people from ethnic minorities had higher rates of post-traumatic stress.

Another study (Tunnard *et al*, 2005) mapped the services available to meet the mental health needs of children and young people held in YOIs. This was a national study, covering all 19 young offender establishments in England and Wales. Health care staff reported that the majority of children in the YOIs had some form of mental health need, and the common view was that a high proportion of the children had significant mental health problems. There was also considerable co-morbidity, where children experience two or more mental health problems at the same time.

All sites referred to the damaging and distressing previous life experiences of many of the children. They commented that these experiences both contributed to their offending behaviours and underlay their mental health problems.

All sites were caring for children whose mental health needs arose from the experience of being in prison. These included actual and threatened self-harm, anxiety, depression, bullying, and outbursts of anger. These arose from being locked up, from boredom, and because they missed their family and loved ones, including sometimes their own babies, or other young relatives. They arose also from the upset caused when a relative did not visit; from worry that a parent's inappropriate behaviour at a review might have an adverse impact on the child's stay in custody;

from concern about the safety of others at home (especially where children had the role of protecting their mother and younger siblings from domestic violence), and from worries about the safety and well-being of parents with mental health or substance misuse problems.

Many other children had severe and entrenched mental health needs linked to longer-term problems or traumatic experiences. They included asylum seekers and children with past experiences of neglect and rejection; children with histories of physical and sexual abuse, some of whom were worried that younger siblings at home were being exposed to similar abuse, and those with problems stemming from loss, bereavement and family separation and dislocation.

Most sites made the point that diagnosis of specific disorders is difficult with this age group. Concerns were also expressed about the number of children in custody with learning disabilities, and the particular difficulties they experienced coping with life in custody.

What is being done?

All the YOI sites said that mental health promotion activities were provided by a range of different departments and on-site or visiting agencies. They all also provided some specific interventions for the young people with identified mental health needs: in particular, cognitive behaviour therapy, bereavement counselling, and what they described as 'a sympathetic ear'. In relation to offending behaviour programmes, all provided anger management courses.

About half the sites had recently expanded their repertoire of mental health interventions to include activities such as art, music and drama therapy, relaxation, acupuncture, and occupational therapy.

A few sites had developed particular responses for vulnerable children. Some related to specific needs, such as dialectical behaviour therapy for those at risk of self-harm; speech and language therapy for those with communication problems; mental health groups to help young people with a particular condition, and small, separate units for young people unable to cope on the main wings. Some took a holistic approach and were piloting programmes to improve children's thinking skills or their abilities to apply what they learnt to daily life. Still others focused on developing skills for life beyond custody – cooking, parenting and other life skills.

Staff working in YOI mental health in-reach teams commented on the difficulty of trying to deliver a 'pure' intervention in a YOI, because they were not able to monitor the child's behaviour between sessions and because children were often there for a short time only. A related concern was that prison was not a sufficiently safe place to begin therapeutic work, and that children might suddenly be moved to another establishment, without the opportunity for child and therapist to end their work well. There were frequent comments, too, about interventions put on hold because staff shortages made it impossible to free up the staff needed.

There were some clear gaps in the type of interventions provided. In particular there was a lack of interventions for children who had committed sex offences, and for those with learning difficulties or a severe mental illness that prevented them from joining in other activities. There was also no joint work with children and their parents.

What is being done – in the community

Emily is 14. The police became involved after domestic abuse problems at home. She was fearful of being involved in the violence and was also being bullied at school and was truanting. The police put her in touch with the local Rapid Action Project (RAP), run by the Rainer voluntary organisation. Through this Emily had weekly family counselling sessions, providing her with the opportunity to discuss her worries and to work with her mother on the changes needed in their lives.

This community-based intervention programme was developed to offer emotional and practical help to young people at risk of becoming serious offenders. It is provided by independent youth workers based in police stations. The target children are those who have received a police reprimand, or are engaged in offending behaviour while still at primary school, or who live with domestic violence, or are at risk of school exclusion. Results so far are impressive: significant improvement in progress at school, an improvement in ways of coping with anger, and no need for further contact with the police.

What is being done – in custody

Tom is 15 and has been placed in a YOI. It is his first time in custody. He has taken a long time to settle in and often reports to the health care centre with minor injuries. The wing officers have noticed that he hangs around the phone, keeps his distance from the other boys, and seems quiet and withdrawn most of the time. He picks at his arms and looks tired and anxious.

The health care manager invites him to come to her drop-in clinic and gets him talking about his home and family. Tom tells her that he spends the night awake, worrying about his mum and younger sister because he used to look after them and he's not sure how they are coping without him. A recent phone call home upset him. He is worried that his mum will be drunk when she comes for his next review meeting and he thinks this will mean that his release date will be put back.

The health care manager helps Tom ring his mum to talk about his worries, and continues to keep in touch with his mum herself, phoning to reassure her that Tom is safe. She also gets Tom to join the relaxation group she is running for boys who have sleep difficulties, and she encourages the wing staff to think about ways of involving Tom in after-school activities. If his difficulties persist, she will call on the specialist mental health team from the local child and adolescent mental health service (CAMHS) who provide an in-reach service to the YOI.

What is being done – after release

Wayne is 17 and has just left a YOI where he has served two Detention and Training Orders following a long history of offences. He has little contact with his family and cannot return home. He has low self-esteem and substance misuse problems and finds it very difficult to talk about his situation. The local YOT that is supervising him is part of the national pilot programme called Resettlement Aftercare Provision (RAP). The programme provides a tailored plan to address the needs of the individual, and funds towards the activities required.

Wayne's YOT support worker makes a plan with Wayne about what they need to work on together. They include:

- helping him settle into the temporary accommodation that the RAP housing worker has found for him before his release
- applying for more permanent housing
- working out what education or training opportunities he wants to pursue
- working on resolving issues with his family, and where he can get help to move on from his past traumas and build a good future for himself.

Wayne also needs help with managing his money, both in the long-term and until his benefits come through. It is critical that Wayne finds some kind of activity that helps him avoid slipping back into heavy drug and alcohol use, now that he is free of them both following his spell in custody. The RAP worker encourages him to get involved in several art projects and voluntary work with animals, both of which he really enjoys. He gradually starts to come out of his shell and to make friends with other young people involved in similar activities. The worker keeps in touch with his mother, who is delighted with Wayne's progress, which in turn boosts his confidence.

What else needs to happen?

Contact with the youth justice system can provide children – and their families – with a unique opportunity to improve their health and well-being and life chances. These opportunities need to be grasped, and the gains not lost. Continuity of care is vital as children move in and out of custody and between secure establishments. Needs must be responded to, not just assessed, and services that are put into place must follow the child through the system.

Responding to the needs of this group of children presents particular challenges for agencies, because of the complexity of factors involved. Individual establishments are all very different in size and how they operate, children move frequently between sites and may come from all over the country, local CAMHS arrangements and resources vary hugely, and health and social care commissioners and providers have different remits and responsibilities. The Department of Health has published a framework to guide commissioners responsible for promoting the mental health of children in the youth justice system (Department of Health, 2007).

Research is beginning to show the direction of travel for responding to these children's mental health needs. There is growing consensus on the approaches most likely to alter the trajectories of young offenders. Rutter and colleagues (1998) found that custody has negligible impact as a deterrent, and that beneficial effects on behaviour are most likely when:

- education and training open up new opportunities once the young person is released
- help is offered with drug misuse, and drugs are not available during their stay in custody
- a pro-social ethos with good relationships and models for behaviour is maintained
- there are chances for making a change in mind-set, leading to a greater sense of self-efficacy and control over life
- strong and regular links with families are encouraged.

Getting the ethos right is probably the most important thing to tackle. And there is evidence that a combination of strong leadership and staff expertise can produce a caring and child-centred environment for this vulnerable group of children. Key features of such an environment include:

- appointing custody staff with a particular interest in working with adolescents
- offering training in counselling to custody staff
- encouraging staff to use foster care approaches
- staff wearing everyday clothes rather than prison uniform
- using children's first names
- creating opportunities for all staff to listen to the children
- encouraging children to 'look out' for one another
- keeping health files open, to encourage children to come back at any time
- ringing children's families and encouraging contact, and
- using visiting time for family work and discussion.

There is no question that children and young people in secure settings present some of the most challenging behaviours and problems for health and social care services. However, research and practice wisdom provide clear messages about what works. If services build on these achievements and initiatives, in both community and custody settings, there is a chance that children in or close to custody will escape what has sometimes seemed to be an unavoidable trajectory, and will then develop to their full potential.

References

Department of Health (2004) *National service framework for children, young people and maternity services.* London: Department of Health.

Department of Health (2007) *Promoting mental health for children held in secure settings: a framework for commissioning services.* London: Department of Health.

Harrington R, Bailey S with Chitsabesan P, Kroll L, Macdonald W, Sneider S, Kenning C, Taylor G, Byford S, Barrett B (2005) *Mental health needs and effectiveness of provision for young offenders in custody and in the community.* London: Youth Justice Board for England and Wales.

HM Inspectorate of Prisons for England and Wales (1997) *Young prisoners: a thematic review by HM Chief Inspector of Prisons for England and Wales.* London: Home Office.

Rutter M, Giller H, Hagell A (1998) *Antisocial behaviour by young people.* Cambridge: Cambridge University Press.

Social Exclusion Unit (2002) *Reducing re-offending by ex-prisoners.* London: Office of the Deputy Prime Minister.

Tunnard J, Ryan M, Kurtz Z (2005) *Mapping mental health interventions in the juvenile secure estate. Report for the Department of Health.* London: Department of Health.

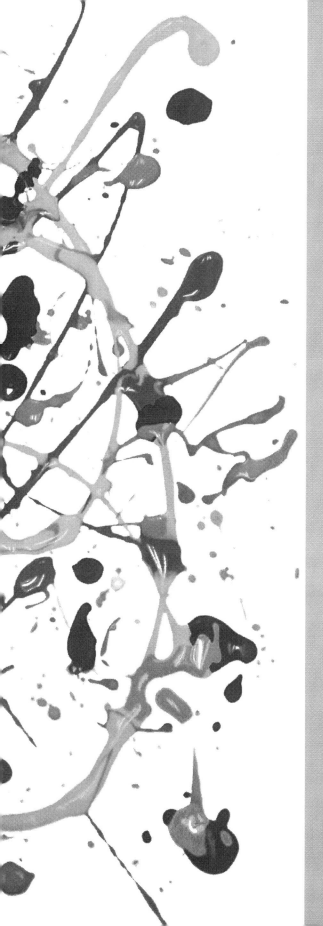

Part V

Diagnoses and treatments

Depression and bipolar disorder

Andrew Cotgrove and Tim McDougall

Key points

- Approximately one in 100 pre-pubertal children and around three per cent of post-pubertal adolescents will have a depressive disorder

- Risk factors for depression include genetic, biological and psycho-social vulnerabilities; stressful life events can also act as a trigger for an episode of depression

- Treatments include cognitive behavioural therapy and medication, although there are concerns about the safety of SSRI antidepressants

- Diagnosis of bipolar disorder before puberty is rare; the peak age of onset is in late adolescence and the teenage years

- Drugs are the mainstay treatment for bipolar disorder in children and adolescents, and they should be offered psychological support.

Key words
Depression; Bipolar disorder; Management; Psychological therapy; Medication

Depression and bipolar disorders can cause considerable distress in young people. They can seriously impact on a young person's emotional, educational and social development. These disorders are often under-recognised and under-treated but, if picked up, respond well to a range of interventions.

This chapter focuses on the key features of these disorders, their prevalence, what is known about their causes, and the treatments currently available.

The National Institute of Health and Clinical Excellence (NICE) and the National Collaborating Centre for Mental Health (NCCMH) have carried out separate systematic reviews of the management and treatment of depression in children and young people (NCCMH, 2005), and the management of bipolar disorder in adults, children and adolescents (NCCMH, 2006). What follows is broadly based on these two guidelines.

Depression

Depression is a term commonly used in lay-language to refer to a state of sadness or unhappiness. However, clinically, the term depression refers to a group of symptoms that affect three areas: mood, thinking and activity. Mood changes typically include sadness and/or irritability associated with a loss of pleasure, even in things normally readily enjoyed. Cognitive changes include negative thoughts, such as low self-esteem, loss of confidence, feelings of guilt, and pessimistic views of the future, possibly including suicidal thoughts. There may also be a loss of motivation, loss of interest, and difficulty concentrating or making decisions. Physically, young people may experience disturbed sleep and appetite, reduced energy, and tiredness. Several of these symptoms need to be present for at least two weeks in order to make a diagnosis of depression. In addition, the symptoms need to be of sufficient severity to cause distress or impairment in social, educational, or other important areas of functioning. Depressive disorders can be sub-classified as mild, moderate or severe according to the number of symptoms present.

These key features of depression are true for depressive disorders across the life-span. However, there are some differences in the younger age group in the way the disorder can present. In younger children, low mood may manifest itself in frustration or temper outbursts, and there may be additional physical symptoms such as headaches or stomach aches. Loss of interest, poor concentration and poor attention may also be prominent, as well as separation anxiety, school refusal, or failure to progress academically. Irritability, anxiety, agitation and social withdrawal tend to feature more in older children and adolescents than in adults with a depressive disorder.

Prevalence

In a 12-month period approximately one per cent of pre-pubertal children and around three per cent of post-pubertal adolescents will have a depressive disorder (Angold & Costello, 2001). There is no sex difference in prevalence in pre-pubertal children, but by the mid-teens approximately twice as many girls suffer with depression than boys.

Depression commonly occurs with other mental health disorders in children and adolescents. In one study, 93% of cases of depression presenting to a child and adolescent mental health service (CAMHS) were found to have a comorbid diagnosis (Goodyer *et al*, 1997). Most common of these was separation anxiety disorder (65%), oppositional defiant disorder (44%), conduct disorder (37%), social phobia disorder (37%), panic disorder (25%), and generalised anxiety disorder (25%). Other studies have also found high correlations between depression and attention deficit/hyperactivity disorder (ADHD) and anorexia nervosa.

Risk factors and aetiology

There are many factors that contribute to the onset of depression in an individual young person. These can include genetic, biological and psychosocial vulnerabilities, as well as stressful life events, which can act as a trigger for an episode of depression (Harris & Molock, 2000). The relative influence of these different factors will vary from individual to individual. However, it is clear that young people are at much higher risk of experiencing depression if they have multiple rather than single risk factors. Sixty per cent of young people with depression have experienced an acutely disappointing life event in the month prior to onset, but 90% have already been exposed to two or more ongoing risks – for example, abuse, bereavement, parental discord or genetic/family risk (Goodyer, 2001).

Detection and recognition

While there is no good evidence for routine screening for depression in the community, it is important that professionals in primary care, schools and other community settings are aware of the risk factors. They need to have skills in listening, and to be able to identify key symptoms, offer support to the young person if appropriate, and know when to refer on for more specialist help. If multiple risk factors are present or there are clear symptoms of depression, then a more thorough assessment is indicated. Multiple sources of information should be sought, including information from the child, seen individually, and from the family and the school. Children are often reticent to discuss how they feel in the presence of their parents, for fear of upsetting them, and this may be exacerbated by feelings of guilt and low self-worth. In addition, children seen alone may feel able to disclose a precipitant such as bullying or abuse, which they might not reveal in front of their parents.

A diagnosis of depression may be aided by the use of questionnaires, such as the Recent Mood and Feelings Questionnaire (Angold *et al*, 1987), or standardised interviews such as the K-SADS (Kaufman *et al*, 1997). A full medical history and examination will help to exclude a physical cause for the symptoms, followed by further investigations if indicated. Comorbid difficulties should always be considered.

Treatment

For mild depression, it is appropriate to offer 'watchful waiting' before providing an active intervention. If symptoms persist, advice about exercise and lifestyle can be given, along with a brief psychological intervention, such as non-directive supportive therapy, group cognitive behavioural therapy or guided self-help. These can be provided in Tier 1 or Tier 2 CAMHS, but if the child or young person does not respond to treatment, then referral on to Tier 2 or Tier 3 CAMHS should be considered after two to three months.

Those initially assessed to have moderate to severe depression should be managed within Tier 2 or Tier 3 CAMHS from the outset. First line treatment for this group is a specific psychological intervention offered for about three months. This can include individual cognitive behavioural therapy, interpersonal therapy or family therapy. If there is no response after four to six sessions, a review of the diagnosis should be conducted, particularly addressing any additional comorbid difficulties. Only then should consideration be given to the prescription of fluoxetine, an antidepressant medication. Fluoxetine should normally be started at a dose of 10mg daily, and only increased to 20mg after a week. There should be regular checks for side-effects, especially increased impulsivity, urges to self-harm or suicidal thoughts.

Occasionally consideration may need to be given to referring on to a Tier 4 inpatient CAMH service. Indications for this include high recurrent risk of self-harm or suicide, significant ongoing self-neglect, or the need for an intensity of treatment and/or supervision that is not available elsewhere.

The NICE guidelines state that ECT can be considered for those with intractable, severe and life-threatening symptoms.

Use of antidepressants

Early in this decade, antidepressants, and in particular selective serotonin reuptake inhibitors (SSRIs), were increasingly being used as the mainstay of treatment for depression in young people. A wave of adverse publicity started in 2003 when the UK Committee on Safety of Medicines concluded that all SSRIs were contra-indicated, with the exception of fluoxetine, for children and young people aged under 18 years, due to the risk of suicide. It then became apparent that previous studies reporting negative results of SSRIs had remained unpublished, and those that were published were presented far more positively than the evidence justified. However, subsequent studies have consistently shown SSRIs to have significant benefits, while the risk of increased suicidality, for fluoxetine at least, appears small. While the debate continues (Cotgrove & Timimi, 2007), on balance the evidence would currently seem to indicate that antidepressants do have a role in the treatment of depression in young people, but that parents and young people should be told of the risks and benefits, so that they can make an informed choice about treatment.

Course and prognosis

Around 10% of children and young people with depression recover within three months without need for treatment. A further 40% recover within the first year. Of the remaining 50% who are still depressed, about 20%–30% remain depressed at two years (Harrington & Dubicka, 2001). However, recurrence rates are high; one long-term follow-up study (Fombonne *et al*, 2001a) found that over 60% of children diagnosed with major depressive disorder had a recurrence later in life. A small but significant number of cases go on to develop bipolar disorder. At 20-year follow-up, the rate of attempted suicide was 44% and completed suicide 2.5% (Fombonne *et al*, 2001b).

The influence of treatment on the course of the disorder is not fully known, but it appears to lessen the likelihood of symptoms lasting for longer than 12 months.

Bipolar disorder

Bipolar disorder, formerly known as 'manic depression', is a chronic and recurring mood disorder affecting up to one per cent of the general population (Mackin & Young, 2005). People with bipolar disorder experience profound, cyclical changes to their mood and behaviour. Despite being relatively common, this disorder sometimes goes unrecognised, misdiagnosed and untreated.

Little is known about what causes bipolar disorder. Various explanations based on psychosocial, biological and genetic research have been offered, and there is some consensus among researchers and clinicians that a combination of genetic, neurohormonal and psychosocial factors are at play.

Prevalence

While there are major differences in the rates of diagnosis of bipolar disorder in the US and UK, diagnosis of children before puberty is relatively rare. The peak age of onset is in late adolescence and during the teenage years (Weissman *et al*, 1996; Johnson *et al*, 2000). Epidemiological studies consistently report the lifetime prevalence to be approximately one per cent, with up to a fifth of adults with bipolar disorder experiencing their initial symptoms before the age of 19 (Harrington *et al*, 1994). Although the symptom profile may differ, bipolar disorder affects boys and girls approximately equally (Lloyd *et al*, 2005).

Clinical features

While there are some differences in the major classification systems used to diagnose bipolar disorder, essentially there needs to be at least two discrete mood episodes, one of which must be mania or hypomania (a milder form of mania).

The characteristic features of depression in bipolar disorder are the same as those described above for depression. Mania is characterised by a distinct period of abnormally and persistently elevated, expansive or irritable mood, lasting at least one week, and featuring three (or more) of the following manic symptoms (four if the mood is only irritable) to a significant degree:

- inflated self-esteem or grandiosity
- decreased need for sleep
- more talkative than usual or compulsion to keep talking
- flight of ideas or subjective experience that thoughts are racing
- distractibility (attention too easily drawn to unimportant or irrelevant external stimuli)
- increase in goal directed activity (either socially, at work or school, or sexually) or psychomotor agitation
- excessive involvement in pleasurable activities with a high risk of negative consequences.

The combination of hypomania or mania, grandiose and elated mood, and increased drive and decreased need for sleep can lead to psychosis and physical exhaustion if left untreated and unmanaged.

While the hallmarks of bipolar disorder are episodes of both depressed and elated mood, the most common experience for people with this illness is low mood (Judd *et al*, 2002; Post *et al*, 2003; Lewinsohn, 2003). For children and adolescents presenting with a first episode of depression, it may not be possible to distinguish between those who will go on to develop recurrent depressive episodes (unipolar depression), and those who go on to develop bipolar disorder. For the treatment of acute depression in bipolar disorder, the good practice and prescribing guidelines outlined earlier in this chapter apply.

Diagnosis

The assessment, treatment and management of children and adolescents should be led by specialist child and adolescent mental health services (CAMHS). However, frontline professionals such as teachers, school nurses and GPs play a crucial role in recognising the early signs of the disorder, as well as promoting recovery, preventing relapse and promoting social inclusion for children and adolescents already diagnosed with bipolar disorder (Taylor *et al*, 2006; Hamrin & Pachler, 2006).

The diagnosis of bipolar disorder in children and adolescents is subject to controversy and debate. This is due to overlap with other psychosocial disorders of childhood (Biederman *et al*, 2000), symptoms of attention deficit hyperactivity disorder (ADHD) (Biederman *et al*, 1996; Geller & Luby, 1997; Geller *et al*, 1998), and the rarity of severe cases of child and adolescent bipolar disorder (Emslie *et al*, 1994). These not only make the diagnosis of children and adolescents challenging; they also mean that drawing up the subsequent treatment plan can be problematic. The accurate diagnosis of children and adolescents is also difficult because some of the diagnostic markers of bipolar disorder, such as grandiosity, over-activity and pleasure-seeking behaviour, vary according to age and developmental level. What may be considered a feature of bipolar disorder in an adult may not be so in a child. For example, it is not unusual for children to behave in an elated, giddy or grandiose way – the appropriateness of the context requires careful consideration.

Given the overlap between bipolar disorder and other psychosocial disorders of childhood, alternative explanations for the symptoms and behaviour should always be considered. For example, a child or adolescent who is sexually disinhibited or hyper-vigilant may have experienced sexual or physical abuse (Geller & Luby, 1997). Similarly, the effects of substance misuse, particularly stimulants, can produce manic-like symptoms similar to those seen in a bipolar episode. For this reason, it is important to seek information about drug and alcohol use. Less commonly, undiagnosed learning disabilities and organic causes such as excited confusional states in young people with epilepsy may also explain what first appear to be manic symptoms.

Clearly defined episodes of elated mood, grandiosity and cycling of mood should be used to distinguish bipolar disorder from other childhood disorders such as ADHD and conduct disorder. The presence of mood cycles should be used to distinguish bipolar disorder from schizophrenia, which is rarer than bipolar disorder in children and adolescents (NCCMH, 2006). In severely mentally ill children and adolescents, early diagnosis is crucial, and this should be subject to regular review by a child mental health specialist with expertise in bipolar disorder.

It is generally agreed that bipolar disorder exists along a continuum of severity, ranging from severe, chronic or persistent mood disturbance to normal mood fluctuations. For this reason, classification systems used to diagnose mental disorders distinguish between bipolar I disorder, where people suffer from full blown manic episodes with or without periods of major depression, and bipolar II disorders, where the person experiences less severe or profound depressive episodes and where mood is mildly elated but not manic.

Assessment

A comprehensive assessment by experienced clinicians is needed before a diagnosis can be made and appropriate care, treatment and management planned. Given the overlap between bipolar disorder and other psychosocial disorders of childhood, it is important to consider alternative diagnoses when children and adolescents are being assessed. A detailed developmental and neuro-developmental history, including birth history and speech and language development, as well as information about attachment, behaviour and any sexual, physical or emotional abuse, is crucial. A thorough assessment should include a comprehensive mental state examination, a medical assessment to exclude organic causes, and further neuropsychological and neurological interventions as appropriate.

Children and adolescents should be offered individual appointments in addition to joint meetings with their parents or carers and other significant adults such as teachers. Stressors and vulnerabilities in the child or adolescent's social, educational and family environments, including the quality of interpersonal relationships, should be explored, as this may yield important information to support or exclude a diagnosis of bipolar disorder.

As children and adolescents are vulnerable to exploitation or abuse, particularly during manic episodes, their levels of disinhibition and risk from others should be assessed. It is also important to assess risk to others arising from disinhibited, reckless and impulsive behaviour during manic episodes.

Treatment

Drugs are the mainstay of treatment for bipolar disorder in children and adolescents (NCCMH, 2006; Hamrin & Pachler, 2006). However, there is a lack of high quality evidence for the psychopharmacological treatment of this condition.

When treating acute manic, hypomanic and mixed episodes, antipsychotics such as olanzapine, quetiapine and risperidone are generally first line treatments, although lithium can also be used in these circumstances. For long-term treatment of child or adolescent bipolar disorder, so-called mood stabilisers such as lithium, sodium valproate, carbamazepine or olanzapine should be used. The choice should depend on gender, previous response to treatment, what is known about manic versus depressive relapse, history of adherence, and physical factors such as presence of obesity, renal disease and diabetes. Sodium valproate should not be prescribed routinely for girls and young women of childbearing age. This is due to the risk of polycystic ovary disease and because valproate is teratogenic and can damage the foetus during pregnancy (Rasgon, 2004).

Most of the drugs that are used to treat bipolar disorder can result in weight gain (Hamrin & Pachler, 2006). For children and adolescents, this presents additional health risks and personal issues about body image. It is important that children and adolescents who are taking medication have their weight carefully monitored, and access to health promotion information and healthy lifestyle choices should be encouraged.

There are no high quality studies on the management of acute depression in children and adolescents with bipolar disorder. There are the same concerns about the side effects of antidepressants as described above, as well as particular concerns about their use for bipolar depression, as there is a risk that antidepressants may induce a 'switch' to mania.

As well as medication, children and adolescents with bipolar disorder should be able to access psychological support. As described in the previous section, this is primarily cognitive behavioural therapy for moderate depressive episodes, or psychological interventions in conjunction with an antidepressant for severe or persistent depressive symptoms (NCCMH, 2005).

It is also important to support children and adolescents during the management of behavioural disturbance associated with manic episodes. To help reduce the negative consequences of manic symptoms, children and adolescents should be encouraged to avoid excessive stimulation, to delay taking important decisions, and to establish a structured routine in which levels of activity are reduced.

Many people with bipolar disorder experience early warning signs for several days or weeks before becoming seriously unwell. Relapse prevention involves helping young people and their parents or carers to recognise these early warning signs and take appropriate action. This includes monitoring and adjusting medication as necessary.

Children and adolescents who exhibit seriously disturbed behaviour should only be admitted to hospital if the risks associated with community treatment are too high, to avoid disruption to family, education and social functioning. However, if the young person is suicidal, vulnerable to exploitation or presenting a risk to others, an inpatient admission may be the safest alternative.

Course and prognosis

Although there is wide variation in relation to number of episodes and severity of symptoms, for most people bipolar disorder is a chronic and recurrent condition (Mackin & Young, 2005). Early detection is important, both in terms of implementing an appropriate treatment and management plan and in terms of improving outcomes and minimising harm caused by repeated episodes of illness. There is uncertainty about long-term outcomes for bipolar disorder in children and adolescents, but it is generally assumed that recovery is more likely if the child is living in a consistently supportive environment, and appropriate support is available for parents or carers (NCCMH, 2006).

Conclusion

Childhood bipolar disorder can cause severe disturbances in personal, social and education functioning. Professionals working in front-line children's services are well placed to support children and adolescents with bipolar disorder during first contact with primary care services, through engagement with specialist child and adolescent mental health services, and in accessing early intervention and crisis services.

References

Angold A, Costello EJ (2001) The epidemiology of depression in children and adolescents. In: Goodyer IM (ed) *The depressed child and adolescent* (2nd edition). Cambridge: Cambridge University Press.

Angold A, Costello EJ, Pickles A *et al* (1987) *The development of a questionnaire for use in epidemiological studies of depression in children and adolescents*. London: Medical Research Council Child Psychiatry Unit.

Biederman J, Mick E, Faraone SV *et al* (2000) Paediatric mania: a developmental subtype of bipolar disorder? *Biological Psychiatry* **48** 458–466.

Biederman J, Farone S, Mick E *et al* (1996) Attention deficit hyperactivity disorder and juvenile mania: an overlooked comorbidity? *Journal of the American Academy of Child and Adolescent Psychiatry* **35** (8) 997–1008.

Cotgrove A, Timimi S (2007) Should young people be given antidepressants? *British Medical Journal* **335** 750.

Emslie G, Kennar B, Kowatch R (1994) Affective disorders in children: diagnosis and management. *Journal of Child Neurology* **10** 42–49.

Fombonne E, Wostear G, Cooper V *et al* (2001a) The Maudsley long-term follow-up of child and adolescent depression: 1. Psychiatric outcomes in adulthood. *British Journal of Psychiatry* **179** 210–217.

Fombonne E, Wostear G, Cooper V *et al* (2001b) The Maudsley long-term follow-up of child and adolescent depression: 2. Suicidality, criminality and social dysfunction in adulthood. *British Journal of Psychiatry* **179** 218–223.

Geller B, Luby J (1997) Child and adolescent bipolar disorder: a review of the past 10 years. *Journal of the American Academy of Child and Adolescent Psychiatry* **36** 1168–1176.

Geller B, Williams M, Zimerman B *et al* (1998) Prepubertal and early adolescent bipolarity differentiate from ADHD by manic symptoms, grandiose delusions, ultra-rapid or ultradian cycling. *Journal of Affective Disorders* **51** 81–91.

Goodyer I, Herbert J, Secher SM, Pearson J (1997) Short-term outcome of major depression: I. Comorbidity and severity at presentation as predictors of persistent disorder. *Journal of the American Academy of Child and Adolescent Psychiatry* **36** (2) 179–187.

Goodyer IM (2001) Life events: their nature and effects. In: Goodyer IM (ed) *The depressed child and adolescent*. Cambridge: Cambridge University Press.

Hamrin V, Pachler M (2006). Paediatric bipolar disorder: evidence based psychopharmacological treatments. *Journal of Child and Adolescent Psychiatric Nursing* **20** (1) 40–58.

Harrington R, Bredenkamp D, Groothues C *et al* (1994) Adult outcomes of childhood and adolescent depression: III. Links with suicidal behaviours. *Journal of Child Psychology and Psychiatry* **35** 1309–1319.

Harrington R, Dubicka B (2001) Natural history of mood disorders in children and adolescents. In: Goodyer IM (ed) *The depressed child and adolescent*. Cambridge: Cambridge University Press.

Harris TL, Molock SD (2000) Cultural orientation, family cohesion, and family support in suicide ideation and depression among African American college students. *Suicide and Life Threatening Behavior* **30** 340–353.

Johnson J, Cohen P, Brooks J (2000) Associations between bipolar disorder and other psychiatric disorders during adolescence and early adulthood: a community based longitudinal investigation. *American Journal of Psychiatry* **157** 1679–1681.

Judd L, Akiskal H, Schettler P *et al* (2002) The long-term natural history of the weekly symptomatic status of bipolar I disorder. *Archives of General Psychiatry* **59** 530–537.

Kaufman J, Birmaher B, Brent D *et al* (1997) Schedule for affective disorders and schizophrenia for school-age children – present and lifetime version (K-SADS-PL): initial reliability and validity data. *Journal of the American Academy of Child and Adolescent Psychiatry* **36** 980–988.

Lewinsohn P, Seeley J, Klein D (2003). Bipolar disorders during adolescence. *Acta Psychiatrica Scandinavica* **418** 47–50.

Lloyd T, Kennedy N, Fearon P *et al* (2005) Incidence of bipolar affective disorder in three UK cities: results from the AESOP study. *British Journal of Psychiatry* **186** 126–131.

Mackin P, Young A (2005) Bipolar disorders. In: Wright P, Stern M, Phelan M (eds) *Core psychiatry.* Edinburgh: Elsevier Saunders.

NCCMH (2005) *Clinical guideline 28. Depression in children and young people: identification and management in primary, community and secondary care.* London: NICE.

NCCMH (2006) *Bipolar disorder: the management of bipolar disorder in adults, children and adolescents in primary and secondary care. Appendix 19: consensus conference on the diagnosis of bipolar I disorder in children and adolescents.* London: BPS.

Post R, Denicoff K, Leverich G (2003) Morbidity in 258 bipolar outpatients followed for one year with daily prospective ratings on the NIMH life chart method. *Journal of Clinical Psychiatry* **64** 680–690.

Rasgon N (2004) The relationship between polycystic ovary syndrome and antiepileptic drugs: a review of the evidence. *Journal of Clinical Psychopharmacology* **24** 322–334.

Taylor C, McDougall T, Wellman N (2006) Bipolar disorder: the nurse's role. *Mental Health Practice* **10** (2) 10–12.

Weissman M, Bland R, Canino G (1996) Cross-national epidemiology of major depression and bipolar disorder. *Journal of the American Medical Association* **276** 293–299.

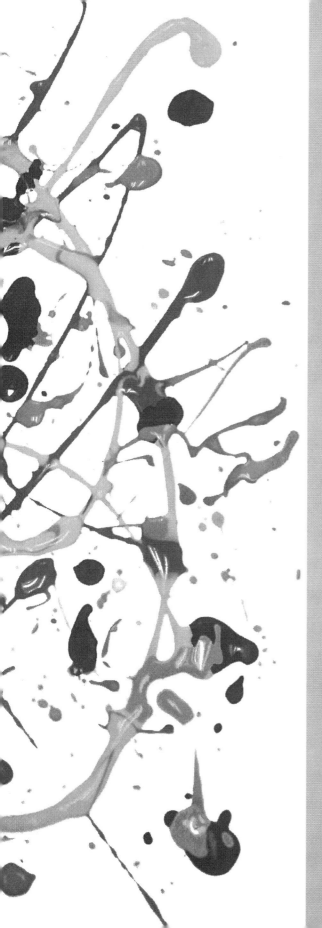

Early intervention in psychosis for children and adolescents

Eric Davis

Key points

- Children and young adults aged 14–35 can benefit from early intervention for early onset psychosis

- Reduced duration of untreated psychosis results in better clinical outcomes for the young person

- Treatments should include psychological, social, occupational and medical interventions

- the family/carers should be involved and supported

- Services should be delivered wherever possible in a non-stigma setting; if hospitalisation is needed, duration of stay should be kept to a minimum.

Key words
Early intervention; Schizophrenia; Duration of untreated psychosis; At-risk mental state; Relapse prevention

E arly intervention (EI) services for young people with first-episode psychotic symptoms are a comparatively recent feature of mental health service provision, having emerged only within the past two decades, and most strongly in the past 10. Their development was influenced by a number of factors. First, it is estimated that some 80% of first episode psychosis emerges between the ages of 16 and 30, and on average at 22 years. Second, it is recognised that the longer the duration of untreated psychosis (DUP), the worse the outcome is for children, adolescents and young adults. Typically, it takes between one and two years for psychosis and schizophrenia-like difficulties to be identified and diagnosed (Edwards & McGorry, 2002; Perkins *et al*, 2005). This can be due to several factors: most notably, lack of knowledge about mental health and mental health services, ambiguous early symptoms, and stigma (Davis *et al*, 2007), which all contribute to delay in accessing appropriate professional help. There is also an initial 'prodromal' phase, or at-risk mental state (ARMS), of up to three years for schizophrenia and slightly less for bipolar disorder, during which the symptoms of psychosis begin to manifest (Jackson *et al*, 2003), and when intervention can be effective in averting the development of full psychosis (Morrison *et al*, 2007; Nelson & Yung, 2007).

This chapter concerns itself with schizophrenia; bipolar disorder is discussed elsewhere.

The requirement on mental health trusts to introduce EI services is spelled out in the *Mental Health Policy Implementation Guide* (MHPIG) published in 2001 by the Department of Health, which expands on the National Service Framework (NSF) for Mental Health (Department of Health, 1999). EI is intended for people aged 14–35 years with first episode psychotic symptoms, and should be provided for the first three years of illness. The NSF for Children, Young People and Maternity Services (Department of Health, 2004) also underlines the importance of developing EI teams. By the end of 2007, there were 160 EI teams in place in England, covering some 7,000 new cases of psychosis (only slightly fewer than the national target of 7,500 new cases set by the Department of Health).

Clinical symptoms

The very early signs of psychosis in children are often missed. This can be because of its rarity pre-age 12 (Kumra *et al*, 2001), or because psychosis may simply not be suspected in children.

Pre-illness, children's functioning may be affected by developmental delays in language and reading, and physical factors such as bladder control (Hollis, 2000; Jones *et al*, 1994). Developmental issues are of clear importance when assessing and formulating or diagnosing mental health difficulties in children. For example, visual or auditory hallucinations could be explained by temporal lobe epilepsy, so it is important to exclude this as a potential cause of problems. Screening for autism and Asperger's syndrome may also be required, as poor language and social skills and withdrawn behaviour can be mistaken for psychosis.

Table 1: Clinical features of childhood and adolescent psychosis

- Poor pre-illness functioning (social, intellectual, educational), with greater severity associated with youngest onset
- Lower IQ scores (30% of children with psychosis have learning disabilities)
- Very slow (insidious) onset
- Mainly negative symptoms (eg. apathy, poor language skills, lack of spontaneity)
- Family history of psychosis
- Childhood onset is associated with poorer outcome than adult onset.

Psychosis more frequently manifests in late adolescence and early adulthood. Unlike adult psychosis, which more often presents as a rapid, abrupt departure from the person's usual self, childhood/adolescent psychosis is often slow to manifest. Deteriorating school performance, loss of friendships, and withdrawn and odd/eccentric behaviour can characterise some of the subtle signs of at-risk mental states and early illness changes. Children and adolescents are more likely than adults to experience poor psychological, social and occupational functioning (negative symptoms), rather than positive symptoms, such as hearing voices or holding extreme or exaggerated beliefs.

Outcomes depend very much on early intervention. The Maudsley study (Hollis, 2000) followed up 110 cases of adolescent-onset psychoses and found that half of those whose active psychotic symptoms lasted for less than three months made a full recovery. However, this dropped to just 15% of those who were still experiencing negative or positive psychotic symptoms at six months or longer after diagnosis, underlining the importance of early, active intervention. It also found that adolescents with psychosis generally did not recover as well as adults. Neither gender nor length of pre-psychotic illness appeared to affect psychological outcome. Social functioning was markedly affected – approximately 50% did not achieve close friendships or loving relationships. Again, negative symptoms formed a very important part of the clinical picture.

The national campaign organisation Rethink spells out the impact of untreated psychosis (www.rethink.org): of 100 young people with untreated psychosis, 80% drop out of school or work, between one and two per cent die by suicide, only 50% receive any kind of specialist help, and just 10% receive psychological therapy. One in three seek treatment and are turned away, and of those who do receive treatment, 50% are sectioned, often with police involvement, and 60% are subsequently lost to follow-up.

This underlines the need for specialist early intervention: as stated above, reducing the duration of untreated psychosis (DUP) ought to result in better outcomes (Birchwood *et al*, 1997; Perkins *et al*, 2005).

Early intervention services

The MHPIG (Department of Health, 2001) sets out the main components and principles of care required of an EI team or service (see table 2). The Gloucestershire Recovery in Psychosis (GRIP) EI service, which was launched in 2003 and is part of Gloucestershire Partnership NHS Trust, is based on this framework. Its core clinical work with children aged 14–17 and young adults aged 18–35 is described here in order to illustrate how the framework can translate into effective services on the ground. The service currently comprises a team of 10 staff, which is multidisciplinary in nature, including psychology, nursing, psychiatry and social work, although the numbers will increase as the service expands to encompass the entire county over the next two years. The team carries an average caseload of 15 service users. It covers a population of 200,000 currently, rising to 580,000 once expansion is completed in 2008–2009.

Table 2: Key features of an early intervention service (Department of Health, 2001)

An early intervention service should be able to:

- reduce the stigma associated with psychosis and improve professional and lay awareness of the symptoms of psychosis and the need for early assessment
- reduce the length of time young people remain undiagnosed and untreated
- develop meaningful engagement, provide evidence-based interventions and promote recovery during the early phase of illness
- increase stability in the lives of service users, facilitate development and provide opportunities for personal fulfilment
- provide a user-centred service ie. a seamless service available for those from age 14 to 35 that effectively integrates child, adolescent and adult mental health services and works in partnership with primary care, education, social services, youth and other services
- ensure that the care is transferred thoughtfully and effectively at the end of the treatment period.

Evidence indicates that the following principles of care are important:

- culture, age and gender sensitive
- family orientated
- meaningful and sustained engagement based on assertive outreach principles
- treatment provided in the least restrictive and stigmatising setting
- separate, age-appropriate facilities for young people
- emphasis on normal social roles and service user's development needs, particularly involvement in education and achieving employment
- emphasis on managing symptoms rather than the diagnosis.

Raising awareness of psychotic illness

The GRIP team has adopted a number of ways to communicate and liaise with a range of local services, such as schools, GPs, Connexions, and non-statutory youth agencies that cater for disadvantaged and homeless children (Reed & Stevens, 2007; Adams *et al*, 2007). It has been helped in this by robust links to colleagues in the child and adolescent mental health services (CAMHS) within the same trust, who are able to provide supporting information about adolescent mental health issues and useful community and inpatient links.

One unusual method of raising public and professional awareness was the opportunity to link with an innovative drama-based awareness-raising project, On the Edge, (Roberts *et al*, 2007). This was a mental health education programme designed to support early intervention by increasing public and professional knowledge and understanding of early psychosis, reducing the stigma associated with mental health issues and improving awareness of avenues to help. The target audience was young people aged 14–22 years in schools and colleges. By attending one of the theatre events staged as part of the national tour in Gloucester, GRIP made important contacts that have helped in subsequent mental health care through more rapid and accurate referrals for help. Roberts *et al* (2007) also developed an excellent information resource pack that we have used in local awareness-raising work. Passy and Dawe (2006) provide a detailed report concerning the development of these materials.

The most common source of referrals to GRIP are GPs and primary care professionals, and non-statutory agencies. We encourage prompt referral even when there is only suspicion of psychotic symptoms. We also encourage self-referral and carer referrals direct to GRIP, to remove barriers to service entry.

Transition issues

The Departments of Health and Education and Skills (2006) have stipulated that good EI practice will be facilitated by close collaboration between adult services and CAMHS. Historically, the transition of care from CAMHS to adult mental health services has been problematic, with adult services not able to treat young people aged under 18, and some CAMHS feeling unable/unwilling to provide a diagnosis of psychosis when a young person is aged under 18. GRIP and local CAMHS have worked together to achieve good, continuous care. Tiffin and Hudson (2007) attest to the importance of managing transition issues. Locally, clinicians are available from differing cultures and gender-separate inpatient services are available for younger people.

Early detection

Early detection can also mean working with young people at ultra high risk (UHR) or in an at-risk mental state (ARMS) (see, for example, Nelson & Yung, 2007; Morrison *et al*, 2007; Borgmann-Winter *et al*, 2006). Essentially, this work attempts to identify and provide treatment to children and young people at high risk of developing a subsequent and frank episode of psychosis. Morrison *et al* (2007) have found that cognitive therapy (CT) significantly reduces the likelihood of children (16 and 17 years old in this study) and young adults progressing to full-blown psychosis. CT is a form of therapy that assumes that thought problems can become negative and fixed, resulting in lowered mood and reduced activity levels, which can further compromise confidence and self-esteem in a psychological vicious cycle. By working cognitively with such thoughts, the vicious cycle can be challenged.

GRIP uses CT when working with children who are at UHR or in an ARMS. We also use the Comprehensive Assessment of At-Risk Mental States (CAARMS) (Yung *et al*, 2005) and/or the Structured Interview for Prodromal Symptoms (SIPS) (Miller *et al*, 1999) tools, which both contain useful questions for exploring mental health states in the earliest stages of difficulty.

Assessment

Interviews both for early detection and wider assessment are usually conducted jointly with a CAMHS colleague. The comprehensive assessment for a suspected first episode of psychosis (FEP) includes as a minimum:

- psychiatric history
- mental state examination (aided by structured and recognised scales such as the KGV (Lancashire, 1994) and/or Positive and Negative Syndrome Scale (PANSS) (Kay & Opler, 1987)
- risk – including suicide risk
- social functioning and resource assessment
- psychological assessment
- occupational assessment
- family/support assessment (eg. Smith *et al*, 2007)
- service user's aspirations and understanding
- contribution from people important to the service user (eg. teachers, friends, family).

A comprehensive care plan is then formulated in consultation with the young person and their carers that documents the range of interventions that will be carried out by GRIP and its partners.

Interventions
Watching brief

If there is uncertainty about the diagnosis, the team works with the child and his/her family for up to six months using a 'watching brief'. This allows opportunity to clarify presence of symptoms, and assess psychological, social and education/work functioning. If the young person has experienced a psychotic episode, work can begin. All service users are tracked so none are 'lost to follow up', with the vast majority of work taking place in low stigma settings such as the person's home, GP practice, school or at GRIP's base in a local resource centre. At no stage does failure to engage with treatment lead to case closure.

Medication

It is important to prescribe the right medication at the optimal dose. Edwards and McGorry (2002) suggest 'start low and go slow' when prescribing for the first time. For the vast majority of children with a suspected or actual FEP, this will be the first time they have been prescribed powerful psychotropic (consciousness-altering) medication (they are said to be 'drug-naïve'). Walker and colleagues (2001) and Hollis (2005) discuss the challenges associated with the pharmacological management of childhood psychosis. First, onset in young people is associated with greater severity of symptoms than in adults. Second, the side effects of medication can often present greater difficulties to young people, because the medication can exacerbate underlying negative and cognitive deficits. Also, neurodevelopmental factors, such as the maturation of the central nervous system, mean that the way medication is absorbed/metabolised by children may differ from adults, and side effects may also be more serious because of these metabolic differences. Movement disorders, agitation, weight gain, prolactin difficulties (milk production and breast enlargement), sedation, raised or lowered blood pressure, sexual difficulties and cardiac problems can occur. Because of this, compliance needs to be carefully addressed. Third, most of the evidence for efficiency (from research trials) and effectiveness (from routine clinical practice) comes from research with adults and may not apply to children. For example, children with psychosis may also experience clinical depression, but there is little evidence for the efficacy or effectiveness of antidepressants (except fluoxetine) with children, whereas a wider range of antidepressants are therapeutically acceptable to use with adults.

Nevertheless, the newer antipsychotics such as risperidone, olanzapine, quetiapine and aripiprazole exhibit greater effectiveness and fewer side effects than other medications such as haloperidol. If two of the newer medications do not work, or are less than optimally effective, then clozapine is recommended, as it has produced very good results in otherwise medication non-responsive children (Hollis, 2005).

GRIP maintains close contact with psychiatrist colleagues in CAMHS. The majority of children on our caseload are in receipt of one of the newer antipsychotics. However, a number are prescribed clozapine, with generally good or better results than the previous medication regime. The use of standard side effects monitoring tools such as the Liverpool University Neuroleptic Side Effects Rating Scale (Day *et al*, 1995) and Drug Attitude Inventory (Hogan *et al*, 1983) help us to work with compliance issues, as these tools promote discussion about the taking of medication.

Psychological therapies

Cognitive behavioural therapy (CBT) is offered as standard to GRIP service users (Chadwick *et al*, 1996). We have also offered this to carers who are struggling with the stresses of looking after a person with a serious mental health difficulty. As with CT in early detection described above, CBT aims to challenge distorted, unhelpful and fixed patterns of negative thinking that can lead to further erosion of self-confidence and self-esteem. Correspondingly, the gentle resumption of activities is also encouraged, as enhanced self-esteem is known to be connected to successful task/activity completion and the development of greater coping strategies (Baguley & Baguley, 1999).

Family involvement and support

A significant volume of research attests to the effectiveness of family work (Barrowclough & Tarrier, 1997; Smith *et al*, 2007). Generally, outcomes are improved if the families and/or significant others are helped to cope with the stress of dealing with a serious mental health difficulty. A combination of active problem-solving work, provision of accurate and timely information, examination of communication styles and the development of techniques for stress management are all thought to help as 'active ingredients' in family work, and to improve outcomes for children (and adults) with psychosis. Generally, our contact with parents and significant others begins from the point of referral (Reed & Stevens, 2007). Regular and flexible contact with the family and significant others is maintained throughout our involvement with the child or young person, until the point of discharge.

Another aspect of GRIP that is useful is a carers group that runs over 10 weeks. It covers a number of issues, such as 'What is psychosis?' medication, psychological treatments, the Mental Health Act and stress management (Davis, Reed *et al*, 2007). Encouragingly, the carers group has become self-sustaining and mutually supportive. The carers (mainly parents) meet monthly for support and to exchange information and experiences.

Pathways to education and occupation

Looking to the future, we try to adopt an approach somewhere between realism and optimism. We aim to achieve functional recovery. If full recovery can be attained, this means adopting an assertive approach to supporting children back into school, training or work. The team works with the local education re-integration service to try to help children get back to school. For older children, links have been established locally with Connexions and non-statutory youth agencies such as Cheltenham Community Projects and a mental health informed employment agency, ARENA, which offer work experience and placements. These might include car maintenance, plastering, office work and dealing with computers. We always try to get the child or young person back into education, training or work before resorting to claiming benefits, because receipt of benefits can act as a disincentive to this (Boldison *et al*, 2007).

Treating co-morbidity

Children will often experience other difficulties alongside psychosis: for example, substance misuse (van Nimwegen *et al*, 2005) and depression and anxiety (Escher *et al*, 2003; Fombonne *et al*, 2001a; Fombonne *et al*, 2001b). Again, CBT is our treatment of choice for depression and anxiety. Substance misuse is addressed by using motivational interviewing, a technique that seeks to explore the young person's ambivalence to the use of illicit drugs, and, through talking about the issues, motivate them to change their behaviour (Zweben & Zuckoff, 2002).

Relapse prevention plan

Once a psychotic episode has been formally identified it is important to focus on relapse prevention. Another CBT technique that can be helpful is to identify the early warning signs (EWS) of a relapse – the individual's 'relapse signature'. Smith (2003) has developed a very useful pack to identify EWS, which we routinely use. Davis, Undrill and Samuels (2007) discuss ways of working with EWS incorporating medication adherence and cognitive therapy. Any such relapse prevention work should include a crisis plan with practical information such as who should be contacted if/when such an event occurs.

Inpatient and respite care

We aim to avoid hospitalisation wherever possible. If it is needed, then the team has access to two 'hospitals in the community' that cater for older children (16 and 17years). For younger children, and more seriously unwell older children, out of county referrals are necessary. However, the aim is always to transfer children to the least restrictive and lowest stigma setting as soon as possible. The GRIP team and CAMHS colleagues liaise with hospital staff from admission through to discharge, and work closely with the family throughout this process.

Discharge from GRIP

We work with children for as long as is required. If the young person still needs care within an EI environment on reaching age 18, we offer a further three years of intervention. However, if children are well and remaining stable they can be discharged to primary care. If the young person remains unstable and needs assertive outreach because of engagement issues, then we refer them to an assertive outreach team as required. If they are still unwell and experiencing significant negative symptoms, then we may refer them to continuing care. If the young person leaves home, or moves area prior to or at age 18+, then we will liaise, whenever possible, with services in the area to which they have moved.

Evaluation

It is important that EI services are evaluated. Edwards and McGorry (2002) suggest that evaluation encompasses both 'quality control' and outcome assessment, in order to provide evidence to satisfy management and funding bodies, inform and influence other clinicians and policy makers, and ensure resources are deployed efficiently and for the purposes for which they were intended.

Evaluation can also help a team or service retain focus on its vision and, as part of this, can generate new and useful data for performance management. The GRIP team has conducted a rigorous evaluation (Davis *et al*, 2005) that shows service outcomes have improved, and user and carer satisfaction levels have increased. The service was recognised in the CSIP/NIMHE 10 High Impact Changes report (2006).

Conclusion

Early intervention in psychosis is now recognised as able to lessen the impact of the illness and produce better long-term outcomes for children and young people at risk. Interventions need to address psychological, social, family and education/occupation issues. Raising awareness of the incidence and signs of psychosis is important to ensure young people are referred as soon as practicable to expert, designated EI services that, working closely with CAMHS, can ensure they receive timely, focused treatments, and so avert life-long disability and social exclusion.

References

Adams S, Bishop L, Bellinger J (2007) Recovery through sports in first-episode psychosis. In: Velleman R, Davis E, Smith G, Drage M (eds) *Changing outcomes in psychosis: collaborative cases from practitioners, users and carers.* Oxford: BPS Blackwell.

Baguley I, Baguley C (1999) Psychosocial interventions in the treatment of psychosis. *Mental Health Care* **2** 314–317.

Barrowclough C, Tarrier N (1997) *Families of schizophrenic patients: cognitive behavioural intervention.* Cheltenham: Stanley Thornes.

Birchwood M, McGorry P, Jackson H (1997) Early intervention in schizophrenia. Editorial. *British Journal of Psychiatry* **170** 2–5.

Boldison S, Davies R, Hawkes H, Pace C, Sayers R (2007) Employment, mental health and PSI: occupation is everyone's job. In: Velleman R, Davis E, Smith G, Drage M (eds) *Changing outcomes in psychosis: collaborative cases from practitioners, users and carers.* Oxford: BPS Blackwell.

Borgmann-Winter K, Calkins ME, Kniele K, Gur RE (2006) Assessment of adolescents at risk of psychosis. *Current Psychiatry Reports* **8** 313–321.

CSIP/NIMHE (2006) *10 high impact changes for mental health services. Case study 9b: Demonstrating the impact of a whole system approach to early intervention.* Leeds: CSIP/NIMHE.

Chadwick P, Birchwood M, Trower P (1996) *Cognitive therapy for voices, delusions and paranoia.* Chichester: John Wiley & Sons.

Davis E, Morgan J, Parris R, Riley G (2005) *Mental health service response to first-episode psychosis in Gloucestershire.* Unpublished report. Available from the first author: davis@ericlaura.freeserve.co.uk

Davis E, Reed M and GRIP carers (2007) *First-episode psychosis: improving carers' well-being through a psycho-educational support group.* Presentation delivered at Working with Families – Developing Caring Partnerships conference, 19–20 March, Stratford-upon-Avon.

Davis E, Undrill G, Samuels L (2007) Relapse prevention in bipolar disorder with staff who are also service users. In: Velleman R, Davis E, Smith G, Drage M (eds) *Changing outcomes in psychosis: collaborative cases from practitioners, users and carers.* Oxford: BPS Blackwell.

Davis E J, Velleman R, Smith G, Drage M (2007) Psychosocial developments: towards a model of recovery. In: Velleman R, Davis E, Smith G, Drage M (eds) *Changing outcomes in psychosis: collaborative cases from practitioners, users and carers.* Oxford: BPS Blackwell.

Day J, Wood G, Dewey M, Bentall R (1995) A self-rating scale for measuring neuroleptic side-effects: validation in a group of schizophrenic patients. *British Journal of Psychiatry* **166** 650–653.

Department of Health (1999) *The national service framework for mental health: modern standards and service models.* London: Department of Health.

Department of Health (2001) *The mental health policy implementation guide.* London: Department of Health.

Department of Health (2004) *National service framework for children, young people and maternity services.* London: Department of Health.

Department of Health/Department for Education and Skills (2006) *Report on the implementation of standard 9 of the national service framework for children, young people and maternity services.* London: Department of Health/Department for Education and Skills.

Edwards J, McGorry P (eds) (2002) *Implementing early intervention in psychosis: a guide to establishing early psychosis services.* London: Martin Dunitz.

Escher S, Delepsaul P, Romme M, Buiks A, van Os J (2003) Coping defence and depression in adolescents hearing voices. *Journal of Mental Health* **12** (1) 91–99.

Fombonne E, Wostear G, Cooper V, Harrington R, Rutter M (2001a) The Maudsley long-term follow-up of child and adolescent depression: 1. Psychiatric outcomes in adulthood. *British Journal of Psychiatry* **179** 210–217.

Fombonne E, Wostear G, Cooper V, Harrington R, Rutter M (2001b) The Maudsley long-term follow-up of child and adolescent depression: 2. Suicidality, criminality and social dysfunction in adulthood. *British Journal of Psychiatry* **179** 217–224.

Hogan T, Awad A, Eastwood R (1983) A self-report scale predictive of drug compliance in schizophrenics: reliability and discriminative validity. *Psychological Medicine* **13** 177–183.

Hollis C (2000) Adolescent schizophrenia. *Advances in Psychiatric Treatment* **6** 83–92.

Hollis C (2005) Paediatric psychopharmacology in schizophrenia. *Psychiatry* **4** (11) 49–51.

Jackson A, Cavanagh J, Scott J (2003) A systematic review of manic and depressive prodromes. *Journal of Affective Disorders* **74** (3) 209–217.

Jones P, Rogers B, Murray R *et al* (1994) Child development risk factors for adult schizophrenia in the British 1946 birth cohort. *Lancet* **344** 1398–1402.

Kay SR, Opler LA (1987) The positive and negative syndrome scale (PANSS) for schizophrenia. *Schizophrenia Bulletin* **13** 507–518.

Kumra S, Shaw M, Merka P, Nakayama E, Augustin R (2001) Childhood-onset schizophrenia: research update. *Canadian Journal of Psychiatry* **46** 923–930.

Lancashire S (1994) *Revised KGV assessment tool.* London: Institute of Psychiatry.

Miller TJ, McGlashan TH, Woods SW *et al* (1999) Symptom assessment in schizophrenia prodromal states. *Psychiatry* **70** 273–287.

Morrison AP, French P, Parker S, Roberts M, Stevens H, Bentall R P and Lewis S (2007) Three-year follow-up of a randomised controlled trial of cognitive therapy for the prevention of psychosis in people at ultra-high risk. *Schizophrenia Bulletin* **33** (3) 682–687.

Nelson B, Yung AR (2007) When things are not as they seem: detecting first-episode psychosis upon referral to ultra high risk ('prodromal') clinics. *Early Intervention in Psychiatry* **1** 208–211.

Passy R, Dawe J (2006) *On the edge: a theatre in education programme – final report.* Exeter: Exstream Theatre Company. Available from www.exstream.org.uk

Perkins DO, Hongbin G, Boteva K, Lieberman JA (2005) Relationship between duration of untreated psychosis and outcome in first episode schizophrenia: a critical review and meta-analysis. *The American Journal of Psychiatry* **162** (10) 1785–1804.

Reed M, Stevens C (2007) Shared caring for a first episode of psychosis: an opportunity to promote hope and recovery. In: Velleman R, Davis E, Smith G, Drage M (eds) *Changing outcomes in psychosis: collaborative cases from practitioners, users and carers.* Oxford: BPS Blackwell.

Roberts G, Somers J, Dawe J, Passy R, Mays C, Carr G, Shiers D, Smith J (2007) On the Edge: a drama-based mental health education programme on early psychosis for schools. *Early Intervention in Psychiatry* **1** 168–176.

Smith G, Gregory K, Higgs A (2007) *An integrated approach to family work for psychosis: a manual for family workers.* London: Jessica Kingsley.

Smith J (2003) *Early warning signs: a self-management training manual of individuals with psychosis.* Worcestershire: Worcestershire Community and Mental Health NHS Trust.

Tiffin PA, Hudson S (2007) An early intervention in psychosis service for adolescents. *Early Intervention in Psychiatry* **1** 212–218.

van Nimwegen L, de Haan L, van Beveren N, van den Brink W, Linszen D (2005) Adolescence, schizophrenia and drug abuse: a window of vulnerability. *Acta Psychiatrica Scandinavica* **111** (s427) 35–42.

Walker G, Wiltshire C, Anderson J, Storm V (2001) The pharmacologic treatment of the early phase of first-episode psychosis in youths. *Canadian Journal of Psychiatry* **46** 803–809.

Yung AR, Yuen HP, McGorry PD *et al* (2005) Mapping the onset of psychosis: the comprehensive assessment of at risk mental states (CAARMS). *Australian and New Zealand Journal of Psychiatry* **39** 964–971.

Zweben A, Zuckoff A (2002) Motivational interviewing and treatment adherence. In: Miller WR, Rollnick S (eds) *Motivational interviewing.* New York: Guilford Press.

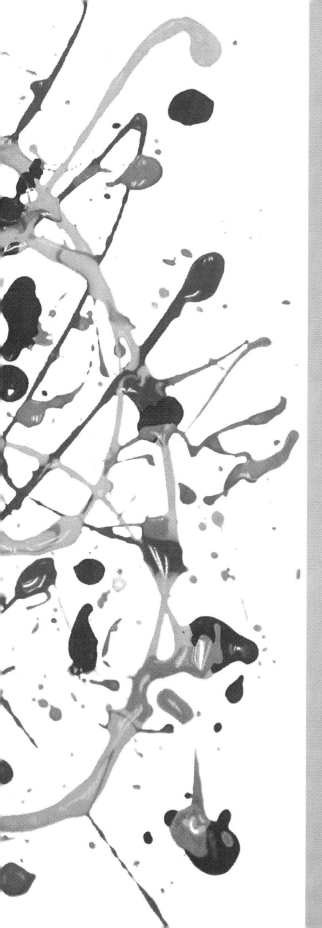

Attention deficit/ hyperactivity disorder

Kapil Sayal

Key points

- Attention deficit/hyperactivity disorder (ADHD) affects an estimated 2%–5% of children and young people, and is more common among boys

- Primary clinical features include inattentiveness, over-activity and impulsiveness

- It is commonly treated with medication, often in combination with psychosocial interventions

- Concerns have been raised about the validity of the ADHD diagnosis and the treatment of young children with powerful stimulants

- All those who work with children are in a position to recognise children with features of ADHD and facilitate referral for specialist assessment and treatment.

Key words
Attention deficit/hyperactivity disorder; Diagnostic criteria; Behavioural problems; Neuro-developmental disorder; Methylphenidate

This chapter aims to summarise the key literature relating to attention deficit/ hyperactivity disorder (ADHD). First, it outlines the main features and diagnostic description of ADHD. Second, it summarises epidemiological information in terms of its prevalence, correlates, associated difficulties, and longer-term outcomes. Third, it outlines some of the controversies about this disorder. Finally, it describes the diagnostic process and different approaches to managing ADHD. It aims to help the reader develop an understanding of ADHD and to assist in practice in terms of identifying children who may need an ADHD assessment.

Diagnostic description

ADHD is described in the fourth edition of the Diagnostic and Statistical Manual of Mental Disorders (DSM-IV) (American Psychiatric Association, 1994), which is the main diagnostic classification system used in the US. It is the term used to describe behaviour in children that fulfils particular criteria. It involves three main features: inattentiveness, over-activity and impulsiveness. These behaviours need to have started before the age of seven years. Three other factors are crucial in distinguishing children who have ADHD from other children who might behave in an inattentive, overactive or impulsive way from time to time. First, these behaviours should have been present for at least six months (ie. they have persisted over time); second, they should be abnormal for the child's developmental age (ie. they are out of keeping with the child's level of learning and functioning); and third, they lead to functional impairment for the child that is pervasive across different situations.

In the UK, there has been a considerable shift in clinical diagnostic practice and the public's understanding of attentional and hyperactivity problems and disorders over the past decade. Traditionally, the main diagnostic classification system used in the UK and Europe is the 10th edition of the International Classification of Diseases (ICD-10) (World Health Organisation, 1992). This describes a narrower diagnostic category of hyperkinetic disorder, where all three core features (inattentiveness, over-activity and impulsiveness) need to be present and be pervasive across at least two different situations, such as home and school. Like ADHD, these behaviours need to persistent over time and be abnormal for the child's developmental age. However, the age of onset is before the age of six years. Another key difference is that the DSM-IV system allows for different sub-types of ADHD: namely, predominantly inattentive, predominantly hyperactive/impulsive, and combined (both inattentive and over-active/impulsive) sub-types. The first set of clinical guidance for ADHD published by the National Institute for Health and Clinical Excellence (NICE, 2000) focused on hyperkinetic disorder and conceptualised this as a severe combined sub-type of the broader ADHD. The forthcoming (2008) NICE clinical practice guidelines focus on ADHD, underlining the shift in conceptualisation over the last decade. This broadening of the diagnostic criteria has also fuelled controversy about the validity of the disorder, because of the increase in the numbers of children who meet the diagnostic criteria (see below).

Key behaviours

Key behaviours related to hyperactivity include restlessness (for example, difficulties in keeping or sitting still; getting up and down, running or wandering around unnecessarily, and climbing furniture), fidgeting (for example, moving parts of the body while seated), and descriptions of the child being 'always on the go'. Other behaviours include being very talkative and noisy and difficulties in playing quietly and being able to calm down.

Key behaviours related to impulsivity include difficulties in waiting turn, frequent interrupting of others, and blurting out answers. These features are associated with risky behaviours, such as crossing roads without looking or climbing heights.

Features of inattention include being easily distractible, difficulties with concentrating on activities for the expected time (given the situation under consideration and the child's developmental level), making careless mistakes, appearing not to listen, avoiding tasks that require concentration, having problems following instructions and finishing things, being forgetful and disorganised, and frequently losing things.

All these behaviours can occur at home or school and, as outlined above, are persistent, impairing, and out of keeping with the child's developmental level.

Impact of ADHD

ADHD can result in a range of difficulties for children. It can adversely affect their development in terms of emotional well-being, friendships, family relationships, education, and functioning into adulthood. It is also a risk factor for the development of other problems. Academically, it is associated with educational under-achievement, relationship difficulties with peers and teachers, problems adjusting to the greater demands for self-organisation at secondary school level, and disciplinary problems (including exclusion and dropping out from school (Barbaresi *et al*, 2007). In terms of mental health, it can lead to poor self-esteem and other behavioural problems, including oppositional defiant and conduct disorders. Further mental health difficulties into adolescence and adulthood are outlined below.

The presence of ADHD in a child can have considerable impact on family life. Family difficulties can include parental relationship difficulties and marital discord, maternal depression, and a negative impact on parents' employment and family finances (Sayal *et al*, 2003). There can be wider family relationship difficulties, including effects on siblings and negative parent–child interaction. The family may be at risk of restricted social activities and few social relationships.

Prevalence of ADHD

The tighter diagnostic criteria for hyperkinetic disorder mean that its prevalence rate is estimated to be about one per cent of school-aged children (Green *et al*,

2005). In contrast, the broader criteria for ADHD mean that the majority of studies have estimated the prevalence rates of ADHD at between four per cent and eight per cent (Faraone *et al*, 2003). There is, however, marked variation in estimates, ranging from two per cent to 18% (Ford *et al*, 2005; Polanczyk *et al*, 2007). These estimates vary because of differences in methodology, such as the measures used for the research, the choice of sample under study (such as age range or population sample), and the way in which diagnostic criteria are interpreted and where cut-off points are set (for example, whether teacher ratings are obtained, and how teacher and parent ratings are combined to determine the total number of symptoms or the presence of pervasive impairment).

When similar methodology is used in terms of measures and interpretation of DSM-IV criteria, prevalence rates of ADHD are broadly similar across countries. However, the recognition rate of children with ADHD varies enormously across countries, tending to be higher in western countries, and particularly in the US. Recognition rates are affected by many factors, including levels of service provision, access to and availability of services, social and political attitudes towards ADHD, and cultural beliefs about the causes of and treatments for childhood behavioural problems. In a cross-cultural comparison, Chinese parents were found to be more likely than English parents to rate their sons as having higher levels of hyperactivity (Leung *et al*, 1996). Despite these differences in subjective perceptions, the Chinese boys had lower levels of activity than the English boys when assessed objectively.

Associated problems

Associated problems are often described as 'comorbidity', which means the presence of more than one disorder. About one-third of children with ADHD have an additional (comorbid) disorder. Most commonly, these include oppositional defiant disorder (in younger or primary school age children), conduct disorder (in adolescence), emotional disorders (such as anxiety or depressive disorders), tic disorders (such as Tourette's syndrome) and global or specific learning disorders (such as reading or developmental co-ordination disorders).

Many of these comorbid disorders can also resemble ADHD, with the risk that, in the absence of a comprehensive and careful assessment, other disorders can be misdiagnosed as ADHD. These look-alike disorders include other developmental difficulties, such as undiagnosed global or specific (including speech and language problems) learning disorders, social communication disorders (autism, Asperger's syndrome), oppositional defiant or conduct disorders, and emotional disorders.

Causes and correlates of ADHD

ADHD is more common in boys than girls; the gender difference is estimated to vary between 2:1 to 4:1 in the population (Ford *et al*, 2004; Gaub & Carlson, 1997). Data from a large UK population-based survey have indicated that, unlike other child and adolescent mental health disorders, ADHD was not associated with any of the range of family factors that were investigated (Ford *et al*, 2004), or with any school or neighbourhood factors. It is conceptualised as a neuro-developmental disorder and is often associated with other neuro-developmental difficulties (such as cerebral palsy, epilepsy, and co-ordination difficulties) and poorer reading ability (Ford *et al*, 2004). These findings support the conceptualisation that ADHD has an underlying biological basis. Clinical practice also suggests that environmental and family factors can exacerbate difficulties and impairment.

In terms of possible causes, a large body of research indicates that the aetiology of ADHD is complex and likely to involve a variety of factors. Genetic studies have consistently found strong evidence of a genetic contribution and that ADHD is highly heritable (average heritability is around 0.8), and more likely to be found in closer biological relatives than more distant relatives. Research has also suggested that certain candidate genes might be implicated. Nevertheless, there is no clear or predictable pattern of transmission across generations. Neuro-anatomical and neuro-psychological studies demonstrate consistent group differences (between children who do and do not have ADHD) in terms of the volume of particular regions of the brain and performance on tests measuring specific functions, such as executive function, delay aversion and response inhibition. Other, more environmental risk factors may also play a role, perhaps interacting with a genetic vulnerability. These include maternal use of tobacco, alcohol, or other psychoactive substances during pregnancy, prematurity, birth complications, and head injury.

Outcomes

Symptoms of ADHD often persist into adolescence or adulthood. Longitudinal studies suggest that around two-thirds of affected children have persistent symptoms associated with significant clinical impairments, implying a prevalence of at least one per cent for ADHD in adults. As ADHD diagnostic criteria were written with children in mind, persisting difficulties in adulthood may not meet these criteria. These difficulties can also contribute to poor social adjustment and personality problems in adulthood. Other outcomes include the development of other psychiatric disorders, substance misuse (research suggests up to a five-fold increase in risk), antisocial and criminal behaviours, relationship difficulties, a lack of involvement in social activities and social exclusion, and employment problems (Klein & Mannuzza, 1991; Taylor *et al*, 1996; Willoughby, 2003). Adults with undiagnosed ADHD may also present for the first time to health or criminal justice services, because of behaviours linked to these difficulties.

Diagnosis

In terms of care pathways, parents and teachers are usually the first adults who notice ADHD-type behaviours in children. Depending on the child's age, parents most commonly discuss their concerns with teachers, health visitors, or GPs.

Research has found that those children with ADHD who are referred to specialist health services are more likely than those who are not to have more severe levels of hyperactivity. They are also more likely to have comorbid problems and to have parents who have mental health problems. The problems also tend to have a greater impact (burden) on the family (Sayal *et al*, 2003).

Although there is now considerable professional consensus about the recognition and management of children with ADHD, many children with ADHD remain undiagnosed. A national survey in 1999 found that only one in three children with ADHD had seen specialist health services in their lifetime (Sayal *et al*, 2006). NICE guidance (2000) recommends that assessments for ADHD should only be carried out by specialists (a child and adolescent psychiatrist or a paediatrician with expertise in ADHD) and, ideally, be multidisciplinary in nature. It emphasises that the assessment should be comprehensive, involving the child, parent, and the child's school, and holistic, taking into account family, social, environmental, and cultural factors. This requirement for detailed specialist assessments reflects the risks associated with inaccurate diagnoses. Particular emphasis should also be placed on the identification of any comorbid and associated psychosocial problems, as these can influence the child's response to treatment and their outcome.

Although parents might regard their child as being overactive or inattentive, their interpretation of this term may differ from the diagnostic description. In a UK population-based survey, 3.4% of parents reported their child as being hyperactive, but less than a quarter of these children had ADHD, when assessed using a research diagnostic interview (Ford *et al*, 2005). When parental reports about teachers' complaints about inattentiveness, over-activity and impulsiveness were incorporated, the confirmation rate rose to almost two-thirds. If a parent raises concerns about their child having ADHD, all professionals who work with children are in a position to make further enquiries and possibly observe the child in an everyday setting. Key points include the nature of the child's behaviours, whether they are pervasive across settings, how long they have been present, and any related difficulties in terms of peer relationships, academic progress, activities, and family life. With parental permission, information can be obtained from the child's school. The compilation of this information from a number of sources and discussion with the parent and child may help determine whether a referral to specialist services for a diagnostic assessment is required.

Treatment

There is considerable evidence based on randomised controlled trials that stimulant medication (methylphenidate, one version of which is marketed as Ritalin) is an effective treatment for ADHD. A large-scale randomised trial carried out by the MTA Co-operative Group (1999) in the US has strongly influenced clinical practice. This compared the effects of four treatment approaches (including drug treatment and intensive psychosocial intervention separately and in combination) over 14 months in 579 children with combined type ADHD. This found that carefully monitored and adjusted medication was more effective for ADHD symptoms than behavioural treatment alone. It was also much more effective than routine usual treatment (mainly medication) in the community (ie. from the primary care 'paediatrician' or family GP). The addition of medication to the intensive behavioural treatment intervention provided considerable advantage but, surprisingly, behaviour therapy added little value to medication, despite its highly intensive nature.

However, the psychosocial intervention in combination with medication was of benefit to children with comorbid disorders, highlighting the importance of the availability of a range of treatment approaches.

In clinical practice, a combination of approaches including psycho-education for the child, family, and school, behavioural management strategies at home and school, and family and dietary interventions (where indicated) may be of benefit. Decisions about the choice of treatment should be made jointly with the child and the family and their views and preferences fully taken into account. Some families may not want medication. Where there are concerns about side effects with stimulant medication, other medications such as atomoxetine are available. Detailed clinical guidelines recommending best practice in the US and Europe have been published (American Academy of Child and Adolescent Psychiatry, 2007; Taylor *et al*, 2004).

Controversies about ADHD

Descriptions of children with ADHD have been found going back to at least the mid 19th century. However, the number of children diagnosed as having ADHD and receiving treatment has increased greatly in recent years (Bramble, 2003). This may reflect a greater awareness about ADHD among clinicians, referrers, teachers, and parents, as well as changes in diagnostic criteria.

These recent increases in rates of diagnosis and use of treatments have led to concerns about the medicalisation of childhood behaviour problems, the risk of over-diagnosis, the effects on the child of labelling and stigma, and the use of stimulant medication to treat the condition, particularly in the US, where diagnosis rates are also higher (see, for example, Radcliffe & Newnes, 2005). In recent years, increases in treatment rates have been most marked among girls, teenagers (Olfson *et al*, 2003), children with inattentive symptoms and, most controversially, pre-school children (Zito *et al*, 2000). It has been argued and debated (Timimi & Taylor, 2004) that ADHD is simply a 'cultural construct' – that its diagnosis reflects different levels of tolerance of and concerns about children's behaviours within different cultures and societies. It is also argued that many children can show inattentive, overactive or impulsive behaviours from time to time, that many children grow out of these ADHD-type behaviours, and that different levels of these behaviours are found across the population.

Another point of controversy is the point at which the diagnostic cut-off (where the behaviours are seen to be outside the normal range) is applied. This has led to concerns about the validity of the ADHD diagnosis as a disorder. However, similar approaches to cut-offs are used with other medical conditions, such as high blood pressure (hypertension) or high levels of blood glucose (diabetes) to indicate the point at which the condition can lead to adverse consequences.

Conclusions

ADHD is a common disorder in childhood that is often associated with other mental health and developmental difficulties and can lead to adverse outcomes. Although recognition rates have increased in recent years, many children with ADHD remain undiagnosed. All professionals working with children are well placed to notice possible symptoms and to make further enquiries of parents and other professionals such as teachers.

References

American Academy of Child and Adolescent Psychiatry (2007) Practice parameter for the assessment and treatment of children and adolescents with attention deficit/hyperactivity disorder. *Journal of the American Academy of Child and Adolescent Psychiatry* **46** 894–921.

American Psychiatric Association (1994) *Diagnostic and statistical manual of mental disorders* (4th edition) (DSM-IV). Washington, DC: APA.

Barbaresi WJ, Katusic SK, Colligan RC, Weaver AL, Jacobsen SJ (2007) Long-term school outcomes for children with attention-deficit/hyperactivity disorder: a population-based perspective. *Journal of Developmental and Behavioral Pediatrics* **28** 265–273.

Bramble D (2003) Annotation: the use of psychotropic medications in children – a British view. *Journal of Child Psychology and Psychiatry* **44** 169–179.

Faraone SV, Sergeant J, Gillberg C, Biederman J (2003) The worldwide prevalence of ADHD: is it an American condition? *World Psychiatry* **2** 104–113.

Ford T, Goodman R, Meltzer H (2004) The relative importance of child, family, school and neighbourhood correlates of childhood psychiatric disorder. *Social Psychiatry and Psychiatric Epidemiology* **39** 487–496.

Ford T, Sayal K, Meltzer H, Goodman R (2005) Parental concerns about their child's emotions and behaviour and referral to specialist services: general population survey. *British Medical Journal* **331** 1435–1436.

Gaub M, Carlson CL (1997) Gender differences in ADHD: a meta-analysis and clinical review. *Journal of the American Academy of Child and Adolescent Psychiatry* **36** 1036–1045.

Green H, McGinnity A, Meltzer H, Ford TJ, Goodman R (2005) *Mental health of children and young people, Great Britain 2004*. London: Palgrave MacMillan.

Klein RG, Mannuzza S (1991) Long-term outcome of hyperactive children: a review. *Journal of the American Academy of Child & Adolescent Psychiatry* **30** 383–387.

Leung PW, Luk SL, Ho TP, Taylor E, Mak FL, Bacon-Shone J (1996) The diagnosis and prevalence of hyperactivity in Chinese schoolboys. *British Journal of Psychiatry* **168** 486–496.

MTA Co-operative Group (1999) A 14-month randomized clinical trial of treatment strategies for attention-deficit/hyperactivity disorder. *Archives of General Psychiatry* **56** 1073–1086.

NICE (2000) *Guidance on the use of methylphenidate (Ritalin, Equasym) for attention deficit/hyperactivity disorder (ADHD) in childhood.* Technology appraisal guidance no.13. London: NICE.

Olfson M, Gameroff MJ, Marcus SC, Jensen PS (2003) National trends in the treatment of attention deficit hyperactivity disorder. *American Journal of Psychiatry* **160** 1071–1077.

Polanczyk G, de Lima MS, Horta BL, Biederman J, Rohde LA (2007) The worldwide prevalence of ADHD: a systematic review and metaregression analysis. *American Journal of Psychiatry* **164** 942-948.

Radcliffe N, Newnes C (2005) *Making and breaking children's lives.* Ross-on-Wye: PCCS Books.

Sayal K, Taylor E, Beecham J (2003) Parental perception of problems and mental health service use for hyperactivity. *Journal of the American Academy of Child and Adolescent Psychiatry* **42** 1410–1414.

Sayal K, Goodman R, Ford T (2006) Barriers to the identification of children with attention deficit/hyperactivity disorder. *Journal of Child Psychology and Psychiatry* **47** 744–750.

Taylor E, Chadwick O, Heptinstall E *et al* (1996) Hyperactivity and conduct problems as risk factors for adolescent development. *Journal of the American Academy of Child and Adolescent Psychiatry* **35** 1213–1226.

Taylor E, Dopfner M, Sergeant J *et al* (2004) European clinical guidelines for hyperkinetic disorder – first upgrade. *European Child and Adolescent Psychiatry* **13** (s1) I7–30.

Timimi S, Taylor E (2004) ADHD is best understood as a cultural construct. *British Journal of Psychiatry* **184** 8–9.

Willoughby MT (2003) Developmental course of ADHD symptomatology during the transition from childhood to adolescence: a review with recommendations. *Journal of Child Psychology & Psychiatry* **44** 88–106.

World Health Organisation (1992) *International statistical classification of diseases and related health problems.* 10th revision. Geneva: WHO.

Zito JM, Safer DJ, dos Reis S, Gardner JF, Boles M, Lynch F (2000) Trends in the prescribing of psychotropic medications to preschoolers. *Journal of the American Medical Association* **283** 1025–1030.

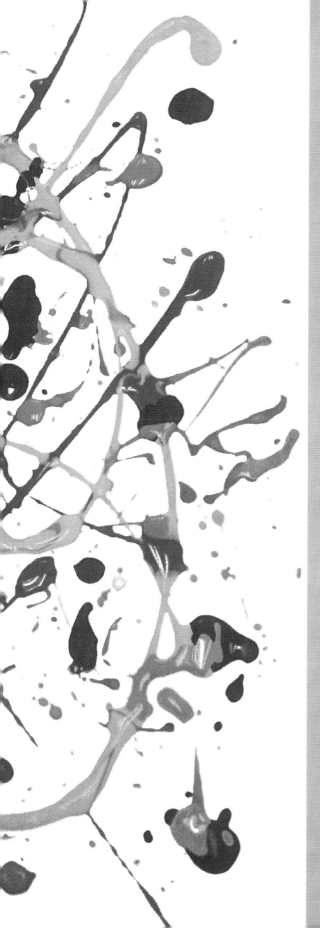

Attitudes matter: working with children and young people who self-harm

Jude Sellen

Key points

- One in 12 young people in the UK self-harm

- Self-harm is often an important coping mechanism

- Young people say staff do not listen to them and their needs

- Current models of response to self-harm focus too heavily on getting the young person to stop self-harming

- Staff working in children's services need training and support to recognise and manage their own emotional response to self-harm, in order to be able to respond better to young people.

Key words

Self-harm; Suicide; Staff support; Staff training; Risk management

Fact: Two children in every classroom self-harm (Camelot Foundation/Mental Health Foundation, 2006).

Fact: One in 12 young people self-harm (Camelot Foundation/Mental Health Foundation, 2006).

Fact: 25,000 young people present to hospitals each year, following an episode of self-harm (Fox & Hawton, 2004).

Fact: The highest rate of self-harm is among 13–15 year old girls (Meltzer *et al*, 2001).

Fact: In 1998 21% of prison suicides were by people under 21 years (Home Office, 2003).

Fact: One young person attempts suicide every 30 minutes (Stenager, 2000).

Fact: Attempted suicide by young men has tripled since 1985 (ONS, 2003).

Such facts have been greeted by newspaper headlines declaiming: 'New figures reveal 170,000 people a year – mostly teenagers and young adults – are hospitalised after harming themselves in despair' (*The Independent*, 27 July 2004), and 'Teenagers' epidemic of self-harm. A new study suggests that one in 12 British children deliberately hurt themselves – the highest rate in Europe' (*The Observer*, 26 March 2006).

Yet where do these alarming statistics, and the media response, leave frontline staff who are seeking to support young people who self-harm, and the young people themselves?

In 2006 the Camelot Foundation and the Mental Health Foundation published the findings of their national inquiry into self-harm among young people (Camelot Foundation/Mental Health Foundation, 2006). Their aim was 'to draw this hidden problem into the light; to understand it as thoroughly as possible, and to identify how young people can be helped and supported to find less damaging ways of dealing with their distress'. The inquiry sought the views both of frontline staff and young people. It found an apparent lack of awareness among frontline staff both of the extent of the problem and of how best to respond. It also found that the support and supervision offered to staff were often inadequate; that information and help both for staff and young people were difficult to access, and that training about self-harm and mental health in general among staff working in children's services was very patchy. It also, importantly, observed that self-harm generates a powerful emotional response in those working with young people.

The young people reported that, in the main, they experienced unhelpful responses from adults, and that they would more often talk to their friends – who often did not know how best to respond. They also said they would rarely ask for help directly; they wanted professionals to be honest if they did not understand; they wanted to talk to someone who did not over-react and knew how to help them, and they felt that the subject should be talked about more in schools.

The combination of these findings from staff and service users led to a series of recommendations, including the need to increase the availability of information about self-harm in a range of media, and to ensure all staff working in children's services have access to adequate training and support.

Responsive services

All too often these young people who self-harmed reported unsupportive and unsympathetic responses from adults and staff in the education, health and social care services when they sought help.

'My doctor looked at me differently once I told her why I was there. It was as if I were being annoying and wasting her time.'

'A&E isn't usually a positive experience. The last time I had a blood transfusion the consultant said I was wasting blood... he asked whether I was proud of what I had done... Some nurses have tried to offer acceptance and treat me clinically only – that's been a relief.'

'Self-harm is not tackled in schools or anywhere else. If they didn't make it such a dirty subject people would come forward a lot more quickly to get help.'

Despite the apparent increasing recognition, within both research and practice, that self-harm is an expression of mental distress, staff are often left holding uncomfortable feelings, and often remain uncertain how best to support young people. So when and how should staff respond, and what gets in the way?

Equally, young people who self-harm continue to say they do not feel heard and/or listened to by those seeking to support them. Having discussed and reflected on this in my working relationships with young people over many years, it occurs to me that what they are in fact saying is: 'They [the staff] do not listen to themselves.'

To support young people who self-harm, staff need to be adequately supported – not only by having access to information about self-harm and the purpose it serves for many young people, and the pros and cons of the various psychosocial models of intervention, but also by having opportunities to reflect on their own feelings about and attitudes to self-harm, and the impact these have in turn on their capacity to engage and work with young people who self-harm.

When a young person is unable to express their feelings verbally, as is frequently the case with young people who self-harm, there is, arguably, an even greater need for the member of staff to feel comfortable with their own feelings. Should the young person 'pick up' some discomfort that is neither articulated nor acknowledged by the worker, the young person may become suspicious and, indeed, anxious as to the capacity of the worker to engage with them in an honest way or offer any support.

Irrespective of the content of the dialogue between the worker and the young person, this can lead to the young person feeling that they are not heard. This is not to suggest that a member of staff should be trying to reach a point where they feel comfortable when sitting with someone who has either self-injured and/or taken an overdose. I simply argue that this experience should not leave the member of staff feeling disempowered and/or inadequate, and that if those feelings are provoked, they should be supported within their work setting. The member of staff should first be provided with an opportunity to address their own, understandable attitudes to this complex and distressing area of work, and second, helped to acknowledge that many of the emotions they are feeling are likely to mirror those felt by the young person (eg. feelings of inadequacy and disempowerment).

The challenge for staff, therefore, is how best to unravel the complexities of the emotions provoked within the dynamic of the relationship between them and the young person they are seeking to support. Involving the young person in this process is crucial, and extends far beyond debates about frequency of self-harm and working towards self-harming safely and/or ceasing to self-harm in a particular way.

What happens when we do not manage our own attitudes and feelings? What strategies do we adopt to protect ourselves, but which in fact reduce our capacity to be effective?

I first knowingly met a young woman who self-harmed some 25 years ago. She told me of her long history of self-harm and asked me to give her a reason why she should not kill herself. At the time I was working as a trainee counsellor/ resource officer in the Greater Manchester Council of Alcoholism (as it was then called; now of course it would be alcohol misuse). The reception counter acted as a divide between me and this young woman as she showed me the scars on her arms and asked me this question. My mind went blank, I had an uncomfortable sick feeling in my stomach and an overpowering sense that I needed to say something positive and come up with some rationale for why she should choose to live (I remember also, to my shame, thinking how unattractive she was and scantily dressed). I started to panic. I suggested that we make our way through to one of the small counselling rooms. En route my panic receded and I started to remember (with some excitement) what I'd learned on a recent course on 'working with aggressive behaviour'. We'd been told that, when entering a room with a client (service user), we should ensure that they sat at the far end of the room, and that we, the worker, ensured our chair was near the door, in case there was a need to escape. I also started to recall other points gleaned from that course – where possible, pictures should be permanently fixed to the walls so clients (service users) couldn't remove them and hurl them at you. I also used this walk from the reception to the counselling room to think about what I might offer this young woman to drink. So, having arrived in the room, ensured that she was seated at the far end, noted to my relief that the pictures were screwed to the wall, and fumbled with a coffee table to place a suitable barrier between us, my sense of panic returned. She didn't want anything to drink; she repeated the question: 'Give me a reason to live.'

I chose to manage my feelings through distraction. We all too often seek to replace uncomfortable feelings through engaging in a range of thoughts and/or activities that take us away from those that are uncomfortable. Many of you reading this may be thinking, 'That's obvious,' but how many of you have had an opportunity, in training and/or in supervision, to explore the emotions evoked when supporting someone who self-harms, let alone discuss how to work with these feelings within your working relationship with the young person?

Working alongside the young person

The training and support I offer to staff working in children's services (see Sellen, 2006) has taken inspiration from Karl Menninger, an American psychiatrist writing back in the 1930s. Menninger argued that self-harm is 'a recognition towards self-destructiveness examined as a misdirection of the instinct for survival'. In his landmark book, *Man Against Himself*, published in 1938 (Menninger, 1938), he further argued that, in supporting people who self-harm, 'attitudes are more important than facts'.

The (more recent) publication *Beyond Fear and Control: Working with young people who self-harm* (Spandler & Warner, 2007), usefully explores the value of 'working alongside' young people who self-harm, and accepting the young person's choice to use self-harm as a way of coping with distress. More and more services are adopting this approach across the UK, but they remain the minority. The concept of 'working alongside' is underpinned by an acceptance of self-harm as the young person's coping strategy. This places the relationship between the young person and the worker on a positive footing as it provides a non-judgmental mode of engagement. The parameters for the engagement come out of this relationship – that is, the young person and the worker discuss and agree the nature of the support to be offered and the time frame. This model of engagement is, crucially, underpinned by a focus on 'process' rather than 'solution'; a focus on 'process' will bring more positive outcomes for the young person and the member of staff.

For there is a danger, when working with young people who self-harm, that the search for a 'solution' starts from the premise that a successful outcome would be for the young person to stop self-harming, and that the focus of the work becomes practical advice – first aid and short-term harm minimisation strategies. This can, again, remove the need for the member of staff to explore the impact of their attitudes and feelings within the working relationship – and (crucially) closes off opportunities for the young person to explore their own feelings about and attitudes to their self-harming behaviours.

In recent years, I have been increasingly struck by the number of times members of staff and young people who self-harm have asked me (this is a direct quote from a young woman of 15 who self-harms): 'Why is it that sometimes, when everything is going really well, I harm myself, and it can be really bad?'

Or consider the following exchange between several young people who self-harm. The names have been changed, but the scenario is real.

Susan: I sold a picture of mine the other day.
Ellie: Cor, that's amazing.
John: How much did you get for it then?
Susan: One hundred and fifty quid (pause) But you know something, I'm more proud of these (she points at the numerous scars on her upper and lower arms) than that, do you know what I mean?
Ellie (looks round at members of the group): Yeah I know what you mean.
Susan: I can't explain it.
Ellie: I can, it's like when something really good happens, you've got farther to fall then haven't you, at least when you cut yourself nobody can take that away from you.
Susan: That's right. But it's weird isn't it? I wish I could be normal.
Ellie: Yeah, but what's normal?

If we look at the first example, adopting a 'solution-focused' model, where either the reduction of self-injury or its cessation could be the desired outcome, sets up both the young person and the worker for failure if self-injury does happen. However, adopting a 'process' model offers more opportunity for reflection both before, during and after the act of self-injury.

Why would someone harm themselves after they've had a really good time? In order to understand this, I believe it is important to look at the young person's emotional development from birth (some research would advocate pre-birth) right up to the present day. How many positive experiences has the young person had that have engendered within them feelings of warmth, excitement, self-worth and pleasure? Equally, how many events and/or encounters with people have provoked feelings of sadness, being alone, despair, self-loathing, and fear?

Consider how you feel when you see a sunrise. What feelings does it evoke? Do you notice any difference in your feelings? Do you feel a sudden whoosh of warmth that lingers even when the initial impact has receded, you have returned to your normal emotional equilibrium, and the image has faded? What if your emotional equilibrium has been significantly impaired during your emotional development, such that you have become much more 'comfortable' with feelings of fear, loss and anger, and you are less familiar with feelings of warmth? This can lead to a significant imbalance in our emotional responses to external stimuli. Imagine you have an internal pendulum – to achieve optimal levels of emotional well-being, most of us strive to expose ourselves to a balance of external stimuli, recognising that exposure to stimuli that provoke extreme highs or lows has a significant impact on our overall capacity to manage our private and public lives.

Now let's go back to thinking about the young person who self-harms, who has had exposure to limited positive emotional encounters but has accumulated many negative emotional experiences – for example, the young person who is separated from their siblings at age eight, and has had 16 placements, and as many changes of school, between the ages of eight and 14 years. Many of the moves from placement to placement result, at least in their minds, from their disruptive behaviour, and reinforce their perception that they are unable to develop healthy and positive relationships, which in turn reduces their sense of self-worth. They have had a number of negative experiences in their relationships with peers. They then have a period of being 'settled', during which their self-harming behaviours significantly reduce. However, the underlying factors that caused the significant imbalance to their internal emotional balance remain unaddressed, dormant. They then have a fun day out in which they experience both their peers and staff/carers interacting positively and offering warm responses throughout the day; there is a lot of laughter, the young person feels happy, optimistic. They then return home. What happens?

For many young people, the swing of their internal pendulum is experienced as enormous, even painful; sensations of anxiety and discomfort can come tumbling in. If the young person has a history in which they have learnt to manage these sensations through self-injury/overdose, it is not surprising that they will feel a sense of relief, even comfort, from the sensation of disassociation often reported as accompanying an act of self-injury. It is therefore important, where possible, to pre-empt this scenario through discussion with the young person. It is likely that previous examples of behaviour that fall within a wider definition of 'self-harm' – sexual risk-taking behaviour, substance misuse etc – may emerge.

This is in no way to simplify the act of self-harm, as there can be many, highly complex causation factors, but the frequent experience for some young people is that we jump too quickly to label them with a diagnosis and/or behaviour trait that further compounds their negative sense of self. This process of labelling can also serve to disempower frontline staff – it can encourage them to believe a young person needs specialist intervention, when in fact specialist workers often point to the lack of appropriate community resources and non-crisis support for young people who self-harm.

What we need is the mainstreaming and embedding of creative training initiatives across all children's services that encourage opportunities for staff to examine their own attitudes and feelings about self-harm. However, what staff do is inevitably dictated by the context within which they work, and current health and social care provision is profoundly influenced by national policy directives and national targets, and by the imperative to provide measurable outcomes from services and interventions. This, in turn, has resulted in an increased emphasis on solution-focused models of intervention, whose outcomes are readily quantifiable, and the abandonment of longer-term psychotherapeutic models of care. There's nothing wrong with trying to find solutions to problems, but the solution-focused approach can often move our attention away from the importance of 'process' and, as I argue above, 'process' (rather than 'solutions') can be key to working with young people.

In contrast, the current trend has been accompanied by a plethora of risk management tools and training for frontline staff that have, arguably, increased the anxiety both of frontline staff and their managers to 'get it right'.

This is not to suggest that there are not service providers who seek to address the often complex needs of young people by offering long-term and creative solutions, yet examples of this are rare, and most models of care look to match risk with short-term reactive solutions. It also reduces the opportunities for the young person to be supported in a holistic way, resulting in frustration for service users and staff alike.

To restate, fundamental to the way of working put forward in this chapter is a recognition that we all (young people and staff alike) have to consistently reflect on our own attitudes and how in turn these impact on the choices we all make. Furthermore, this position recognises young people as actors in their own lives as opposed to victims.

Fact: Stop treating young people who self-harm like freaks.
Fact: It's important to involve young people who self-harm in the design of their services.
Fact: See beyond the label.
Fact: Self-harm is not attention-seeking.
Fact: Young people want self-harm to be talked about in schools.
Fact: Young people do not encourage each other to self-injure.
Fact: Young people are very supportive of each other.
Fact: More A&E nurses and doctors should receive self-harm training.
Fact: Think about young people's lives as a whole.

References

Camelot Foundation/Mental Health Foundation (2006) *Truth hurts: report of the national inquiry into self-harm among young people.* London: Mental Health Foundation.

Fox C, Hawton K (2004) *Deliberate self-harm in adolescence.* London: Jessica Kingsley Publishers.

Home Office (2003) *Prison statistics England and Wales 2002.* London: Home Office.

Meltzer H, Harrington R, Goodman R *et al* (2001) *Children and adolescents who try to harm, hurt or kill themselves.* London: Office for National Statistics.

Menninger K (1938) *Man against himself.* New York: Harcourt Brace.

ONS (2003) *Death rates from suicide by gender and age 1971–1998.* London: ONS.

Sellen J (2006) *See beyond the label: empowering young people who self-harm. A training manual.* London: YoungMinds.

Spandler H, Warner S (2007) *Beyond fear and control: working with young people who self-harm.* Ross-on-Wye: PCCS Books.

Stenager EN (2000) Physical illness and suicidal behaviour. In: Hawton K, van Heeringen K (eds) *International handbook of suicide and attempted suicide.* Chichester: John Wiley & Sons.

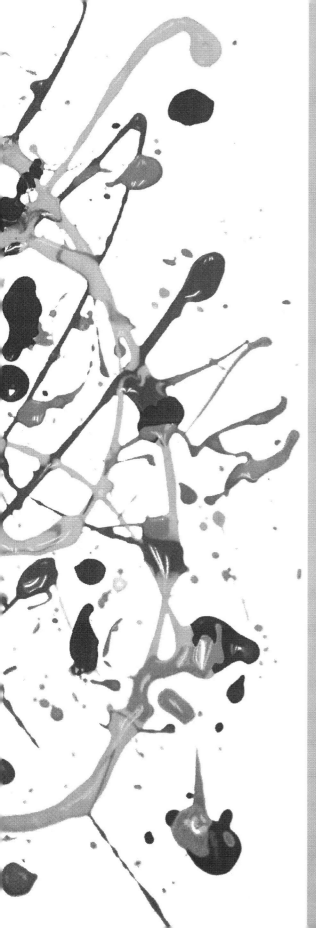

Eating disorders

Marion E. Roberts and Janet L. Treasure

Key points

- Eating disorders affect 4.8%–12.5% of the female population, and occur more rarely (10%–15% of female rates) in males

- Many young people suffer from partial, or sub-threshold, eating disorders that, while less dangerous to life and health, also cause a significant amount of distress

- Young people with anorexia often consider their eating disorder to be a solution rather than a problem, making identification and treatment more difficult

- Family therapy has been found successful in improving outcomes for children and adolescents with anorexia

- Bulimia has been found to respond well to cognitive therapies.

Key words
Anorexia nervosa; Bulimia nervosa; Binge eating disorder; Cognitive therapy; Family therapy

Despite what is portrayed in the media, eating disorders are not an attention-seeking game played by white, middle-class female adolescents. Nor are they the idiosyncratic eating habits of naturally thin celebrities, or the girl who checks the small print on the packaging of every food item she buys at the supermarket (she may simply have a food allergy).

The eating disorders anorexia and bulimia nervosa are serious, often long-term, psychological illnesses, whose effects can be disastrous for both the individual affected and their family and friends (Whitney *et al*, 2005). By depriving themselves of the food their body needs to survive, young people with anorexia are at serious risk of death. Prolonged bulimia can lead to irreversible damage to the digestive system, due to laxative abuse or self-induced vomiting. Of all medical conditions, eating disorders are ranked 15th in terms of 'life lived with disability'. Anorexia has the highest death rate of all psychiatric conditions.

In this chapter we will explore the types of eating disorders (diagnostic categories), how common eating disorders are (incidence), what can contribute to the development of an eating disorder (risk factors), and evidence-based approaches to treatment. It is hoped that this chapter will give readers a basic understanding of anorexia and bulimia nervosa, so that they will be equipped at least to recognise those at risk with whom they have contact in their daily working lives, and work sympathetically with them to ensure they get the specialist treatment they may need.

Diagnostic categories
Figure 1. Diagnostic categories for eating disorder

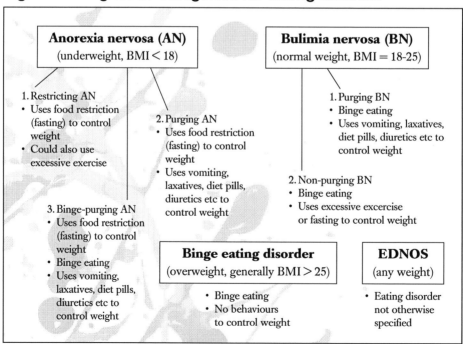

As can be seen in figure 1, different sub-types make up both anorexia and bulimia nervosa, as outlined in the Diagnostic and Statistical Manual of Mental Health Disorders (DSM-IV-TR) (APA, 2000). It may seem that these conditions overlap considerably, and, indeed, many patients with an eating disorder swap between diagnostic categories (particularly if they have a long duration of illness). Perhaps the most defining difference between anorexia and bulimia nervosa is whether the patient is underweight (body mass index (BMI) [kg/m2] < 18), or at a normal weight (BMI between 18 and 25).

The normal weight of people with bulimia is sustained through regular (at least twice a week, but it can be many times a day) binge eating episodes, where the individual feels distressed and out of control with the large amounts of food they are consuming. These binges are compensated for by purging the food (by self-induced vomiting and/or laxatives), or using non-purging methods, such as excessive exercise or dietary restriction. In most cases, people with bulimia seem to have normal eating patterns to those around them.

In addition to their eating problems, women with bulimia often present with significant impulsive behaviours, as evidenced by high rates of alcohol and drug use, self-harm, and borderline personality disorder. Those with bulimia also have higher rates of post-traumatic stress disorder than those with anorexia (Kaye *et al*, 2004), indicating that their lives are perhaps more chaotic and traumatic than the lives of those with anorexia.

Amy struggles with her body weight and shape and tries to be strict with herself about what she eats. She skips breakfast but has lunch and dinner so that she will not arouse any suspicions. Amy makes sure she has smaller portions than the rest of her family, and will not let herself snack between meals. However, Amy loves chocolate, and a couple times a week the cravings get too much for her. She goes to the supermarket on her way home from school, buys a couple of king-size bars of chocolate, a tub of chocolate ice cream, and some packets of chocolate biscuits. She races up to her room and eats them all. Amy feels guilty and sick afterwards, and worries that she will become fat after eating all that food. She has never been able to make herself sick so she re-focuses on her strict eating plan, and goes for a long run later that night. Amy has a BMI of 23.8.
Diagnosis = Bulimia (non-purging)

Anorexia nervosa is easier to identify than bulimia, as excessive restriction of food results in being obviously underweight. People with anorexia often develop strict rules and rituals around eating, such as the way they prepare food, the order in which food is eaten, and which cutlery may be used. While some sufferers simply restrict their food, others also engage in the compensatory behaviours seen in bulimia nervosa, such as self-induced vomiting and laxative abuse (purging anorexia). The binge/purge subtype of anorexia occurs more rarely. Here the binge episodes occur less frequently than in bulimia nervosa, allowing the patient to maintain their low weight, but these episodes are otherwise very similar to those seen in bulimia.

In general, the personality type of those with anorexia is different to that of young people with bulimia. While both eating disorders are accompanied by high rates of depression, people with anorexia tend to be high achievers, displaying perfectionist tendencies that are often present from childhood (Brecelj-Anderluh *et al*, 2003). High rates of anxiety disorders, particularly obsessive-compulsive disorder and social phobia, are also seen in anorexia (Godart *et al*, 2006; Kaye *et al*, 2004).

Claire couldn't believe what she saw in the mirror – she was so fat! It must have been the extra tomato and the bit of cheese she had at lunch. She usually didn't eat cheese, but her dad was watching her. The cheese was right in front of her, and he kept pushing her to have some. Now all she could think of was getting rid of it before her body absorbed the calories. Claire knew her dad would be watching the bathroom for a while after the meal, so she made herself sick in one of the small bags she kept hidden in her room. She would flush it later. Claire was grateful that the family still had the exercise machine in the lounge, and she headed downstairs to work out. Claire has a BMI of 15.4. Diagnosis = Anorexia (purging)

Binge eating disorder (BED), a condition where an individual engages in binge eating without any compensatory behaviours, has been found in both normal weight and overweight/obese individuals. To date, BED does not have its own category in the DSM-IV (APA, 2000), but is classified under Eating Disorder Not Otherwise Specified (EDNOS), and marked for further study. Growing evidence suggests that BED may be a clinically useful formal diagnosis for inclusion in DSM-V.

The category of EDNOS is used when patients do not fit all the criteria for the eating disorders anorexia and bulimia nervosa as outlined in the DSM-IV (APA, 2000). Nearly half of cases presenting to community eating disorder clinics fall into this category (Button *et al*, 2005). Examples of EDNOS include someone of normal weight who engages in purging behaviours but does not binge ('purging disorder'), or someone with anorexia whose weight is not low enough to merit full diagnosis (ie. her periods have not stopped). This difficulty with classification is especially obvious in the child and adolescent population, prompting some researchers to develop modified criteria for children and adolescents with eating disorders (Nicholls *et al*, 2000).

It is difficult to discuss those with EDNOS as a category, given that it represents such a mixed bag of disordered eating behaviours. For the purposes of this chapter we will focus on the two main categories of eating disorders: anorexia and bulimia nervosa, along with the emergent BED.

Incidence

The often quoted statistic for the incidence of eating disorders among western females is 0.3% lifetime for anorexia, and one per cent lifetime for bulimia. However, research findings indicate that eating disorders can affect 4.8%–12.5% of the female population at a clinical level (Wade *et al*, 2006). Community studies have found disordered eating behaviour in up to a third of female university students (Roberts, 2006). Chamay-Weber and colleagues (2005), in a systematic review, note that many adolescents suffer from partial, or sub-threshold, eating disorders (EDNOS), and that, while they do not reach diagnostic criteria, they still suffer to a significant degree.

The incidence of anorexia nervosa increased substantially in the mid 20th century, leveling off in the 1970s. However, the age of sufferers has continued to drop, with girls as young as six years old admitted for treatment. Bulimia, however, entered the DSM relatively recently, in the 1980s, resulting in an (unsurprising) increase in prevalence, which has only recently leveled off (Currin *et al*, 2005). Incidence of bulimia is five times higher in cities than rural areas, whereas no such difference is found in incidence of anorexia (van Son *et al*, 2006). This may be due to the easier access to sources of high-calorific foods in urban areas.

While one might assume that eating disordered behaviour would differ between females and males, in fact nearly all aspects are the same. The prevalence of eating disorders in males is approximately 5%–10% of that of females. However, a review of male eating disorders found that incidence rates considerably increase when partial criteria are applied to adolescent boys, and these partial syndromes often predict full blown cases in adulthood (Muise *et al*, 2003).

BED has been found in up to 6.6% of the general population (Grucza *et al*, 2007). However, there is little research investigating how often this new category is found in the adolescent population. A review has indicated that up to 25% of female children and adolescents say they have experienced an occasion of binge eating with loss of control at some point in their life (Marcus & Kalarchian, 2003). However, a study formally assessing 186 obese adolescents aged 10–16 years referred for weight loss treatment found that only one per cent met criteria for BED (Decaluwe & Braet, 2003).

Risk factors

Perhaps the most obvious risk factor for an eating disorder is a cultural one, particularly noticeable in the more affluent western world. Young women are faced with more pressure than ever before to be thin, with messages from the media and the catwalk constantly pushing unrealistic and unhealthy body images. These pressures are understandably predictive of eating pathology, and are felt in girls as young as age five (Dohnt & Tiggemann, 2006). But the media cannot be held solely responsible for eating disorders. Anorexia and bulimia nervosa are in truth the result of a complex interaction of multiple factors: cultural, environmental, psychological, and biological.

Risk factors in anorexia nervosa

Anorexia and bulimia nervosa share many risk factors, such as gender, ethnicity, genetics, childhood anxieties, aversive life events, acculturation, and negative self-evaluation. However, there are a number of risk factors exclusive to anorexia. Following an extensive review of the literature, Jacobi and colleagues have outlined specific risk factors, weighted by potency, for each of the conditions (Jacobi *et al*, 2004). Specific to anorexia are obsessive-compulsive personality traits throughout childhood and adolescence (medium potency), perfectionism in late adolescence (medium potency), and high level of exercise at approximately age 13 (high potency).

Although present in anorexia and bulimia, understanding the genetic or heritable aspects of anorexia has been a crucial step forward in the last decade of research. Eating disorders are often found to 'run in families', with the relative risk for developing anorexia of 11.2 for female relatives of those with anorexia, and 12.3 for female relatives of those with bulimia (Schmidt, 2005). Susceptibility genes for anorexia such as brain-derived neurotropic factor (BDNF), along with the serotonin system (5-HT), have been identified in molecular genetics (Collier & Treasure, 2004). These relatively new advances in our understanding of the genetic risk of anorexia require further exploration and replication.

Risk factors in bulimia nervosa

Like anorexia, a number of specific risk factors have been identified for bulimia nervosa. Childhood obesity from as early as age four, along with parental obesity, are medium potency risk factors (Jacobi *et al*, 2004). Dieting behaviour in mid adolescence is, perhaps surprisingly, a high potency risk factor for bulimia, but not anorexia. Additional parental factors such as parental alcohol and drug use, parental depression, parental criticism (high expectations, comments on weight, low contact with the adolescent) and adverse family experiences factor as specific risks for bulimia.

Bulimia would seem to be influenced by genes to a lesser extent. The relative genetic risk for developing bulimia is considerably lower than it is for anorexia, reported at 4.2 for female relatives of those with anorexia, and 4.4 for female relatives of those with bulimia (Schmidt, 2005).

Given BED is not yet an established category, only a few studies have assessed risk factors in this population. While it seems BED shares many risk factors with bulimia, significantly more research for this group is required for the evidence base to approach that of anorexia and bulimia.

Maintaining factors

Schmidt and Treasure (2006) recently outlined a detailed model of maintaining factors in anorexia nervosa. Four factors are proposed:

1   perfectionism/cognitive rigidity/obsessive-compulsive traits (often seen in childhood, also reflected in the high rate of co-occurring obsessive-compulsive disorder and obsessive-compulsive personality disorder in anorexia)
2   experiential avoidance (essentially avoiding emotion and emotional memories, which is aided by the maintenance of a low weight)
3   pro-anorectic beliefs (positive thoughts about the value of the eating disorder)
4   response of close others (see 'Support for carers' below).

The model proposes that these four factors interact to encourage the patient to continue the eating disorder behaviours, and that addressing each of these points in specialist therapy will achieve a more positive outcome. These factors avoid cultural aspects of the disorder, such as weight and shape related pressures.

Evidence-based psychological treatment

Without question, the earlier that someone with an eating disorder is identified and provided with appropriate specialist treatment, the greater their chance of a quick and full recovery. However, a barrier to delivering speedy treatment is that people with anorexia often consider their eating disorder to be a solution rather than a problem, and often keep their abnormal eating patterns secret. Motivation to change is therefore a key issue in treatment. Where the young person with anorexia is still living at home with their parents, there may be tension as the family seeks to get help for their visibly unwell child, and he or she remains unwilling to accept there is a need to change.

There is a limited number of randomised controlled trials (RCTs – the 'gold standard' research design for assessing different treatments) investigating treatment outcomes for anorexia, bulimia and BED. Only a small number of RCTs focus on treatment outcome for adolescents with eating disorders. None of these address medication treatment.

Treatment for adolescent anorexia nervosa

Family therapy has been recognised as the most promising form of therapy for children and adolescents with anorexia nervosa, as recommended by the National Institute for Clinical Excellence guidelines (grade B) (NICE, 2004). James Lock and colleagues (2001) have produced a manual describing this style of family therapy (the 'Maudsley model'). A number of RCTs have compared various 'doses' of family therapy for adolescents, with all forms producing a good outcome.

Treatment for adolescent bulimia nervosa

Only recently have we begun to see evidence of effective treatment for adolescent bulimia. Two recent case series have indicated the potential for tailored cognitive behavioural therapy (CBT) in the adolescent population (Lock, 2005; Schapman-Williams *et al*, 2006). A Maudsley model-based family approach has also since been recently developed (le Grange & Lock, 2007). The first RCT of adolescent bulimia, published by Schmidt and colleagues, found CBT guided self-care (supported by a professional) to be more effective at six-month follow-up than family therapy (Schmidt *et al*, 2007). Unfortunately this difference was not maintained 12 months later but, given the smaller direct cost of treatment for the self-care group, this is an encouraging finding.

All in the family

Many people still believe that families 'cause' anorexia, despite the lack of evidence to support such beliefs. There is, however, a growing amount of research showing families are essential to their child's recovery. Professor Janet Treasure, consultant psychiatrist and head of the South London and Maudsley NHS Foundation Trust eating disorder services, and her team at Institute of Psychiatry have started to focus on what families or 'carers' (parents, siblings etc) of those with an eating disorder can contribute to treatment and recovery.

The Maudsley team are developing and testing support for carers of people with eating disorders in different formats – workshops, workbooks and DVDs, and a web-based programme. These provide carers with relevant information and skills to help them cope with care-giving and reduce their distress, which may in turn improve their child's compliance with treatment and outcome.

A book, *Skills-Based Learning for Caring for a Loved One with an Eating Disorder: the new Maudsley model* (Treasure *et al*, 2007b), forms the basis of the workshops and DVDs for carers. It includes detailed techniques and strategies that aim to improve carers' ability to build continuity and consistency of support and is based on the results of research and personal experience.

These workshops have only been running for the last few years, and evaluation of their effectiveness in reducing the impact of the eating disorder is ongoing. However, feedback from carers indicates that the workshops are helpful and effective in improving carer well-being and reducing the burden of care. Many carers repeat the course, or a different carer from the same family will attend a subsequent course.

In the words of one carer: '[The course] was absolutely invaluable as a support mechanism… getting hold of the book was a real turning point and it definitely gave me the confidence to care for her.'

Treatment for adolescent binge eating disorder

No treatment trials for adolescent BED have been published to date. The limited trials available in the adult literature suggest that a combination of medication and behavioural therapy may be a promising treatment. However, these studies suffer from small sample sizes (Brownley *et al*, 2007).

Cognitive remediation therapy

Cognitive remediation therapy, a new, novel approach to treating severe cases of anorexia, is currently being trialled (Tchanturia *et al*, 2007). This pre-therapy focuses less on what the patient is thinking (as standard psychological interventions do), and instead takes a step back to look at how the patient thinks. This approach is based on findings that those with eating disorders process information in a more detailed or piecemeal way (Lopez *et al*, in press), and display rigid thinking and behavioural patterns (Roberts *et al*, 2007). Use of CRT in an outpatient setting, where direct feedback on neuropsychological performance is given to the patient, is also being trialed and is receiving positive feedback from patients.

Support for carers

The role of the caregiver has only recently been explored in the treatment of eating disorders. Given that family therapy has been identified as best for adolescents with an eating disorder, it makes sense to give parents tools and knowledge, so that the home environment can facilitate recovery as much as possible. The Maudsley carers workshops (Treasure *et al*, 2007a) use various animals as metaphors for behaviour patterns, to help family members to recognise and step out of some of the patterns of behaviour that can maintain the problem (eg. kangaroo = over-protective parent wanting to carry child in pouch; rhinoceros = angry parent, getting frustrated and wanting to 'stomp' the eating disorder out of child). The user-friendly manual for carers is available to the public (Treasure *et al*, 2007b). An RCT investigating the impact of carer training on patient outcome is currently underway.

Conclusion

Children and adolescents with an eating disorder have the best chance of full recovery with early identification and treatment. Family therapy is the best treatment for adolescent anorexia. A preferred treatment for adolescent bulimia has not yet been identified, with treatment trials for bulimia only in the past few years producing results. Involving the family in treatment is essential.

References

APA (2000) *Diagnostic and statistical manual of mental disorders – revised (DSM-IV-TR)*. Washington DC: American Psychiatric Association.

Brecelj-Anderluh M, Tchanturia K, Rabe-Hesketh S, Treasure J (2003) Childhood obsessive-compulsive personality traits in adult women with eating disorders: defining a broader eating disorder phenotype. *American Journal of Psychiatry* **160** 242–247.

Brownley KA, Berkman ND, Sedway JA, Lohr KN, Bulik CM (2007) Binge eating disorder treatment: a systematic review of randomized controlled trials. *International Journal of Eating Disorders* **40** 337–348.

Button EJ, Benson E, Nollett C, Palmer RL (2005) Don't forget EDNOS (eating disorder not otherwise specified): patterns of service use in an eating disorders service. *Psychiatric Bulletin* **29** (4) 134–136.

Chamay-Weber C, Narring F, Michaud P-A (2005) Partial eating disorders among adolescents: a review. *Journal of Adolescent Health* **37** 417–427.

Collier D, Treasure J (2004) The aetiology of eating disorders. *British Journal of Psychiatry* **185** 363–365.

Currin L, Schmidt U, Treasure J, Jick H (2005) Time trends in eating disorder incidence. *British Journal of Psychiatry* **186** 132–135.

Decaluwe V, Braet C (2003) Prevalence of binge-eating disorder in obese children and adolescents seeking weight-loss treatment. *International Journal of Obesity* **27** 404–409.

Dohnt H, Tiggemann M (2006) The contribution of peer and media influences to the development of body satisfaction and self-esteem in young girls: a prospective study. *Developmental Psychology* **42** 929–936.

Godart N, Berthoz S, Rein Z, Perdereau F *et al* (2006) Does the frequency of anxiety and depressive disorders differ between diagnostic subtypes of anorexia nervosa and bulimia? *International Journal of Eating Disorders* **39** 772–778.

Grucza RA, Przybeck TR, Cloninger C (2007) Prevalence and correlates of binge eating disorder in a community sample. *Comprehensive Psychiatry* **48** 124–131.

Jacobi C, Hayward C, De Zwaan M, Kraemer HC, Agras W (2004) Coming to terms with risk factors for eating disorders: application of risk terminology and suggestions for a general taxonomy. *Psychological Bulletin* **130** 19–65.

Kaye WH, Bulik CM, Thornton L, Barbarich N, Masters K (2004) Comorbidity of anxiety disorders with anorexia and bulimia nervosa. *American Journal of Psychiatry* **161** 2215–2221.

le Grange D, Lock J (2007) *Treating bulimia in adolescents: a family-based approach*. New York: Guilford Press.

Lock J (2005) Adjusting cognitive behavior therapy for adolescents with bulimia nervosa: results of case series. *American Journal of Psychotherapy* **59** 267–281.

Lock J, Grange DL, Agras WS, Dare C (2001) *Treatment manual for anorexia nervosa: a family-based approach*. New York: Guilford Press.

Lopez C, Tchanturia K, Stahl D, Happe F, Booth R, Holliday J, Treasure J (in press) An investigation of central coherence in women with anorexia nervosa. *International Journal of Eating Disorders*.

Marcus MD, Kalarchian MA (2003) Binge eating in children and adolescents. *International Journal of Eating Disorders* **34** s47–s57.

Muise AM, Stein DG, Arbess G (2003) Eating disorders in adolescent boys: a review of the adolescent and young adult literature. *Journal of Adolescent Health* **33** 427–435.

NICE (2004) *Eating disorders: core interventions in the treatment and management of anorexia nervosa, bulimia nervosa and related eating disorders.* London: National Institute for Clinical Excellence.

Nicholls D, Chater R, Lask B (2000) Children into DSM don't go: a comparison of classification systems for eating disorders in childhood and early adolescence. *International Journal of Eating Disorders* **28** 317–324.

Roberts ME (2006) Disordered eating and obsessive-compulsive symptoms in a sub-clinical student population. *New Zealand Journal of Psychology* **35** 45–54.

Roberts M, Tchanturia K, Stahl D, Southgate L, Treasure J (2007) A systematic review and meta-analysis of set shifting ability in eating disorders. *Psychological Medicine* **37** 1075–1081.

Schapman-Williams AM, Lock J, Couturier J (2006) Cognitive-behavioral therapy for adolescents with binge eating syndromes: a case series. *International Journal of Eating Disorders* **39** 252–255.

Schmidt U (2005) Epidemiology and aetiology of eating disorders. *Psychiatry* **4** 5–9.

Schmidt U, Treasure J (2006) Anorexia nervosa: valued and visible – a cognitive-interpersonal maintenance model and its implications for research and practice. *British Journal of Clinical Psychology* **45** 343–366.

Schmidt U, Lee S, Beecham J *et al* (2007) A randomised controlled trial of family therapy and cognitive behaviour therapy guided self-care for adolescents with bulimia nervosa and related disorders. *American Journal of Psychiatry* **164** 591–598.

Tchanturia K, Davies H, Campbell IC (2007) Cognitive remediation for patients with anorexia nervosa: preliminary findings. *Annals of General Psychiatry* **14** 1–6.

Treasure J, Sepulveda AR, Whitaker W, Todd G, Lopez C, Whitney J (2007a) Collaborative care between professionals and non-professionals in the management of eating disorders: a description of workshops focused on interpersonal maintaining factors. *European Eating Disorders Review* **15** 15–24.

Treasure J, Smith G, Crane AM (2007b) *Skills-based learning for caring for a loved one with an eating disorder: the new Maudsley method.* London: Routledge.

van Son GE, Van Hoeken D, Bartelds AI, Van Furth EF, Hoek HW (2006) Urbanisation and the incidence of eating disorders. *British Journal of Psychiatry* **189** 562–563.

Wade TD, Bergin JL, Tiggemann M, Bulik CM, Fairburn CG (2006) Prevalence and long-term course of lifetime eating disorders in an adult Australian twin cohort. *Australian and New Zealand Journal of Psychiatry* **40** 121–128.

Whitney J, Murray J, Gavan K, Todd G, Whitaker W, Treasure J (2005) Experience of caring for someone with anorexia nervosa: qualitative study. *British Journal of Psychiatry* **187** 444–449.

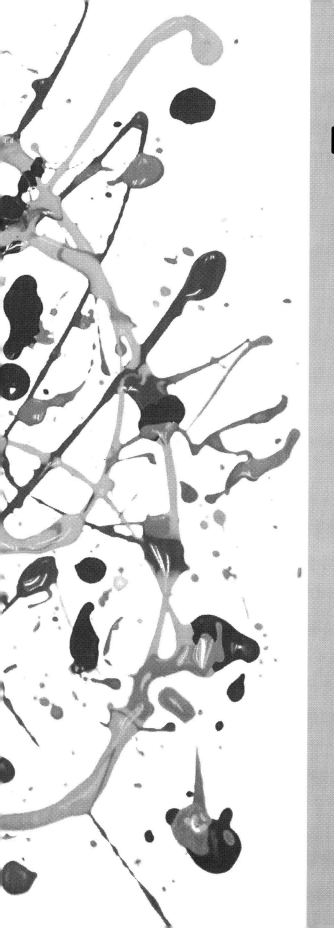

Index

Subject index

Note: The following abbreviations have been used: ADHD for attention deficit/hyperactivity disorder; BME for black and minority ethnic; DfES for Department for Education and Skills; DCSF for Department for Children, Schools and Families; DoH for Department of Health

Author index